Current Issues in Economics and Finance

Bandi Kamaiah · C.S. Shylajan
S. Venkata Seshaiah · M. Aruna
Subhadip Mukherjee
Editors

Current Issues in Economics and Finance

Springer

Editors
Bandi Kamaiah
Department of Economics
University of Hyderabad
Hyderabad
India

M. Aruna
Department of Economics
IBS Hyderabad
Hyderabad
India

C.S. Shylajan
IBS Hyderabad
Hyderabad
India

Subhadip Mukherjee
Department of Economics
IBS Hyderabad
Hyderabad
India

S. Venkata Seshaiah
IBS Hyderabad
Hyderabad
India

ISBN 978-981-10-5809-7 ISBN 978-981-10-5810-3 (eBook)
DOI 10.1007/978-981-10-5810-3

Library of Congress Control Number: 2017950019

Printed on acid-free paper

This Springer imprint is published by Springer Nature
The registered company is Springer Nature Singapore Pte Ltd.
The registered company address is: 152 Beach Road, #21-01/04 Gateway East, Singapore 189721, Singapore

Preface

This book is a collection of selected papers presented at Fifth International Conference on Applied Econometrics organized by IBS Hyderabad, a constituent of the ICFAI Foundation for Higher Education (IFHE). The conference was held during July 22–23, 2016. It was organized in collaboration with The Indian Econometrics Society (TIES), New Delhi.

This volume consists of 13 research papers selected out of 52 papers presented at the conference. The papers were selected based on their quality in terms of contemporary topic, newness in the methodology, and themes. It covers topics related to current issues in economic growth and development, international trade, macroeconomic and financial stability, monetary policy, intellectual capital and financial performance, productivity performance of Indian banks, corporate social responsibility, and agriculture and food security. All papers have followed an empirical approach to address research issues. Part I covers papers related to fiscal policy, monetary policy, and financial integration. Part II deals with issues related to international trade and economic growth. Part III covers topics related to productivity and firm performance, and finally, Part IV covers issues related to agriculture and food security.

In the opening chapter, Nikita Pahwa analyzes the impact of internal and external debt on economic growth in India by employing Auto Regressive Distributed Lag (ARDL) technique of co-integration. The results of the study indicate that there is a negative effect of both internal and external debts on Indian economy. M.R. Anantha Ramu and K. Gayithri by using vector error correction method (VECM) examine the composition of fiscal deficit and its impact on GDP. The results of the study indicate that fiscal deficit is adversely affecting the growth. Amrendra Pandey and Jagadish Shettigar examine the empirical relationship between monetary policy variables and industrial production since the onset of economic reforms in India. The study becomes important in the backdrop of recent changes in the RBI's monetary policy stance to target inflation. Anoop S. Kumar and B. Kamaiah analyze the co-movements of nine Asian Forex markets which include China, India, Hong Kong, Malaysia, Indonesia, Singapore, Japan, Taiwan, Thailand, and South Korea using bilateral exchange rate against US dollar from January 3, 2006, to September 4, 2015. They employ wavelet-based methodology to analyze the extent to which the markets are correlated with each other across different timescales.

The second part of the volume consists of two papers on international trade and growth. Laila Memdani examines the link between economic growth and international trade of various countries and examines how it varies across various income groups. Economic integration within regional trading blocs adds the significant value to increase economic growth, trade, investment, etc. Gurpreet Kaur, Vishal Sarin, and Jasdeep Kaur Dhami explore the empirical relationship between export and GDP for BIMSTEC nations by using time series data over 1997–2015 periods.

The third part of the volume contains four papers related to productivity and firm performance. Mohd Anas Raushan and Ahmed Musa Khan empirically investigate the relationship between the value creation efficiency and financial performance measures of selected Indian business process outsourcing (BPO) and knowledge process outsourcing (KPO) firms. The study finds that intellectual capital efficiency has a significant impact on profitability but not on productivity. Value Added Intellectual Coefficient (VAIC™) method is used to measure the value-based intellectual capital performance of the selected companies. Vasiq Nuvaid, Sucheta Sardar, and Sujoy Chakravarty analyze how spending in CSR is related to the ownership pattern and firm performance in India. By using financial data of 176 BSE-listed firms, authors examine how the ownership structure, firm size, and leverage of a firm affect its CSR expenditure over 2010–2015 periods. Jayashree Patil-Dake analyzes the productivity performance of Indian banks in the post-liberalization era with FDI contents. M. Kollapuri examines whether the acquirer banks are more efficient than the target banks in 16 consolidation deals in Indian banking sector during the period 1995–2013.

The last part consists of three papers on agriculture and food security. Madhabendra Sinha and Partha Pratim Sengupta investigate empirically the causal linkage between movements of foreign exchange rate and agricultural performance in India in terms of production and exports in the post-reform period. This chapter explores the underlying long-term co-integrating relationship between foreign exchange rate and agricultural export in India. Bhabani Prasad Mahapatra and Bhagabata Patro examine the nutritional intake using household data on daily food intake which was collected from the villages in Odisha. They discuss the status of nutritional security at household level. Finally, S. Indrakant examines the dynamics of food grain production in Telangana and estimates the contribution of "increase in area under food grains" and "improvement in technology" to the growth of food grain production in Telangana by using simple decomposition technique. Moreover, the chapter also estimates the influence of important determinants on per capita availability of food grains at state and district levels.

Acknowledgements

We are grateful to all the contributors for timely completion of their manuscripts. We would like to take this opportunity to place on record our gratitude to Prof. K.L. Krishna, Former Director and Professor, Delhi School of Economics, who delivered inaugural address and Dr. C. Rangarajan, Former Chairman, Economic Advisory Council to the Prime Minister, and Former Governor of RBI, who delivered a special address at the conference. In addition, we are particularly grateful to Prof. J. Mahender Reddy, Vice-Chancellor, IFHE, for his continuous motivation for the publication of this volume. We thank The Indian Econometrics Society (TIES), New Delhi, for their collaboration in organizing the conference. Finally, this book project would have been impossible without continuous effort by the team from Springer. We thank all team members.

Hyderabad, India

Bandi Kamaiah
C.S. Shylajan
S. Venkata Seshaiah
M. Aruna
Subhadip Mukherjee

Contents

About the Editors

Dr. Bandi Kamaiah is currently Professor and Dean of School of Economics at University of Hyderabad, India, and President of The Indian Econometric Society (TIES). He has held multiple administrative positions as SAP and ASHIS Coordinator, Head of the Department of Economics at University of Hyderabad. He also served as the Head of RBI Endowment Unit, Institute for Social and Economic Change (ISEC), Bangalore. With 140 research papers in international journals of repute, his areas of research interest are monetary and financial economics, applied time series analysis, macroeconomics, and international finance.

Dr. C.S. Shylajan is Professor and Dean Academics at IBS Hyderabad, India. Prior to this, he was a Post-Doctoral Fellow at Indian Institute of Management (IIM) Calcutta. He was also a Visiting Research Fellow at International Centre for Theoretical Physics (ICTP), Trieste, Italy as part of a Research Program sponsored by UNESCO and Beijer Institute, Sweden. His areas of research interest are international economics, macroeconomics, environmental economics, etc. He was the Consulting Editor of *IUP Journal of Public Finance* during 2006–2012. He is currently Associate Editor of *International Journal of Ecology and Development*.

Dr. S. Venkata Seshaiah is Professor and Director at ICFAI Business School, Hyderabad, India. He was a Consulting Editor for *ICFAI Journal of Applied Economics* and he has also edited several books in the area of economic development. He is also a scientific adviser for many national and international journals. His areas of interest are financial economics, capital markets, business strategy, and behavioral economics.

Dr. M. Aruna is Associate Professor with the Department of Economics at IBS Hyderabad. She obtained her Ph.D. from Osmania University and has received short term fellowship from ICSSR, New Delhi. Her research has been published in journals like *Economic and Finance Review*, *Theoretical Economic Letters*, *Energy Review Studies*, *Indian Journal of Economics and Business Economics*, *Business Economics and Finance Review*, and *Journal of Educational Planning and Administration*.

Dr. Subhadip Mukherjee is Assistant Professor in the Department of Economics, ICFAI Business School Hyderabad. He completed the Fellow Programme in Management (FPM) in Economics from IIM Bangalore. His research has been published in journals such as *Economic Modelling* and also in edited volumes published by Springer. His areas of research interest include international trade, applied econometrics especially with respect to microlevel analysis of firms and industries, and development economics.

Part I
Fiscal Policy, Monetary Policy and Financial Integration

Impact of Debt on Short-Run and Long-Run Growth: Empirical Evidence from India

Nikita Pahwa

Abstract This study tries to analyse the impact of internal and external debt on economic growth in India during the period 1980–2014. Employing ARDL technique of co-integration, the study finds the negative impact of both internal as well as external debt on Indian economy in long run, thereby controlling for other variables namely trade openness, investment and population growth. The results of the error correction model (ECM) show that internal debt, external debt, investment, population growth and trade openness affect the economic growth both in short and long run. The relationship between debt (both internal and external) and economic growth turns out to be negative in long run. However, the short-run impact of internal debt is fluctuating; whereas external debt is negatively related to growth.

Keywords Economic growth · Internal debt · External debt · ARDL bound test approach · India

1 Introduction

1.1 Rationale

Debt and its impact on economic growth has been a very controversial topic in economics. There has been no clear consensus among economist about its effect on economic growth. However, it is agreed by all that fiscal deficit and its refinancing through internal and external debt have consequences on economies. Public debt,

N. Pahwa (✉)
Economics, Mysore University, Bangalore, India
e-mail: nikita.pahwa82@gmail.com

B. Kamaiah et al. (eds.), *Current Issues in Economics and Finance*,
DOI 10.1007/978-981-10-5810-3_1

which is summation of internal[1] and external debt,[2] in case of India, has been a matter of concern for Indian economy. The domestic liabilities (of both the Centre and the State) have increased from 38% of GDP in 1980–1981 to 57% in 1990–1991, to 64% in 2000–2001 and currently these liabilities stood as high as 63% in 2014. The post-reform period of Indian economy witnessed an increase in external borrowings from 9% of GDP in 1980–1981 to 11% of GDP in 1990–1991. It further stayed at 9% in 2000–2001 and has seen a decline to 4% of GDP in 2011.

The overall combined debt of both the Centre and the State, inclusive of both internal and external borrowings has increased at alarming rate in post-reform period as compared to pre reform period.[3] During, 1980–1981, total public debt accounted for 47% of GDP, which increased to a drastic 68% in 1990–1991, and 73% in 2000–2001. The public debt increased to its highest of 83% during 2003–2004, however after the implementation of Fiscal Responsibility Budget Management Act 2004 (FRBMA), an act which focused on getting fiscal deficit under desired limits, the borrowing levels started to decline. In 2011, the overall borrowing stood at 66% of GDP, lower than the last decade, but still higher than the pre-reform period.

1.2 Objective

Among mainstream economists, debt has been considered as a burden on society, which affects investment and growth. Ricardian perspective considers government debt as equivalent to future taxes, which implies neutrality of debt to growth, whereas the Keynesian paradigm, considers debt as a key policy perspective for growth. While the focus of neo-classical and Ricardian equivalence approach is on the long run, the Keynesian approach emphasizes on short-run effects of debt. It is in this regard that public debt has implications for economic growth, and hence this becomes a key policy question.

Many studies have tried to test the hypothesis of effect of debt on economic growth in international context, but Indian evidence seems to be very limited in this regard.

This study differs from all other studies on India (Kannan and Singh 2007; Rangarajan and Srivastava 2005; Singh 1999) as it adds other macroeconomic variables like investment, population growth and trade openness (indicated by the sum of both exports and imports), while estimating the impact of debt on growth.

---

[1]Internal debt mostly consists of borrowing through market loans, treasury bills, special securities issued to Reserve Bank of India (RBI) special bearer bonds, other bonds and securities issued to international financial institutions.

[2]External debt component consists of multilateral and bilateral borrowing, which are concessional and non-concessional and government and non-government further, also includes borrowings from IMF, long-term borrowings, short-term and commercial borrowings.

[3]India adopted reforms of liberalization, globalization and urbanization in 1991.

Second, this study employs advanced time series techniques of autoregressive distributed lag model (ARDL), co-integration approach and post-estimation techniques (CUSUM test, Ramsey RESET test, White test, LM test) to validate the relationship between debt and growth. Third, various recent studies such as by Bal and Rath (2014) have analysed the same relationship between domestic and external debt and economic growth, for latest period, however they have used different control variables as compared to this study.[4] This study has tested the consistency of the model by using various post-diagnostic checks for autocorrelation, heteroskedasticity, omitted variable biasness, functional form of the model as well as structural break, which was not included in the study by Bal and Rath (2014).

The study is subdivided into these further subsections: Sect. 2 provides a detailed literature review on the subject, Sect. 3 provides the details of research methodology, data sources and model specification. Section 4 discusses results and findings, and finally, Sect. 5 concludes the study.

2 Review of Literature

Classical economists Ricardo, Mill, and Smith viewed public debt as a destructive factor for economic growth. In Ricardian view, government debt is equivalent to future taxes (Ricardo 1951; Smith 1937). Hence, the shifts between taxes and deficits do not lead to any wealth effects. An increase in debt does not increase consumption, as consumers are forward looking and they save for future rise in taxes and hence total savings in the economy are not affected. In Ricardian view, an increased private savings matches government dis-saving. Hence, total savings, investments and interest rates remain unchanged in this case, thereby leaving national income unaffected. Buchanan (1958) suggested that debt today is postponement of taxes to future, which leads to a shift in tax burden for future generations. Barro (1978) argues that a shift of taxes to future is not necessarily a burden due to the phenomenon of operative intergenerational transfers (Barro and Sala-i-Martin 2003).

However, according to Keynesian economist, investment saving liquidity preference money supply (IS-LM) theory suggests that an increase in government debt which is induced by deficit financing, eventually increasing the level of income, thereby increasing transaction demand for money and prices. As per Keynesian theory if private investors consider the impact of government securities to be positive on net wealth, the deficit will amplify the private consumption expenditure,

[4]Other control variables included total factor productivity, exports, labour force, investment, debt service. Model by Bal and Rath (2014) differs from the model in this study as they took both external and internal debt in one equation of growth. However, both these debt variables are expected to have a very strong correlation and hence my model has two separate equations to test the impact of each of these debt factors on growth.

transaction demand, interest rates and prices. Expansionary fiscal policy, in this case, ends up strengthening economic growth. On the other hand, monetarist argues that debt has negative impact on economic growth, by raising the interest rates, which eventually crowds out private investment. In addition, debt overhang theory suggests that if future debt gets larger than the repayment capacity of the economy, the expected debt service cost will discourage domestic and foreign investments, which will harm the economic growth.

Many studies have tested the relationship between debt and economic growth. Empirical analysis differs in its results, from country to country. Sheikh et al. (2010), in their study on Pakistan, observed that domestic debt servicing had negative impact on economic growth, as compared to the positive impact of domestic debt on growth. The study applied ordinary least square (OLS) technique for the period 1972–2009. Another country specific study on Nigeria by Adofu and Abula (2010), tested the impact of domestic debt on growth, and concluded that negative relationship exists between the two variables. The study further recommended the government to reduce its outstanding domestic debt in the economy. In a panel of 59 developing countries, for the period 1970–2002, study pointed out the negative relationship between debt and growth. Similarly, Kumar and Woo (2010) studied 38 advanced and emerging economies, during the periods 1970 and 2007, and have concluded inverse relationship between initial debt and economic growth. Qureshi and Ali (2010) found high level of public debt negatively affected the economic growth in Pakistan, during 1981–2008.

Concerning India, very few studies have tried to test the impact of debt on growth. Among few of them such as Singh (1999) explored the relationship between domestic debt and economic growth, by applying co-integration technique and granger causality test for the period of 1959–1995. The study supports the Ricardian equivalence hypothesis for India. However, this study only undertook public debt as function of economic growth. Another study by Barik (2010) extended this analysis by increasing the number of control variables in the main equation of debt on growth. This study also examines the indirect effect of public debt on investment and how it further affects growth. Using the basics of augmented Solow growth model, this study supports the Ricardian equivalence hypothesis for India, for the period 1980–2010. Hence, very limited, but the evidence has proved the relevance of Ricardian equivalence in Indian context. Kannan and Singh (2007) showed the impact of high debt and fiscal deficit on interest rates, output, inflation and the trade balance. Rangarajan and Srivastava (2005) concluded that large interest rates on debt and fiscal deficit adversely affect economic growth. Further, the study established the negative impact of public debt on economic growth.

It is with this spirit, that this study also seeks to ask the similar question of how debt affects growth in Indian economy. This study focuses on individual effect of internal and external debt on growth, controlling for various factors like population growth, investment and trade openness.

3 Research Methodology

3.1 Data Source

This study is considering gross domestic product at market price (GDPmp) as an indicator of economic growth. The data on debt of variables namely internal (INT) and external debt (EXT) were collected from Handbook of Statistics of Indian Economy, by Reserve Bank of India (RBI) (2015–2016). The same dataset also provides the data for total exports and imports[5] of India, with gross fixed capital formation, a measure of investment (INV). All the variables were taken in log form, except population growth, for which population growth (POPGR) is considered in terms of percentage. The data for population numbers were collected from Census of India.

3.2 Model Specification

This paper employs autoregressive distributive lag (ARDL) model or bound testing approach (Pesaran et al 2001), in order to check the existence of short- as well as long-run relationship between internal and external debt with economic growth, controlling for population, investment and trade openness. Bound testing approach or ARDL approach has been applied to this model due to two reasons. First, the time series variables are of mixed order of integration $I(0)$ or $I(1)$, but not $I(2)$. Second, this approach is more suitable for the small and finite sample data like ours. The period of study is from 1980 to 2014, which gives 32 observations for this analysis.

In order to achieve the objective of the current study, the following are the two models for its short- and long-run relationship:

$$\begin{aligned}\text{LnGDPmp} = \beta_0 + \beta_1 \sum_{i=1}^{\rho 1} \text{LnGDPmp}_{t-i} + \beta_2 \sum_{i=0}^{q1} \text{LnINT}_{t-i} \\ + \beta_3 \sum_{i=0}^{q2} \text{LnINV}_{t-i} + \beta_4 \sum_{i=0}^{q3} \text{Popgr}_{t-i} + \beta_5 \sum_{i=0}^{q4} \text{Lnttrade}_{t-i}\end{aligned} \quad (1)$$

$$\begin{aligned}\text{LnGDPmp} = \gamma_0 + \gamma_1 \sum_{i=1}^{\rho 1} \text{LnGDPmp}_{t-i} + \gamma_2 \sum_{i=0}^{q1} \text{LnEXT}_{t-i} \\ + \gamma_3 \sum_{i=0}^{q2} \text{LnINV}_{t-i} + \gamma_4 \sum_{i=0}^{q3} \text{Popgr}_{t-i} + \gamma_5 \sum_{i=0}^{q4} \text{Lnttrade}_{t-i}\end{aligned} \quad (2)$$

[5] Sum of exports and imports is referred as trade openness variable, signified as trade.

The first equation shows the relationship between internal debt and economic growth, controlling for other variables. On the other hand, Eq. 2 mainly tests the relationship between external debts and economic growth, after controlling for other variables. In the above equation, $\rho, q1, q2, q3, q4$ refers to the lag length of respective variables. The AIC criteria are applied to identify the lag length. ARDL model gives the Wald test (F statistics), which helps in identifying the long-run relationship among all the variables. The null and alternate hypotheses are as follows:

$$H_0 = \beta_1 = \beta_2 = \beta_3 = \beta_4 = \beta_5 = 0 \text{ and } H_a \neq \beta_1 \neq \beta_2 \neq \beta_3 \neq \beta_4 \neq \beta_5 \neq 0$$

The computed values of F test statistics are then compared to the critical tabulated values of Narayan (2005). Pesaran et al. (2001) and Narayan (2005). They assumed lower bound critical values are integrated of order zero, whereas the upper bound critical values assumed that explanatory variables are integrated of order one. Hence, if the F statistics is smaller than the lower bound value, the null stated above would not be rejected and the conclusion can be drawn that no long-run relationship exists between variables. However, if the computed F statistics is greater than the upper bound values, existence of long-run relationship among variables is validated. If computed F statistics remains between lower and upper bound values, then the results remain inconclusive.

Once, long-run relationship or co-integration exist, coefficients of the model need to be estimated, which requires running of error correction model (ECM). ECM model provides coefficient for short run as well as long-term relationships, as well as one component of error correction, which describes the speed of adjustment from disequilibrium to equilibrium. ECM models for both the models are presented in Eqs. 3 and 4 below:

$$\begin{aligned} \Delta \mathrm{LnGDPmp} = {} & \alpha_0 + \alpha_i \sum_{i=1}^{\rho 1} \Delta \mathrm{LnGDPmp}_{t-i} + \alpha_j \sum_{j=1}^{q1} \Delta \mathrm{LnINT}_{t-j} \\ & + \alpha_k \sum_{k=1}^{q2} \Delta \mathrm{LnINV}_{t-k} + \alpha_l \sum_{l=1}^{q3} \Delta \mathrm{Popgr}_{t-l} \\ & + \alpha_m \sum_{m=1}^{q4} \mathrm{Lnttrade}_{t-m} + \theta \mathrm{ECM}_{t-1} + \varepsilon_t \end{aligned} \tag{3}$$

$$\begin{aligned}\Delta \text{LnGDPmp} = \delta_0 + \delta_i \sum_{i=1}^{\rho 1} \Delta \text{LnGDPmp}_{t-i} + \delta_j \sum_{j=1}^{q1} \Delta \text{LnEXT}_{t-j} \\ + \delta_k \sum_{k=1}^{q2} \Delta \text{LnINV}_{t-k} + \delta_l \sum_{l=1}^{q3} \Delta \text{Popgr}_{t-l} \\ + \delta_m \sum_{m=1}^{q4} \text{Lnttrade}_{t-m} + \mu \text{ECM}_{t-1} + \varepsilon_t\end{aligned} \quad (4)$$

In the equation above, α_i, α_j, α_k, α_l, α_m and δ_i, δ_j, δ_k, δ_l, δ_m are short-run coefficients. Whereas θ and μ, represents long-term coefficient of speed adjustment, which is expected to be negative and significant.

4 Results and Findings

One of the pre-conditions to go ahead with the ARDL or bound test approach is to check the stationarity of the data. If the order of integration of all the series is $I(1)$ or $I(0)$ or both, bound test can be applied. Applying the unit root test with Augmented Dickey Fuller (ADF) approach as well as Phillips Perron (PP) approach, the following are the results presented in Tables 1 and 2 (Phillips and Perron 1988).

The ADF and PPerron test are conducted at intercept level, intercept with trend as well as at first difference. Internal debt (Lnint) turned out to be stationary at level in Tables 1 and 2, at 1%. Except internal debt all other variables are stationary at first difference. Given we have a mix of $I(0)$ and $I(1)$, bound test or ARDL approach is applied further.

Bound test results or ARDL is required to establish if there exist long-term relationship among variables or not and eventually to estimate the coefficients of long-term series. Table 3 reports the results of bound testing of Eq. 1, as specified earlier. As the F statistics of 6.72 is greater than the upper bound value at 1% (4.92), 5% (3.97) a 10% (3.53) level of significance, we fail to accept the null hypothesis of joint significance of all coefficients to be zero. Hence, it can be concluded that there exists a long-term relationship with internal debt and GDP growth. Furthermore, other variables like population growth, investment and trade openness are also co-integrated with economic growth in India. Similar results of long-run co-integration between external debt with economic growth are represented in Table 4, where the F statistic (12.59) is significantly higher than the upper bound values at 1% (4.92), 5% (3.97) and 10% (3.53) level of significance.

Table 1 Augmented Dickey Fuller (ADF)—at levels and first difference

Variable	At level				At first difference			
	Intercept		Intercept and trend		Intercept		Intercept and trend	
	Coefficient	*p* value	Coefficient	*p* value	Coefficient	*p* value	Coefficient	*p* value
LnGDPmp	0.01	0.99	−0.09	0.87	−0.85	0.00*	−0.98	0.00*
LnInt	−0.02	0.01*	−0.11	0.81	−1.07	0.00*	−1.75	0.00*
LnExt	−0.04	0.35	−0.12	0.79	−1.23	0.00*	−1.29	0.00*
Popgr	−0.04	0.79	−0.33	0.33	−1.07	0.00*	−1.07	0.00*
LnTtrade	0.00	0.99	−0.26	0.22	−0.80	0.00*	−0.84	0.00*
LnInv	0.00	0.98	−0.30	0.21	−1.14	0.00*	−1.17	0.00*

* Values being significant at 1%

Table 2 Phillips Perron test—at level and first difference

Variable	At level				At first difference			
	Intercept		Intercept and trend		Intercept		Intercept and trend	
	Coefficient	*p* value	Coefficient	*p* value	Coefficient	*p* value	Coefficient	*p* value
LnGDPmp	0.01	1.00	−0.094	0.89	−0.85	0.00*	−0.98	0.00*
LnInt	−0.02	0.00*	−0.11	0.85	−1.07	0.00*	−1.29	0.00*
LnExt	−0.03	0.43	−0.12	0.81	−1.23	0.00*	−1.29	0.00*
Popgr	−0.04	0.81	−0.33	0.33	−1.07	0.00*	−1.07	0.00*
LnTtrade	0.00	0.99	−0.26	0.21	−0.80	0.00*	−0.84	0.00*
LnInv	0.00	0.98	−0.30	0.21	−1.14	0.00*	−1.17	0.00*

* Values being significant at 1%

Table 3 Bound test approach results: GDP on internal debt (other control variables: population growth, trade openness, investment)

Level of significance	Critical values		*F* statistics	Co-integration
GDPmp (%)	Lower bound I0	Upper bound I1		
1	3.81	4.92	6.72	Co-integration exist between internal debt and GDP growth in India
5	3.05	3.97		
10	2.68	3.53		

Table 4 Bound test approach results: GDP on internal debt (other control variables: population growth, trade openness, investment)

Level of significance	Critical values		*F* statistics	Co-integration
GDPmp (%)	Lower bound I0	Upper bound I1		
1	3.81	4.92	12.59	Co-integration exist between external debt and GDP growth in India
5	3.05	3.97		
10	2.68	3.53		

In order to obtain the short-run and long-run estimates, the running of error correction mechanism (ECM) is required after the co-integration. The results from ECM Eqs. 3 and 4 are presented in Tables 5 and 6, respectively. The main advantage of ARDL model is that it can estimate both the short-run and long-run coefficients simultaneously. The summary of both the short-run and long-run estimates of effects of internal debt on economic growth are shown in Table 5. The impact of internal debt on growth seems to be fluctuating in short run as immediate short-run debt affects growth negatively; however, the lag variable of debt affects growth positively. This makes sense as while in immediate short-run debt affects markets negatively, it is only after a lag of sometime that the positive impact of the debt seems to be in existence. In addition, the positive impact of borrowing will exist in the case where the debt amount is used for productive purposes of creating assets as well as jobs. However, the long-run implication of higher internal debt is clear and negative. An increase in 1% internal debt decreases the GDP by 0.35% in long run.

Similarly, the impact of population growth is fluctuating, like internal debt. Again the long-run impact is clear, with growth in population affecting GDP positively with coefficient of 0.29%. Investment affects GDP positively in both short and long run, with 1% of increase in investment leading to increase in GDP by 0.17 and 0.20% in growth, in both short and long run, respectively. Trade openness affects growth positively in short-run but long-run implication turns out to be

Table 5 Long-run and short-run estimation (GDP and internal debt)

Regressors	Coefficient	*t* test	*p* value
Short-run estimates			
GDP (−1)	0.44	3.16	0.00*
Internal debt	−0.28	−7.31	0.00*
Internal debt (−1)	0.11	2.78	0.01*
Investment	0.17	8.96	0.00*
Investment (−1)	−0.037	−1.19	0.25
Population growth	0.14	2.53	0.02**
Population growth (−1)	−0.14	−2.62	0.01*
Trade openness	−0.03	−1.33	0.19
Trade openness (−1)	0.10	3.94	0.00*
ECM (−1)	−1.55	−7.27	0.00*
Constant	15.45	7.31	0.00*
Long-run estimates			
Internal debt	−0.35	−10.26	0.00*
Investment	0.20	8.09	0.00*
Population growth	0.29	5.97	0.00*
Trade openness	−0.07	−4.89	0.00*

* and ** Values being significant at 1 and 5%, respectively

Table 6 Long-run and short-run estimation (GDP and external debt)

Regressors	Coefficient	*t* test	*p* value
Short-run estimates			
GDP (−1)	−0.46	−4.56	0.00*
GDP (−2)	−0.87	−7.08	0.00*
External debt	−0.15	−8.28	0.00*
External debt (−1)	−0.10	−4.91	0.00*
External debt (−2)	−0.09	−5.61	0.00*
Investment	0.11	4.97	0.00*
Investment (−1)	−0.10	−3.7	0.00*
Population growth	0.29	0.048	0.00*
Population growth (−1)	−0.11	−2.39	0.03**
Trade openness	0.12	4.39	0.00*
Trade openness (−1)	0.08	3.45	0.00*
ECM (−1)	−0.86	−10.23	0.00*
Constant	4.97	10.37	0.00*
Long run estimates			
External debt	−0.09	−2.27	0.04**
Investment	0.40	3.38	0.00*
Population growth	0.50	5.37	0.00*
Trade openness	0.11	2.31	0.03**

* and ** Values being significant at 1 and 5%, respectively

negative. ARDL model has another advantage that it helps in determining the speed of convergence from disequilibrium to equilibrium, by providing the values for error correction term (ECT). The ECT term as depicted by ECT (−1) is negative (−1.55) and is statistically significant (*p* value 0.00), and this shows evidence of long-run causality from independent variables to the dependent variable. The coefficient is −1.55 and shows very high level of convergence to equilibrium. If there is any disequilibrium in GDP growth, the system adjusts back to the equilibrium at the speed of 155%.

Similar results follow in Table 8 for the regression equation of external debt on economic growth, after controlling for other variables. External debt affects the GDP growth negatively and significantly, both in short run and in long run. An increase in external debt by 1% reduces the GDP by 0.15% in short run and 0.09% in long run.

Impact of investment and population growth on GDP remains fluctuating in short run; however, these variables affect the GDP growth positively in long run. Trade openness affects the GDP growth positively unlike the previous equation of internal debt, in both short run and in long run. The value of ECT is negative (−0.86) as well as significant at 1% level (*p* value 0.00), which indicates a high speed of adjustment from disequilibrium to equilibrium. In case of disequilibrium in GDP growth rate, the system adjusts back to equilibrium at the speed of 86%. In conclusion, external debt affects both short-run as well as long-run scenario of growth in economy, negatively.

4.1 Post-Estimation Diagnostic Check

The post-estimation of ARDL model requires checking the model for the problem of heteroskedasticity, autocorrelation, stability, omitted variables biasness and functional form correctness. The diagnostic tests results for internal debt equation on economic growth are in Table 7. To detect the problem of serial correlation, LM test is used. The value of Chi square turned out to be 0.06%, which is less than 0.10 (at 10% significance) hence we fail to reject the null hypothesis of no autocorrelation. Similar values of LM test statistics for external debt to economic growth equation are provided in Table 8. It validates the evidence for no serial correlation for the second equation. The white test, for heteroskedasticity for both the equations gives the *p* values (0.23 and 0.83) for internal and external debt equation, which are greater than 0.01 (at 1% significance level), thereby concluding that null hypothesis of homoscedasticity cannot be rejected.

For sound regression results, it is important to test the normality of error term, and Jarque–Berais test provides the evidence for the same. Given the *p* values in both the equations (0.52 and 0.46) are greater than 0.01 (at 1% level of significance), the null hypothesis of normality of error term is not accepted.

It is often the case with regression equation, which one fails to identify, is the functional form and omission of some key variable in the analysis. To test the main

Table 7 Diagnostic checking (internal debt on economic growth)

Test statistics	Test statistics	LM version	*F* version	Decision
Serial correlation	LM statistic (1)	CHISQ = 0.06	$F = 1.7$ (0.55)	No serial correlation
Stability test	CUSUM test	Structural break stable	Structural break stable	Stable model
Heteroskedasticity	White test	Obs * R = 15.20 (0.23)	$F = 0.98$ (0.52)	Homoskedasticiy
Normality	Jarque–Bera	CHISQ = 1.28 (0.52)	Not applicable	Normality in error term
Functional form and omitted variable bias test	Ramsey RESET test	$t = 1.28$ (0.22)	$F = 1.58$ (0.22)	Good fit
Test statistics	R^2	0.88	*F* statistic	8.19 (0.00)
	Adjusted R^2	0.77	SE =	0.010
			DW statistic =	2.31

Table 8 Diagnostic checking (external debt on economic growth)

Test statistics	Test statistics	LM version	*F* version	Decision
Serial correlation	LM statistic (1)	CHISQ = 0.06	$F = 3.28$ (0.15)	No serial correlation
Stability test	CUSUM test	Structural break stable	Structural break stable	Stable model
Heteroskedasticity	White test	Obs * R = 11.33 (0.83)	$F = 0.44$ (0.94)	Homoskedasticiy
Normality	Jarque–Bera	CHISQ = 1.54 (0.46)	Not applicable	Normality in error term
Functional form and omitted variable bias test	Ramsey RESET test	$t = 1.03$ (0.32)	$F = 1.07$ (0.32)	Good fit
Test statistics	R^2	0.93	*F* statistic	10.8 (0.00)
	Adjusted R^2	0.84	SE =	0.01
			DW statistic =	2.5

results for these two criteria, this study employs the Ramsey RESET test techniques. In Tables 7 and 8, for both equations of internal and external debt to economic growth, the p value of Ramsey RESET test has been noted to be 0.22 and 0.32, which are significantly higher than 0.01 (significance at 1%). This makes us not to reject the null hypothesis of no misspecification in this case.

Furthermore, the R^2, as well as the adjusted R2 values of both the equations, has turned out to be a decent fit for the model. The variation in GDP growth has been explained by internal debt, population growth, investment and trade openness by 77%, where the external debt, with other dependent variables, explains the variation in GDP by 84%. Applying the CUSUM test for structural stability, checks for the problem of structural break in the data. It provides another way of testing the null hypothesis of co-integration. The statistical plots for both the models are presented below in Figs. 1 and 2, which show the CUSUM plots of the regressions are within the critical range, and hence no structural break in data can be identified.

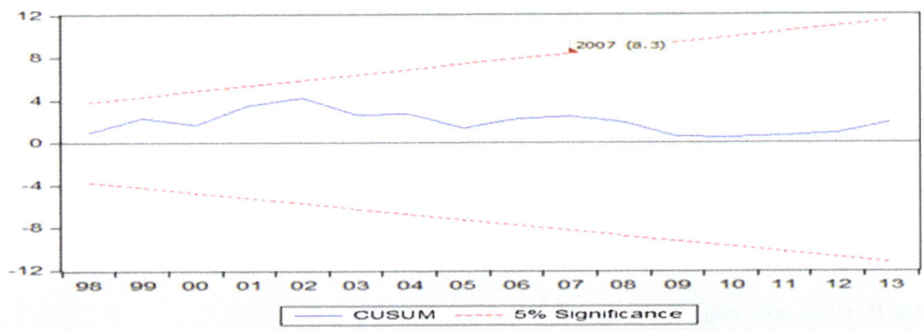

Fig. 1 CUSUM test plot (internal debt to GDP)

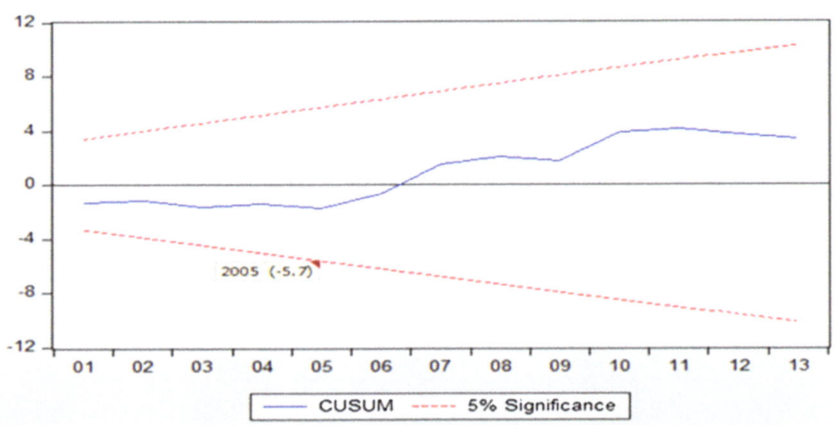

Fig. 2 CUSUM test plot (external debt to GDP). *Note* These are cumulative sum of square for recursive residual, of internal and external debt, on economic growth in India

5 Summary and Conclusion

The purpose of the study is to assess the impact of internal and external debt, separately on economic growth, together with controlling for some other major variables like trade openness, investment and population growth. Conducted for the period from 1980 to 2014, this study employed the ARDL model techniques of times series data. Both the variables of interest, internal as well external debt, turned out to be co-integrated with economic growth of India, both in short run as well as in long run. Both the debt variables are affecting economic growth of the country negatively in long run. Even though, the impact of short-term debt remains fluctuating in short term, the impact of external debt is clearly negative. The conclusion of negative impact of debt on economic growth is in the same line with the various studies conducted for India.

Similarly, these results are not surprising, since most of the government, borrowing and subsequent spending are on consumption expenditure as compared to fewer portions that go for productive capital formation. Furthermore, it is clear from the results of this analysis, that internal debt is more detrimental to economic growth in India as compared to external debt. If higher debt continues, the hypothesis of debt overhang theory might prove to be true for India, whereby if future debt servicing increases beyond country's capacity to pay, the investor's feels discouraged to invest in economy, thereby harming growth subsequently. Given this, Indian economy needs to control the proportion of its debt, in order to avoid negative implications on growth. Another question that is important in the context of the current study is what should be the amount of debt a country can sustain? This requires a detailed sustainability analysis of debt at national and sub-national level, in order to meet the target of fiscal consolidation.

References

Adofu, I., & Abula, M. (2010). Domestic debt and Nigerian economy. *Current Research Journal of Economic Theory*, *2*(1), 22–26.

Bal, D. B., & Rath, B. N. (2014). Public debt and economic growth in India: A reassessment. *Economic Analysis and Policy*, *44*, 292–300.

Barro, R., & Sala-i-Martin, X. (2003). *Economic growth*. Cambridge: MIT Press.

Handbook of Statistics of Indian Economy. (2015–2016). *Reserve Bank of India.*

Kannan, R., & Singh, B. (2007). *Debt-deficit dynamics in India and macroeconomic effect: A structural approach*. Munich Personal RePEc Archive.

Kumar, M. S., & Woo, J. (2010). *Public debt and growth*. IMF working paper WP/10/174.

Narayan, P. K. (2005). The saving and Investment nexus for China: Evidence from co integration tests. *Applied Economics, 37,* 1979–1990.

Pesaran, H. M., Shin, Y., & Smith, R. J. (2001). Bound test approaches to the analysis of level relationships. *Journal Applied Econometrics, 16,* 289–326.

Phillips, P. C., & Perron, P. (1988). Testing for unit root in the time series regression. *Biometrika, 75*(2), 335–346.

Qureshi, M. N., & Ali, K. (2010). Public debt and economic growth: Evidence from Pakistan. *International Research Journal of Finance and Economics, 53,* 100–108.
Rangarajan, C., & Srivastava, D. K. (2005). Fiscal deficits and government debt, implications for growth and stability. Special articles. *Economic and Political Weekly.*
Ricardo, D. (1951). *On the principles of political economy and taxation. The works and correspondence of David Ricardo*. Cambridge: Cambridge University Press with collaboration of M.Dobb.
Sheikh, M. R., Faridi, M. Z., & Tariq, K. (2010). Domestic debt and economic growth in Pakistan: An empirical analysis. *Pakistan Journal of Social Science*, *30*(2), 373–387.
Singh, C. (1999). Domestic debt and economic growth in India. *Economic and Political Weekly, 34*(23), 1445–1453.
Smith, A. (1937). *The wealth of nations*. New York: Random House.

Fiscal Deficit and Economic Growth Relationship in India: A Time Series Econometric Analysis

M.R. Anantha Ramu and K. Gayithri

Abstract High and persistent level of fiscal deficit is one of the major macroeconomic problems in India ever since mid-1980s. Fiscal consolidation is on the forefront of policy discussion since early 1990s to present day context. However, the actual administrative measure to control fiscal deficits in India took place in the year 2003 with enactment of Fiscal Responsibility and Budget Management (FRBM) Act and it brought into force in April 2004. The rationale behind keeping fiscal deficits under control is its adverse effect on macroeconomy and particularly the economic growth. On the one hand, the monetary policy makers in India (Reserve Bank of India) argue that higher fiscal deficits will impede the economic growth and hence requires a control. On the other hand, the fiscal policy makers (Ministry of Finance) argue that deficit spending is indispensable to augment the economic growth. Hence, there exists a puzzle that how fiscal deficit is affecting GDP in India. This paper tries to answer the puzzle by taking up a long-term time series analysis starting from the period 1980–1981 to 2015–2016. By adopting a vector error correction method (VECM), this paper proves that fiscal deficit is adversely affecting the GDP growth and therefore requires a strict control. Based on very few existing literature, paper also argues that if fiscal deficit money spent on capital formation purpose, it promotes growth and hence supports 'Golden Rule' of public finance.

Keywords Fiscal deficit · Economic growth · VEC

JEL Classification E62 · O40 · C32

This chapter has been significantly drawn from ISEC Working Paper, No-367 and MPRA Paper, No-76304 written by the same authors.

M.R.A. Ramu (✉) · K. Gayithri
Centre for Economic Studies and Policy (CESP), Institute for Social and Economic Change (ISEC), Bangalore 560072, India
e-mail: anantharamu.m.r@gmail.com

K. Gayithri
e-mail: gayithri@isec.ac.in

B. Kamaiah et al. (eds.), *Current Issues in Economics and Finance*,
DOI 10.1007/978-981-10-5810-3_2

High level of fiscal deficit is a major macroeconomic problem in India facing by central government and also several state governments. Since early 1990s to present day context, fiscal consolidation is on the forefront of policy discussions in India. However, the actual administrative measure to control fiscal deficits took place in the year 2003 with the enactment of Fiscal Responsibility and Budget Management (FRBM) Act and came into force in April 2004. It has been always argued that higher deficits would adversely affect the macroeconomic stability and hence it should be kept under the control. However, the literature consisting fiscal deficit's relation with macroeconomic variables like economic growth, interest rate, inflation and current account deficit provides mixed evidence. Many studies by Reserve Bank of India (RBI) found that fiscal deficit is the major factor behind persistent and high inflation in India and it was found to be adversely affecting economic growth (RBI 2012; Khundrakpam et al. 2010). However, the central government argues that deficit spending is required to boost the economy.

The relationship between fiscal deficit and economic growth is one of the highly debated issues in the economic literature. However, there is no conclusive evidence in this regard. Theoretically, there exist different perceptions on fiscal deficit and economic growth relationship. As per neo-classical theory, fiscal deficit will adversely affect the economic growth; whereas Keynesian economists argue that deficit spending is required to use the existing unutilised services. Contrary to these theories, Ricardian equivalence negates any such relationship between fiscal deficit and economic growth. Even the existing empirical literature has different conclusions on this relationship. Indian empirical evidences are not exception in this regard. Hence, there is a need for analysing the relation between fiscal deficit and GDP growth on a long-run perspective. This paper makes an attempt to fill the gap in literature by analysing the relationship between fiscal deficit and GDP growth in India over the last 36 years, starting from the period 1980–1981 to 2015–2016.

The paper is organised as follows. Section 1 provides theoretical background to the paper. In Sect. 2, a brief review of available literature is provided. Data and methodological aspects are elaborated in Sect. 3. Obtained results are discussed in Sect. 4 and Sect. 5 concludes with some policy suggestions.

1 Theoretical Background

The text book version of national income identity indicates that total output is summation of four important macroeconomic variables namely, private consumption, government consumption, investment and net exports. The national identity is as follows:

$$Y = C + G + I + (X - M),$$

where Y is total output (gross domestic product or national income), C is consumption expenditure, G is government consumption, I is the investment (gross capital formation), X is exports and M is the imports. From the simple national income identity, it is evident that a rise in 'G' should result in an increase in the national income. However, it depends on how government money is being spent. Government's spending on capital formation is covered under 'I'. The logic of government spending pass through is straightforward. Increase in overall spending by the government, keeping taxes constant, creates employment opportunities and which in turn raises the income level of people and finally results in output rise.

Different schools of economic thought have varied perceptions on the relationship between fiscal deficit and economic growth. The neo-classical theory argues that government dis-savings caused by deficit in budget will have a detrimental effect on economic growth. Increase in government borrowing pushes the interest rate upwards. Higher interest rate adversely affects the private investment and which in turn retards the economic growth rate. High external borrowings to fill the investment gap will adversely affect the exchange rate and trade account by ultimately retarding the economic growth.

As per Keynesian perspective, the government expenditure will have the multiplier effect on the output and employment. Increased government spending will augment the aggregate demand in the economy, which enhances the profitability of private investment and positively affects the economic growth. According to Keynes, deficit spending is necessary when economy is under recessionary conditions in depression. Many policy makers in developing countries argue that deficit financing would be an effective tool to promote economic growth given the large amount of underutilised resources (Nelson and Singh 1994).

Standing apart from the aforementioned theories completely, Ricardo argued that, fiscal deficits are viewed as neutral in terms of their impact on economic growth. In Ricardian perspective, the financing of budget by deficit amount is done only to postpone taxes. The deficit in any current period is exactly equal to the present value of future taxation that is required to pay off the increment to debt resulting from the deficit (Rangarajan and Srivatsava 2005). In other words, government spending must be paid for, whether now or later, and the present value of spending must be equal to the present value of tax and non-tax revenues. The concept of fiscal deficit is irrelevant in the Ricardian perspective.

Basically, above three theories have different perceptions on relationship between fiscal deficit and economic growth.

2 Literature Review

The literature review section is divided into two major heads: first, determinants of economic growth and second, fiscal deficit and economic growth. In the first head, the review has covered major literature analysing the determinants of economic growth. Second head consists literature on fiscal deficit and economic growth relationship. The review covers international as well as Indian literature on the mentioned heads.

2.1 Determinants of Economic Growth

The theoretical and empirical literature on factors determining growth was well captured in a study by Stern (1991). The author found that capital accumulation, human capital, research, and development, innovation, management and organisation and infrastructure are the major determinants of growth. Stern (1991) further argued that there is a high potential for the government action in the growth process.

A classic paper by Barro and Sala-i-Martin (1995) was one of the highly quoted papers in the economic growth literature. In a cross-section analysis on 48 US states, they found that male schooling, life expectancy, human capital, education spending, investment ratio and terms of trade were having significant positive relation with economic growth. Whereas other variables like government consumption, political instability and black market premium found to be adversely affecting economic growth. In a panel regression analysis on 100 countries Barro (1996) proved that human capital, rule of law, terms of trade and investment ratio were playing a significant role in promoting growth whereas inflation and government consumption excluding defence and education spending having negative relation with economic growth. Mankiw et al. (1992) by challenging the endogenous growth model and using augmented Solow type growth model argued that both physical and human capital variables are having significant relation with economic growth. In general, they found that Solow model is consistent with the international evidence if one acknowledges the importance of human as well as physical capital.

In a disaggregated analysis on Chinese economy using cross-sectional data, Chen and Feng (2000) investigate the determinants of growth variations in provinces of China. Variables such as higher education enrolment ratio, industrialisation and investment have showed a positive relation where as other variables such as birth rate, inflation and state owned enterprises moved negatively with GDP growth rate.

Basically, these major literatures depicted that investment, trade and human capital are having significant positive effect on economic growth and inflation, government consumption expenditure, etc., have a deterring effect on growth.

2.2 *Fiscal Deficit and Growth*

Martin and Fardmanesh (1990) examined the impact of different fiscal variables on economic growth for the cross section of 76 developed and developing countries for the period 1972–1981. Along with fiscal deficit they included government expenditure, revenue, non-tax revenue, gross capital formation and population growth. Using cross-sectional linear regression model, it was found that deficit and tax revenue have negative relation with growth, whereas the total expenditure is positively related. However, the sign of total expenditure reverses when they included deficit variable along with the total expenditure. By dividing the countries into low-, middle- and high-income categories they found that the negative relation between deficit and growth holds only for the middle-income countries but not for other two categories (Martin and Fardmanesh 1990). The result seems to be contradictory here because low- and middle-income countries require more government spending in order to utilise the existing unutilised resources.

With the emergence of Keynesian economics, deficit financing concept has become prominent. Keynesian theory argued that deficit spending is required to promote economic growth. However, other mainstream theories such as neo-classical theory argued that fiscal deficits adversely affect economic growth. In order to test the relationship empirically, Nelson and Singh (1994) analysed the deficit growth connection for 70 developing countries using cross-section regression. Author framed the model based on major theories existing on growth and development literature and tested the 'expanding public-sector economic-decline' hypothesis. They found that deficit coefficient even though negative was insignificant indicating no relation with growth rate, and even public investment was found to be insignificant. Revenue, inflation showed negative relation where as other variables were significant and had positive relation with economic growth. However, the ambiguity arises when the capital investment, which is a part of the government expenditure is seemed to be adversely affecting the growth and it requires a proper investigation. In a panel regression analysis, Adam and Bevan (2005) examined relationship between fiscal deficit and economic growth for 45 countries over the period 1970–1999. Government budget variables and other control variables were included in the model. Results were quite interesting. The values of deficit which is less than or equal to 1.5% of GDP was found to be growth enhancing whereas deficit above that threshold level was found to be growth retarding. Seigniorage financing of deficit followed the same result. Debt financing of deficit was found to be having negative effects on per capita growth irrespective of the threshold level. By replacing expenditure for deficit they found that productive expenditure having significant positive relation with economic growth and residual expenditure was having a negative relationship.

Taylor et al. (2012) examined the relationship among fiscal deficit, debt and economic growth for the US economy. Using quarterly data for the period 1961–2011, and adopting VEC method, it was found that primary fiscal deficit has significant and positive effect on economic growth. They found that higher debt affects growth adversely but causality result proved that higher debt-GDP ratio is only the consequence but not the cause of low economic growth. Further, they found that the total expenditure is having a positive relation with GDP whereas tax revenue moved in opposite direction. Authors strongly argue that deficit spending is necessary, particularly in the recession time as it stimulates the economy. Another study by Ferreira and Araujo (2008) on Brazil economy proved that if the deficit money is spent on infrastructure building it will have positive effect on the growth in the long run.

Khundrakpam (2003) has analysed the dynamic interaction between the public sector expenditure and national income for the period from 1960–1961 to 1996–1997 on India. Author tested two major propositions on the relationship between economic growth and government expenditure namely: Wagner's Law of increasing state activity and Keynesian proposition. Former states that higher the output, the higher will be the spending and latter proves the other way round. The long-run coefficients indicated that public sector expenditure, total or the consumption component, have a long-run positive impact on national income. A rise in the share of public sector expenditure in national income leads to a decline in both the national income and its per capita income. Irrespective of the specification, investment in the long run has positively impacted income growth. However, there was no evidence found on Wagner's law in the Indian context. Rather, the relationship between public sector expenditure and national income in India works in the Keynesian fashion. Fiscal deficit is major concern for many of state governments in India. A study on Maharashtra state by Karnik (2002) proved that fiscal deficit and revenue deficit variables both had a negative effect on the growth of state domestic product.

The empirical evidences on the relationship between fiscal deficit and GDP growth are mixed. It was also observed that, in the Indian context, there is no detailed study to examine the relationship between fiscal deficit and economic growth in the long run. Methodologically also this study adopts advanced econometric time series techniques such as vector error correction method. This paper tries to solve the puzzle in the Indian context at a macro level using annual time series data.

3 Data, Variables and Methodology

Trends in deficit indicators and GDP growth is depicted in Fig. 1. The deficit indicators are combined centre and state government fiscal deficits and revenue deficits as percentage of GDP. Growth variable is the growth rate of real GDP at market prices.

Fiscal deficit is almost at a higher rate since 1980s and it reached peak in the early 2000. Revenue deficit which was at a better position in early 1980s started rising in late 1980s and reached a peak level in early 2000. GDP growth is quite fluctuating and a drastic fall can be seen in early 1990s, however, it revived later on.

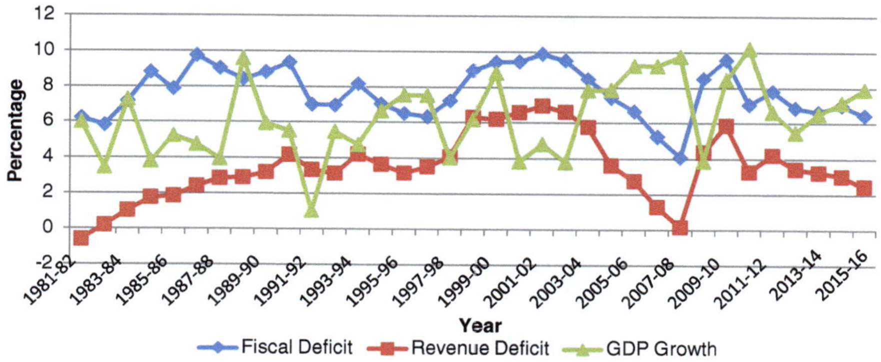

Fig. 1 Trends in deficit indicators and GDP (in %). *Source* RBI Database on Indian Economy (2017)

The government of India enacted FRBM Act in 2003 to control the higher deficits. After the enactment, deficit indicators started behaving well and reached lowest level in 2008. The GDP growth almost reached double digit in that year. However, global financial crisis in late 2008 and general election in the year 2009 made the situation worse again. Presently, Indian government is trying to bring the deficit level to a manageable level by 2017–2018 and putting in efforts to revive the growth. Except for the years in early 1980s, 1990s and also between 1997–1998 and 2000, the inverse relationship can be seen between these two aforementioned variables. The movement of deficit and growth is almost in line with mainstream neo-classical argument.

Considering one variable in growth terms and other variables as percent of GDP may not reveal the true picture of the movement among the variables. In order to capture the movement properly, growth rate of all the three variables namely GDP, fiscal deficit and revenue deficit is considered. The growth of three variables is provided in Table 1. The movement is captured under five different phases and these five different phases are selected based on major policy reforms took place in India particularly from the fiscal policy side. Phase-I is pre-economic reform period and phase-II is post economic reform period. Phase-III is pre FRBM period and in the same period the fiscal deficit and revenue deficit reached its peak level. Fourth phase is the FRBM era and in that period fiscal variables were well under control. The last phase covers the period since 2008 global financial crisis to 2015–2016. However, even from Table 1, the trend is not much clear except for the last two phases where GDP growth and deficit growth move inversely. Hence, we have attempted to capture the behaviour of GDP and fiscal variables over thirty six years using suitable econometric technique.

The purpose of this paper is to find how fiscal deficit is behaving with the economic growth in India. The time period of the study is from 1980–1981 to 2015–2016. As the analysis is limited only to Indian economy at an aggregated level, the time series econometric technique is used for the empirical examination

Table 1 Growth rate of GDP, fiscal deficit and revenue deficit (in %)

Phases	Time period	GDP	FD	RD
I	1980–1981 to 1990–1991	5.57	9.14	22.17
II	1991–1992 to 1996–1997	5.51	−0.16	4.31
III	1997–1998 to 2003–2004	5.62	10.73	15
IV	2004–2005 to 2007–2008	9.06	−8.91	−45.03
V	2008–2009 to 2015–2016	7.05	18.17	277.6

Source RBI Database on Indian Economy (2017)

considering annual data series. The variables for the analysis have been chosen based on theoretical and empirical background. Theoretically, there is an argument that neo-classical theory did not leave much role for fiscal policy but the recent endogenous growth framework had given a fundamental role for the government in affecting the long-term growth performance of any country (Tanzi and Zee 1997). This paper adopts the analytical framework provided by Khundrakpam (2003) with few modifications in variable selection. For the empirical analysis, this paper adopts vector error correction model under the time series technique. Variables included in the model are as follows:

1. Real GDP at market price (GDP): The main intention of this paper is to assess the impact of fiscal deficit on the economic growth rate. However, there will be little variation when we consider growth rate per se that too under the annual data series. Hence in the analysis real GDP at market prices considered as dependent variable, so that the variation can be captured thoroughly.

   Fiscal variables:

2. Tax revenue (TaxRev): Tax revenue receipts of central and state governments.
3. Gross fiscal deficit (GFD): Combined fiscal deficit of centre and state governments. Fiscal deficit is the difference between total expenditure and revenue receipts and non-debt type capital receipts.

   Other variables:

4. Private investment (Inv): Gross capital formation by private sector which includes private corporate sector and household sector.
5. Exchange rate (Exch): It is the nominal exchange rate between Indian rupee and US dollar. This variable is included in order to capture the external sectors effect on growth. Theoretically, it is argued that higher exchange rate results in lowering the value of domestic currency in front of foreign currency. It is expected that higher exchange rate will adversely affects the net exports and it ultimately affects the GDP growth.

Three time dummies namely dummy 1991, dummy 2004 and dummy 2009 have been used in the analysis exogenously to control for the effects of any structural break if it exists.[1] The year 1991 is land mark in Indian economic history as the major economic reforms took place in the same year. In the field of public finance, year 2004 is a prominent year. Government of India enacted FRBM act in 2003 and in order to capture its effect, year 2004 dummy is used in the analysis. The year 2009 dummy is used to capture the effect of recent global financial crisis. However, these dummies will be included in the model if they found to be significant.

A summary descriptive statistics of the variables used in the model is provided in Table 2.

The time series analysis expects the data to be stationary in nature and hence it is important to check whether the data considered are having unit root or not. The Phillips–Perron unit root test is performed for checking the same. The Phillips–Perron unit root test (see Table 3) indicates that all the variables contain unit root and become stationary in the first difference. Hence, the variables considered in the model are $I(1)$ in nature.[2]

As the data indicates all the variables are $I(1)$ in its nature. It is important to check whether there exists a long-run cointegration relation among the non-stationary data or not. The conventional method of testing cointegration was proposed by Engle and Granger (1987). However, this method has several limitations as it does not indicate the number of cointegrating vectors when there are more than two variables. Phillips and Hansen (1990) developed fully modified ordinary least square (FM-OLS) approach to cointegration by including correction factors for endogeneity and serial correlation problems, which existed in the traditional method. As these are single equation methods, the results depend on what variable are used for normalisation of the cointegration relationship (Maddala and Kim 1998). In order to overcome these problems, the system method of cointegration will be used in the present analysis as it enables us to see how many cointegrating vectors are present among the variables and also, the problem of normalisation will not appear. The bi-directional causality will be taken care of and all the variables are treated as endogenous in the system method. Hence, in order to check the existence of cointegration, the method proposed by Johansen and Juselius (1990) has been used here, which overcomes the aforementioned problems like normalisation and others. Johansen cointegration method has two tests to check cointegration; they are λ_{trace} and λ_{max}.

Johansen (1988) procedure relies heavily on relationship between the rank of a matrix and its characteristic roots. Johansen procedure is nothing more than a multivariate generalisation of Dickey Fuller (DF) test. The equation can be written as

[1]Properly specified dummies do not affect asymptotic null distributions (Luktepohl 2004: 116).

[2]The result is same even with battery of unit root tests like ADF test, NG Perron test and KPSS unit root test.

Table 2 Descriptive statistics (in rupees billion)

Variables	Mean	Median	Max	Min	SD	Skewness	Kurtosis
GDP	44,078	34,099	113,575.3	13,435.67	28,949	0.93	2.70
GFD	3311.04	2558.5	7402.741	859.1987	2058.6	0.76	2.28
TAXREV	6996.3	4634.97	194,13.8	1830	5048.5	1.005	2.75
PRIINV	9450.22	5862.86	260,86.24	1229.261	8355	0.80	2.09
EXCH[a]	34.33	38.70	65.46	7.90	16.98	−0.16	1.83

Data Source RBI DBIE (2017) and CSO
[a]Exchange rate is the rate of exchange between Indian rupee and US dollar (absolute number in rupees against US dollar, not in rupees billion)

Table 3 Phillips–Perron unit root test

Variables	Level	First difference
ln(GDP)	4.95	−4.82*
ln(GFD)	−0.75	−6.18*
ln(tax revenue)	0.81	−4.87*
ln(private inv.)	−0.76	−9.16*
Exch	−0.02	−4.69*

*Significant at 1% level; **significant at 5% level; ***significant at 10% level

$$y_t = A_1 y_{t-1} + \varepsilon_t \tag{1}$$

So that

$$\begin{aligned}\Delta y_t &= A_1 y_{t-1} - y_{t-1} + \varepsilon_t \\ &= (A_1 - I) y_{t-1} + \varepsilon_t\end{aligned} \tag{2}$$

$$\Delta y_t = \prod y_{t-1} + \varepsilon_t, \tag{3}$$

where

y_t and ε_t are $(n \times 1)$ vectors
A_1 = an $(n \times n)$ matrix of parameters
I = an $(n \times n)$ identity matrix
$\Pi = (A_1 - I)$

The rank of $(A_1 - I)$ equals number of cointegrating vectors. The equation can be modified to allow for the presence of a drift term.

$$\Delta y_t = A_0 + \prod y_{t-1} + \varepsilon_t \tag{4}$$

where $A_0 = (n \times 1)$ vector of constants.

In line with Augmented Dickey Fuller test, multivariate model can also be generalised to allow for a higher order autoregressive process.

$$\Delta y_t = \prod y_{t-1} + \sum_{i=1}^{p-1} \prod\nolimits_i \Delta y_{t-i} + \varepsilon_t \quad (5)$$

where $\prod = -\left(I - \sum_{i=1}^{p} A_i\right)$ and $\prod_i = -\sum_{j=i+1}^{p} A_J$

If rank $(\Pi) = 0$, matrix is null. If 'Π' is of rank 'n' the vector process is stationary. If rank $(\Pi) = 1$, there is single cointegration vector. If rank is 1 < rank (Π) < n, then there are multiple cointegrating vectors. The rank of matrix is equal to the number of its characteristic roots that differ from zero. If matrix Π obtained and ordered on characteristic roots such that $\lambda_1 > \lambda_2 > \cdots > \lambda_n$, and if the variables in y_t are not cointegrated, the rank of Π will be zero and all of these characteristic roots will equal zero. To test whether the number of characteristic roots that are significantly different from unity or not, Johansen (1988) have provided two test statistics namely λ_{trace} and $\lambda_{\max}$.

$$\lambda_{\text{trace}}(r) = -T \sum_{i=r+1}^{n} \ln(1 - \hat{\lambda}_i),$$

$$\lambda_{\max}(r, r+1) = -T \ln(1 - \hat{\lambda}_{r+1}),$$

where

$\hat{\lambda}_i$ the estimated values of the characteristic roots obtained from the estimated Π matrix.

T number of usable observations.

λ_{trace} tests the null hypothesis that the number of distinct cointegrating vectors is less than or equal to 'r' against the general alternative. $\lambda_{\max}$ tests the null that number of cointegrating vectors is 'r' against the alternative of '$r+1$' cointegrating vectors. If the estimated value of characteristic root is close to zero, $\lambda_{\max}$ will be small. The results obtained using Johansen's method are provided in Table 4.

The result indicates that there exists a cointegration relationship among the variables in all the models selected. Both λ_{trace} and $\lambda_{\max}$ tests confirm the existence of one cointegration relation. After confirming the existence of cointegration relation, we can proceed with the vector error correction (VEC) model for estimating long run and short run relationship among the variables. The estimation procedure of the VEC model is depicted below.

The long run equation of the model is in the following form:

$$\ln \text{GDP}_t = \beta_{10} + \beta_{11} \ln \text{GFD}_t + \beta_{12} \ln \text{TaxRev}_t + \beta_{13} \ln \text{PriInv}_t + \beta_{14}\text{Exch} + e_t \quad (6)$$

Table 4 Johansen cointegration test results

Trend assumption: linear deterministic trend					
Lag order	Hypothesised no of C-Eqns.	Trace stats.	*p* value	Max eigenvalue	*p* value
1, 2	None	118.02	0.0001[a]	62.91	0.000[a]
	At most 1	55.10	0.21	23.20	0.40
	At most 2	31.90	0.39	14.02	0.72

[a]Denotes rejection of hypothesis at 5% level

GDP is normalised to be one in the long run equation. If a variable is a part of cointegration equation with non-zero coefficient, which may thus be normalised to one (Lutkepohl 2004). The next step is to test whether the obtained error is stationary at levels or not. If it is stationary then we can conclude that the variables are cointegrated. However, it has been already proved here with the help of Johansen's method that the data is cointegrated.

The next step is to estimate the error correction model and the model will be as follows:

$$\begin{aligned}\Delta \ln \mathrm{GDP}_t = {} & \alpha_{10} + \alpha_{11}[\ln \mathrm{GDP}_{t-1} - b_{11} \ln \mathrm{GFD}_{t-1} - b_{12} \ln \mathrm{TaxRev}_{t-1} \\ & - b_{13} \ln \mathrm{PriInv}_{t-1} - b_{14} \mathrm{Exch}_{t-1}] \\ & + \gamma_{11} \Delta \ln \mathrm{GDP}_{t-i} + \gamma_{12} \Delta \ln \mathrm{GFD}_{t-i} + \gamma_{13} \Delta \ln \mathrm{TaxRev}_{t-i} \\ & + \gamma_{14} \Delta \ln \mathrm{PriInv}_{t-i} + \gamma_{15} \Delta \mathrm{Exch}_{t-i} + \varepsilon_{1t}\end{aligned} \tag{7}$$

$$\begin{aligned}\Delta \ln \mathrm{GFD}_t = {} & \alpha_{20} + \alpha_{21}[\ln \mathrm{GDP}_{t-1} - b_{21} \ln \mathrm{GFD}_{t-1} - b_{22} \ln \mathrm{TaxRev}_{t-1} \\ & - b_{23} \ln \mathrm{PriInv}_{t-1} - b_{24} \mathrm{Exch}_{t-1}] \\ & + \gamma_{21} \Delta \ln \mathrm{GDP}_{t-i} + \gamma_{22} \Delta \ln \mathrm{GFD}_{t-i} + \gamma_{23} \Delta \ln \mathrm{TaxRev}_{t-i} \\ & + \gamma_{24} \Delta \ln \mathrm{PriInv}_{t-i} + \gamma_{25} \Delta \mathrm{Exch}_{t-i} + \varepsilon_{2t}\end{aligned} \tag{8}$$

$$\begin{aligned}\Delta \ln \mathrm{TaxRev}_t = {} & \alpha_{30} + \alpha_{31}[\ln \mathrm{GDP}_{t-1} - b_{31} \ln \mathrm{GFD}_{t-1} - b_{32} \ln \mathrm{TaxRev}_{t-1} \\ & - b_{33} \ln \mathrm{PriInv}_{t-1} - b_{34} \mathrm{Exch}_{t-1}] \\ & + \gamma_{31} \Delta \ln \mathrm{GDP}_{t-i} + \gamma_{32} \Delta \ln \mathrm{GFD}_{t-i} + \gamma_{33} \Delta \ln \mathrm{TaxRev}_{t-i} \\ & + \gamma_{34} \Delta \ln \mathrm{PriInv}_{t-i} + \gamma_{35} \Delta \mathrm{Exch}_{t-i} + \varepsilon_{3t}.\end{aligned} \tag{9}$$

$$\begin{aligned}\Delta \mathrm{PriInv}_t = {} & \alpha_{40} + \alpha_{41}[\ln \mathrm{GDP}_{t-1} - b_{41} \ln \mathrm{GFD}_{t-1} - b_{42} \ln \mathrm{TaxRev}_{t-1} \\ & - b_{43} \ln \mathrm{PriInv}_{t-1} - b_{44} \mathrm{Exch}_{t-1}] \\ & + \gamma_{41} \Delta \ln \mathrm{GDP}_{t-i} + \gamma_{42} \Delta \ln \mathrm{GFD}_{t-i} + \gamma_{43} \Delta \ln \mathrm{TaxRev}_{t-i} \\ & + \gamma_{44} \Delta \ln \mathrm{PriInv}_{t-i} + \gamma_{45} \Delta \mathrm{Exch}_{t-i} + \varepsilon_{4t}\end{aligned} \tag{10}$$

$$\begin{aligned}\Delta \text{Exch}_t = \alpha_{50} + \alpha_{51}[&\ln \text{GDP}_{t-1} - b_{51} \ln \text{GFD}_{t-1} - b_{52} \ln \text{TaxRev}_{t-1} \\ &- b_{53} \ln \text{PriInv}_{t-1} - b_{54}\text{Exch}_{t-1}] \\ &+ \gamma_{51}\Delta \ln \text{GDP}_{t-i} + \gamma_{52}\Delta \ln \text{GFD}_{t-i} + \gamma_{53}\Delta \ln \text{TaxRev}_{t-i} \\ &+ \gamma_{54}\Delta \ln \text{PriInv}_{t-i} + \gamma_{55}\Delta \text{Exch}_{t-i} + \varepsilon_{5t}\end{aligned} \tag{11}$$

The coefficients α_{11} α_{21} α_{31} α_{41} α_{51} indicate the speed of adjustment to equilibrium and its corresponding value in the bracket is the error correction term. These coefficients must be significantly different from zero if the variables are cointegrated and estimates of these coefficients must not be too large. The γ coefficients indicate the short-term relation. Two lags have been included in the model. As the data is annual, it is expected that impact will be well captured with a lag of two. Taking more lags will lead to loss of degrees of freedom.

4 Result Discussion

The long-term and short-term estimates of VEC model are provided in Table 5. The first part of the table consists of long-term estimates and second part has short-term estimates. R^2 value is high. The LM test result indicates that there is no serial correlation among the error terms, it is homoscedastic and normal. The stability tests (see Appendix 2) indicate that the model is stable and results are reliable.

The long-run estimates suggest that fiscal deficit is having significant negative relation with the GDP. The coefficient value signifies that a 1% increase in fiscal deficit reduces the GDP by 0.31%. This result supports the neo-classical argument. The private investment is significant and positive. A 1% increase in the private investment leads to a 0.87% increase in the GDP. High and significant coefficient value implies the need for high capital investment by the private sector for enhancing the economic growth. It is expected that higher taxes will adversely affect the GDP through private investment channel. One percent increase in the taxes reduces GDP by 0.4%. Higher taxes reduce the private investments and in turn the GDP. Exchange rate is significantly affecting the GDP. A rise in the nominal exchange rate (which measures the depreciation of Rupee) increases GDP by 0.17%. Depreciation of rupee makes Indian goods cheaper in the international market and therefore having a significant and positive impact on trade balance and consequently on the output.

In the short run, the error correction term is negative and significant. It confirms the cointegration among the variables and proves that nearly 9% of the disequilibrium is corrected in a year. Even though insignificant, private investment is having a positive relationship with GDP in both the lags. The relationship between fiscal deficit and GDP in the short run is found to be insignificant. Tax revenue is having a negative relationship with GDP in short term. There is no significant short run relationship is found between exchange rate and GDP. Moreover, the dummy

Table 5 Results—VEC estimates

Long-term estimates[a]

Cointegration Eqn-1:

$$\mathrm{LnGDP} = \underset{[-5.55]}{-0.31\ \mathrm{lnGFD}(-1)} + \underset{[6.59]}{0.87\ \ln \mathrm{PriInv}(-1)} - \underset{[-2.07]}{0.40\ \mathrm{lnTaxRev}(-1)} + \underset{[7.18]}{0.17\ \mathrm{Exch}} + 4.10\ \mathrm{C}$$

Short-term estimates[a]

$$\begin{aligned}\Delta\mathrm{lnGDP} = &\underset{[-2.30]}{-0.09\ \mathrm{ECM}} - \underset{[-1.18]}{0.28\Delta\mathrm{lnGDP}(-1)} + \underset{[0.19]}{0.04\Delta\mathrm{lnGDP}(-2)}\\ &+ \underset{[0.14]}{0.05\Delta\mathrm{lnPriInv}(-1)} + \underset{[1.08]}{0.03\Delta\mathrm{lnPriInv}}\\ &- \underset{[0.20]}{0.004\Delta\mathrm{lnGFD}(-1)} + \underset{[0.79]}{0.01\Delta\mathrm{lnGFD}(-2)}\\ &- \underset{[-1.30]}{0.13\Delta\mathrm{lnTaxRev}(-1)} - \underset{[-2.63]}{0.26\Delta\mathrm{lnTaxRev}(-2)} + \underset{[0.16]}{0.02\Delta\mathrm{Exch}(-1)}\\ &- \underset{[-1.09]}{0.17\Delta\mathrm{Exch}} + \underset{[5.28]}{0.10\ \mathrm{C}} - \underset{[-2.39]}{0.03\mathrm{D91}} + \underset{[4.21]}{0.05\ \mathrm{D04}} - \underset{[0.76]}{0.01\ \mathrm{D09}}\end{aligned}$$

Diagnostic check results

R^2: 0.67; $\bar{R}^2$: 0.41; heteroscedasticity test: χ^2 381.61 (p value 0.39)

LM serial correlation test			Normality test		
Lags	LM stats	p value		χ^2	p value
Lag 1	20.63	0.71	Skewness	5.90	0.31
Lag 2	22.28	0.61	Kurtosis	1.95	0.85
Lag 3	20.63	0.71	Jarque–Bera	7.85	0.64

[a]*t*-values are provided in the brackets []

variables to account for the seasonality or structural shifts might be necessarily considered and properly specified, ensuring that the seasonal dummies do not affect the asymptotic null distributions (Lutkepohl and Kratzig 2004). The exogenous time dummies namely dummy 1991, dummy 2004 and dummy 2009[3] were used in the analysis and both found to be significant.

The result obtained here goes in line with the result obtained by Martin and Fardmanesh (1990) in their cross section analysis. However, results obtained here are in contradict to the results of certain studies like Nelson and Singh (1994) where they found insignificant relation between fiscal deficit and growth and a study by Taylor et al. (2012) where authors found deficit having significant positive relation with growth for the US economy. The results are not strictly comparable with other studies as the time frame, methodology and context are different. The result here confirms that fiscal deficit is having significant and negative relationship with GDP in India.

The result clearly indicated that fiscal deficit is adversely affecting the economic growth. In the Keynesian framework, deficit financing is required in order to use the

[3]Dummy D09 found to be significant in other equations and hence retained in the model.

unutilised resources particularly in less developed and developing countries. It was always suggested that fiscal deficit amount should be spent on capital formation purpose, so that it will have multiplier effect on the growth in the long term. As per the 'Golden Rule' of public finance, whatever may be the amount of fiscal deficit, it should be spent for capital formation purpose but not for the current spending. But in Indian scenario, revenue deficit covers major portion of the fiscal deficit and actual amount left for the capital investment is less. A scenario of effective fiscal deficit is provided in Appendix 1. Except for the year 2008 in many years, revenue deficit covers major portion of fiscal deficit. During 2015–2016, it constitutes around 62% of fiscal deficit. Suppose if we consider central government accounts alone, revenue deficit covers nearly 74% in the year 2012–2013. At state governments level, except for few states like West Bengal and others, remaining states are performing well and have a revenue surplus in their account. But still the combined account is under critical condition.

Few existing studies like (Ramu and Gayithri 2016) prove that fiscal deficit amount spent on capital formation (fiscal deficit net of revenue deficit) will have significant positive impact on the GDP whereas the revenue deficit was found to be adversely affecting the output growth in India. The result supported the 'Golden Rule' that if deficit amount is used on capital formation purposes it promotes economic growth. Hence, Indian government should reduce the revenue deficit component in the fiscal deficit and need to channelize fiscal deficit in entirety towards capital formation.

5 Conclusion

This paper makes an attempt to study the existing gap in the Indian economic literature by analysing long-term relationship between fiscal deficit and GDP growth. Based on the nature of the Indian time series data vector correction method has been used for the analysis.

The results obtained here reveal that fiscal deficit adversely affects GDP supporting the mainstream neo-classical theory and also RBI's view. This result clearly indicates that fiscal deficit should be kept under control and government has to firmly follow fiscal consolidation path. Based on few available literature this paper also argue that portion of fiscal deficit amount spent on capital formation will promote growth and hence, government should take appropriate policy measures to reduce the revenue deficit component under the fiscal deficit and channelize fiscal deficit in entirety towards capital formation. Government investment in infrastructure will have a crowding in effect of private investment. It was also proved in this study that private investment significantly and positively affects GDP. This study strongly suggests to reduce fiscal deficit over time and more importantly, to improve the quality of deficit spending in India.

Appendix 1

Share of FD–RD in gross fiscal deficit

Years	Fiscal deficit (FD)	Revenue deficit (RD)	(In rupees billion)	
			FD–RD	FD–RD as % of FD
1990–1991	535.8	238.71	297.09	55.45
1991–1992	458.5	219.12	239.38	52.21
1992–1993	524.04	236.88	287.16	54.80
1993–1994	709.52	365.29	344.23	48.52
1994–1995	716.39	371.85	344.54	48.09
1995–1996	776.71	379.32	397.39	51.16
1996–1997	872.44	487.68	384.76	44.10
1997–1998	1107.43	627.82	479.61	43.31
1998–1999	1570.53	1106.18	464.35	29.57
1999–2000	1848.26	1213.93	634.33	34.32
2000–2001	1998.52	1388.03	610.49	30.55
2001–2002	2264.25	1593.5	670.75	29.62
2002–2003	2349.87	1629.9	719.97	30.64
2003–2004	2345.01	1594.08	750.93	32.02
2004–2005	2347.21	1147.61	1199.6	51.11
2005–2006	2395.6	993.12	1402.48	58.54
2006–2007	2191.28	553.66	1637.62	74.73
2007–2008	1991.1	96.26	1894.84	95.17
2008–2009	4671.35	2408.65	2262.7	48.44
2009–2010	6046.68	3700.15	2346.53	38.81
2010–2011	5340.32	2492	2848.32	53.34
2011–2012	6849.66	3703.88	3145.78	45.93
2012–2013	6843.95	3439.6	3404.35	49.74
2013–2014	7491.11	3676.11	3815	50.93
2014–2015	8747.18	3808.21	4938.97	56.46
2015–2016	8852.9	3407.54	5445.36	61.51

Data Source RBI Database on Indian Economy (2017)
FD and RD data is combined of Centre and State Governments

Appendix 2: Stability Test of the Model

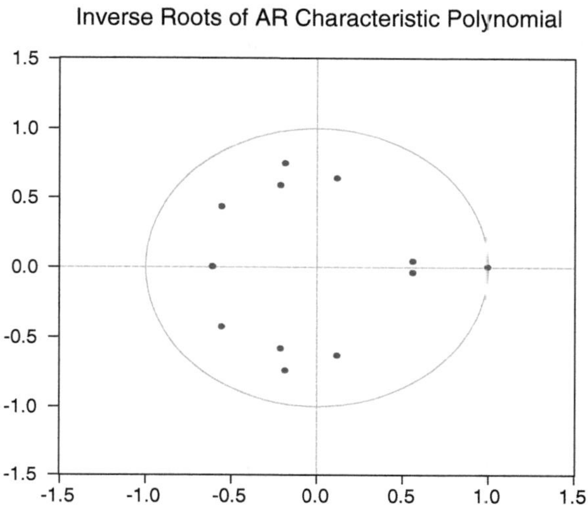

Inverted AR roots are within the unit root circle and signify that model is stable.

Bibliography

Adam, C. S., & Bevan, D. L. (2005). Fiscal deficits and growth in developing countries. *Journal of Public Economics, 89,* 571–597.

Barro, R. J. (1996). *Determinants of economic growth: A cross country empirical study.* NBER working paper no. 5698.

Barro, R. J., & Sala-i-Martin, X. (1995). *Economic growth.* Cambridge: The MIT Press.

Chen, B., & Feng, Y. (2000). Determinants of economic growth in china: Private enterprise, education and openness. *China Economic Review, 11,* 1–15.

Engle, R. F., & Granger, C. W. J. (1987). Cointegration and error correction: Representation, estimation and testing. *Econometrica, 55,* 251–276.

Ferreira, P. C., & Araujo, C. H. V. (2008). Growth and fiscal effects of infrastructure investment in Brazil. In *Fiscal policy, stabilisation and growth—Prudence or abstinence?* (pp. 297–318). Washington, DC: The World Bank.

Johansen, S. (1988). Statistical analysis of cointegration vectors. *Journal of Economic Dynamics and Control, 12,* 231–254.

Johansen, S., & Juselius, K. (1990). Maximum likelihood estimation and inference on cointegration-with application to the demand for money. *Oxford Bulletin of Economics and Statistics, 52,* 169–210.

Karnik, A. (2002). Fiscal policy and growth. *Economic and Political Weekly, 37*(9), 829–831.

Khundrakpam, J. K. (2003). *Public sector spending and economic growth in India.* MPRA paper 51105.

Khundrakpam, J. K., & Pattanaik, S. (2010). Fiscal stimulus and potential inflationary risks—An empirical assessment of fiscal deficit and inflation relationship in India. *Journal of Economic Integration, 25*(4), 703–721.

Lutkepohl, H., & Kratzig, M. (2004). *Applied time series econometrics*. New York: Cambridge University Press.

Maddala, G. S., & Kim, I.-M. (1998). *Unit roots, cointegration and structural change*. London: Cambridge University Press.

Mankiw, G., Romer, D., & Weil, D. N. (1992). A contribution to the empirics of economic growth. *Quarterly Journal of Economics, 107*(2), 407–437.

Martin, R., & Fardmanesh, M. (1990). Fiscal variables and growth: A cross-sectional analysis. *Public Choice, 64*(3), 239–251.

Nelson, M., & Singh, R. D. (1994). The deficit-growth connection: Some recent evidence from developing countries. *Economic Development and Cultural Change, 43*(1), 167–191.

Phillips, P. C. B., & Hansen, B. E. (1990). Statistical inference in instrumental variables regression with I (1) processes. *Review of Economic Studies, 57,* 99–125.

Ramu, M. R. A., & Gayithri, K. (2016). *Relationship between fiscal deficit composition and economic growth in India: A time series econometric analysis* (pp. 1–18). ISEC working paper 367.

Rangarajan, C., & Srivatsava, D. K. (2005). Fiscal deficits and government debt—Implications for growth and stabilisation. *Economic and Political Weekly, 40*(27), 2919–2934.

RBI. (2012). *Fiscal and monetary coordination*. Report on currency and finance 2009–2012.

RBI. (2017). *RBI Database on Indian Economy*. Mumbai: Reserve Bank of India.

Stern, N. (1991). The determinants of growth. *The Economic Journal, 101*(404), 122–133.

Tanzi, V., & Zee, H. H. (1997). Fiscal policy and long run growth. *IMF Staff Papers, 44*(2), 179–209.

Taylor, L., Proano, C., Carvalho, L. D., & Barbosa, N. (2012). Fiscal deficits, economic growth and government debt in USA. *Cambridge Journal of Economics, 36*(1), 189–204.

Relationship Between Monetary Policy and Industrial Production in India

Amrendra Pandey and Jagadish Shettigar

Abstract The purpose of this research paper is to find out the empirical relationship between monetary policy initiatives of Reserve Bank of India and industrial production in India since April 1991–1992 to May 2015–2016. Monetary variables are the broad money and weighted average lending rate (WALR), whereas the industrial production variable is Index of Industrial Production (IIP)-manufacturing. Models used are VECM, ARDL-bound test and VAR. The study has found that there is long-run relationship between the broad money supply and IIP-manufacturing, similarly, changes in WALR have significant and immediate impact on the IIP-manufacturing. Based on these empirical results, it is argued that monetary policy variables and production share a strong relationship and policy to control only inflation may adversely impact the production in the economy.

1 Introduction

One of the most important objectives of the economic policy for a country like India, which has still more than a quarter of its population below the poverty line (BPL) is to attain sustainable economic growth. Monetary policy being an important part of the economic policy may play an important role in achieving this objective. However, RBI (the monetary policy authority) became mainly an inflation targeting central bank, especially since February 2015, with a fixed band of inflation. Economic commentators have questioned this decision by arguing that a monetary policy decision to focus mainly on inflation and ignoring output growth would hamper economic growth of the country. Hence, a few research questions arise such as: (i) *is there long-run relationship between monetary variables and economic growth in India?* (ii) *if there is long-run relationship what is the short run*

A. Pandey (✉) · J. Shettigar
Birla Institute of Management Technology, Greater Noida 201306, India
e-mail: amrendra.pandey@bimtech.ac.in

J. Shettigar
e-mail: j.shettigar@bimtech.ac.in

B. Kamaiah et al. (eds.), *Current Issues in Economics and Finance*,
DOI 10.1007/978-981-10-5810-3_3

dynamic relation between these two economic variables? and (iii) *how much fluctuation in economic growth in India can be explained by monetary variables?* This paper attempts to answer these questions.

Monetary policy initiatives and its impact on the real economy have been at the center of macroeconomic debate for long time. The classical theory of economics being influenced by the quantity theory of money emphasized that in the long-run monetary policy is neutral to income growth. This was an established view till the time of Keynes publication of "The General Theory of Employment, Interest and Money" in 1936, in which he criticized the classical economic thought in the wake of their failure to explain "the great depression" of 1930s. Keynes postulated that money was not neutral to real growth and advanced the view that rise in prices caused decrement in real wages, which in turn stimulated new investment and growth.

But, even the Keynesian view came under severe criticism in the midst of 1970s stagflation in the Organization for Economic Co-operation and Development (OECD) countries. This led to the birth of the concept of "rational expectation" which has criticized the Keynesian view and postulated that under flexible markets, repeated monetary policy shocks would be anticipated by the economic agents and the shocks would only facilitate price rise. This proposition led to the view among central bankers that "output is a real magnitude, not a monetary magnitude" (Friedman and Laidler 2010). It means, monetary policy does not directly affect real output, but it affects indirectly by influencing the expectations of the economic agents. As a result of these conflicting theoretical debates, macroeconomic relationship has been extensively researched globally. Some of the literature reviewed for this study are as follows:

Taylor (1980) using the data from ten countries and rational expectations model showed that due to the contractual nature of the employment agreement there was a trade-off between monetary policy and output.

Bernanke and Gertler (1995) using a VAR model showed that the impact of positive shock to policy interest rate on GDP only became ineffective after 48 months. Similarly, Bernanke and Mihov (1997) using again a VAR model showed that the impact of one unit positive shock to interest rate on GDP was evident even after 10 years.

Ball (1997) arguing for the hysteresis theories of unemployment showed that monetary policy had long lasting impact on the unemployment. Similarly, Roy and Darbha (2000) using the quarterly data from 1970 to 1990 of Indian economy found that money supply was cointegrated to Wholesale Price Index (WPI), Index of Industrial Production (IIP)-manufacturing and agricultural produces. The cointegrating coefficient for IIP-manufacturing was 0.34. Whereas, using a structural vector autoregression (SVAR) the authors found that industrial production response to one unit positive shock in money supply would be positive only in second and eighth quarter, whereas in other quarters it would fall.

Ramachandran (2004) using the Johansen test of cointegration found that money, income and prices in India stood for long-run cointergrating relationship. The coefficient for normalized cointegrating vector with respect to money showed that the coefficient of output was 1.06, which implied that the long run relationship between money supply and output was proportionate. But, one strange phenomenon observed in the short run by the author was that there was a fall in output in response to a positive deviation of money supply from its long run equilibrium level.

Mallick and Agarwal (2007) using the monthly data from March 1993 to March 2005, and autoregressive distributed lag (ARDL) model has shown that interest rate did not have a direct impact on growth. The authors argued that it might be due to the fact that there was poor credit disbursement by the banking system and low credit off-take for productive investment in the country. Whereas, Yadav et al. (2011) using the macroeconomic data from 1991 to 2007 of India had shown that there was no cointegration among the variables, namely real output, money supply, interest rate, exchange rate and price, when real output was considered as the dependent variable. Similarly, the short-run causality result showed that price and interest rate caused the changes in real output.

In a study of the German economy, Schettkat and Sun (2009) concluded the economy with the exception of a few years had worked below its potential level and one of the reasons for the same was the rigid monetary policy followed by the Bundesbank. They argued that structural unemployment in Germany was also due to the asymmetric monetary policy followed by the central bank there. Moreover, the paper argued that at the time when other options did not seem to improve economic conditions, expansionary monetary policy should be followed as inactivity might change the structure of the economy. Similarly, Alexius and Holmlund (2007) using a VAR model on the Swedish economic data had shown that the monetary policy affected growth and unemployment in the Sweden even in the long run.

Using a meta-analysis of 86 studies (De Grauwe and Costa Storti 2008) found that monetary policy affected output even after 5 years. Similarly, Shams (2012) using a cointegration and error correction model (ECM) showed that there was a long-run relationship between monetary policy and growth.

Palamalai et al. (2014) using Indian monthly macroeconomic data from April 1994 to July 2012, and by dividing the period in two parts, before crisis and after crisis showed that output had long-run relationship with money supply, interest rate, prices and exchange rate, during both pre-crisis and post-crisis period. But, variance decomposition of IIP showed that most of the variation in IIP is explained by itself and only 2.5% of the variation is explained by changes in money supply even in the long run. Similarly, impulse response function showed that one unit shock in money supply affected negatively to IIP.

2 Research Methodology

2.1 Data Source

Since monetary policy is a short-term adjustment instrument in political economy of the country, using monthly data is more appropriate. This study intends to test the relationship among monetary aggregates and industrial production during the post-liberalization period. Keeping this objective in mind, monthly data of these variables over the sample period of April 1991–1992 to May 2015–2016 has been examined.

Accordingly, time series data on the wholesale price index (WPI), broad money (M_3) and weighted average lending rates (WALR) have been collected from the database on Indian Economy (dbie) of Reserve Bank of India (RBI). Broad money has been taken as a monetary variable because it has been targeted since 1986 after the recommendations of the Chakravarty Committee in 1985. Similarly, the reason to consider WALR is the fact that it is lending rate and not the weighted average call rate (WACR) (which is official operating target of RBI) which actually affects the demand side of the economy. WPI has been used to measure inflation because RBI communicated indicative level of inflation in WPI terms itself.

IIP-manufacturing instead of GDP has been taken as growth variable, because GDP data is not available on monthly basis. Another reason to consider IIP-manufacturing is the fact that even though manufacturing activity accounts for only 17.4% (at 2011–2012 price) of the total value addition in the economy, it accounts for more than one-third of the production output. This diversion in output and gross value addition (GVA) is not so stark in any other sector of the economy. This shows that the manufacturing provides the demand base for the products of many other growing sectors of the economy, thereby creating substantial backward linkages. Electricity and mining sectors in IIP series have not been included in the present study since they have long gestation period and are less affected by sudden change in the demand side of the economy compared to manufacturing. Another justification for considering IIP-manufacturing is the fact that manufacturing constitute more than 75.0% of the IIP.

WPI series has been converted to the base year of 1981–1982 using conversion rate at 2.478 for 1993–1994 base year and 1.875 for 2004–2005 base year index as provided by the Office of Economic Adviser, Govt. of India, Ministry of Commerce and Industry, Department of Industrial Policy and Promotion (DIPP).

Similarly, manufacturing IIP data have been collected from the data base of '*Ministry of Statistics and Programme Implementation (MOSPI)*', Government of India. Base year of manufacturing IIP has been taken as 1980–1981, and 1993–1994 base year index has been converted to 1980–1981 price using the linking factor of 2.235 and 2004–2005 base year index using the linking factor of 4.97 as provided by the MOSPI.

2.2 Model Specification

It is possible that the time series data being considered in the study will not be stationary individually, but when one or more of the time series data will be regressed on another time series data, the combination may be stationary, i.e., their linear combination will cancel out stochastic trend. This econometric phenomenon is called *cointegration* and in economic terms, it implies that the time series variables have a long run, or equilibrium relation between them.

Before doing further analysis with the time series, stationarity of the data set will be tested for which two tests, namely, augmented Dickey Fuller (ADF) test and Kwiatkowski–Phillips Schmidt Shin Test (KPSS) will be used. After testing the stationarity if the data set is found to be nonstationary then cointegration relationships among the time series variables will be checked. If there is cointegration then impulse responsive function (IRF) and forecast error variance decomposition (FEVD) will be used to analyze the results.

If there is no cointegration relationship among the time series variables then vector auto regression (VAR) will be used for the analysis. All the tests are described below:

2.2.1 Vector Error Correction Model (VECM)

Johansen (1988, 1991), Johansen and Juselius (1990) developed maximum likelihood estimators of cointegrating vectors for an autoregressive process. This approach uses canonical correlation analysis. In the VECM, the variables adjust to their existing long-run relationship. It also explains how long-run error correction term explains the movement in the short run. The general structure of the VECM model used for the analysis is as follows:

$$\Delta y_t = \mu + \alpha\beta' y_{t-1} + A_1 \Delta y_{t-1} + \cdots + A_{p-1} \Delta y_{t-p+1} + \epsilon_t \quad (1)$$

where

$$y_t = \begin{bmatrix} P_t^{\text{IIP}} \\ M_t \\ \text{WALR}_t \end{bmatrix} \quad (2)$$

y_t denotes the variables under consideration. p_t^{IIP} denote manufacturing IIP. M_t denote money supply, WALR_t denote interest rate. Also α denote the vector of adjustment parameter and β is the cointegrating vector and $A_i, i = 1, \ldots, p-1$ are the short-run impact parameters.

2.2.2 Autoregressive Distributed Lag Model (ARDL)-Bound Test

Pesaran et al. (1999, 2001) developed ARDL-bound testing to test the cointegration in a set of time series variables. It has certain advantages over VECM. The advantages are as follows:

- If some of the variables are *I*(0) whereas others are *I*(1) ARDL can be applied.
- There is only single equation to solve, which makes it simple to interpret.
- One of the biggest advantages over other cointegrating tests is that different variables can enter in the equation with different lags.

The steps of the analysis are as follows:

1. This step will involve testing the stationarity of the variables. The variables must not be *I*(2).
2. Then if the variables are either *I*(1) or a mix of *I*(0) and *I*(1), an unrestricted ECM (UECM) will be estimated. The generic UECM is as follows:

$$\begin{aligned} \Delta y_t = B_0 + \sum_{i=1}^{p} B_i \Delta y_{t-i} + \sum_{i=0}^{q} Y_j \Delta x_{1t-j} + \sum_{i=0}^{r} \delta_k \Delta x_{2t-k} \\ + \phi_0 y_{t-1} + \phi_1 x_{1t-1} + \phi_2 x_{2t-1} + \varepsilon_t \end{aligned} \tag{3}$$

3. In the next level, appropriate lag length of the of p, q and r in the Eq. 3 will be selected using Akaike information criteria (AIC) and Schwarz criterion (SC).
4. After selecting the lag lengths, Eq. 3 will be estimated and then the residuals of the model will be tested for the serial correlation independence. The test used for this purpose will be Breusch–Godfrey (B–G) test.
5. After ascertaining that the residuals of Eq. 3 are serially not correlated, 'bound testing' is performed. For this, Wald testing is used. The null hypothesis in the test is, H_0: $\phi_0 = \phi_1 = \phi_2 = 0$ (where ϕ_0, ϕ_1 and ϕ_2 are from Eq. 3). The critical F values for this test are taken from Pesaran et al. (2001).
   As a cross check, 'bound t test' of H_0: $\phi_0 = 0$ is also performed. Critical t values are again taken from Pesaran et al. (2001).
6. In Step 5, if the null hypothesis is rejected then it will be concluded that there is cointegrating relationship between Y, X_1 and X_2. In this case, long-run relationship can be meaningfully estimated between the variables:

$$y_t = a_0 + a_1 x_{1t} + a_2 x_{2t} + v_t \tag{4}$$

7. Now usual ECM will be estimated:

$$\Delta y_t = B_0 + \sum_{i=1}^{p} B_i \Delta y_{t-i} + \sum_{i=0}^{q} Y_j \Delta x_{1t-j} + \sum_{i=0}^{r} \delta_k \Delta x_{2t-k} + \varphi v_{t-1} + \varepsilon \quad (5)$$

where v_{t-1} are the lagged residuals of OSL regression Eq. 5.
If the time series variables will not be cointegrated then VAR will be used. The model is discussed below.

2.2.3 Vector Autoregression (VAR)

Since the criticism of Sims (1980) about the paradigm of simultaneous equation models laid out by Cowles Foundation in the 1940s and 1950s, vector autoregression (VAR) has become a standard instrument for analysis of multivariate time series analysis.

In basic form, a VAR consists of a set of K endogenous variables $y_t = (y_1t, \ldots, y_kt, \ldots, y_Kt)$ for K = 1,…, K. The VAR(p)-process is then defined as

$$Y_t = A_1 Y(t-1) + \cdots + A_p Y(t-p) + CD_t + u_t \quad (6)$$

where A_i are ($K \times K$) coefficient matrices for $i = 1, \ldots, p$ and u_t is a K-dimensional white noise process. The matrix C is the coefficient matrix of potentially deterministic regressors with dimensions ($K \times M$), and D_t is an ($M \times I$) column vector holding the appropriate deterministic regressors, like constant, trend and dummy variables.

3 Impact of Monetary Policy Initiatives on Industrial Production: Descriptive Analysis

The ultimate objective of monetary policy initiatives is to impact interest rate which in turn is likely to affect industrial production. Attempt has been made to find out the monetary policy's impact on industrial production.

Table 1 and Fig. 1 summarizes year wise broad money supply growth, WALR and growth in IIP-manufacturing. From the figure and table, it is clear that monetary policy stance of RBI since 1991–1992 has three phases, i.e., contractionary monetary policy stance since 1991–1992 to 1997–1998, expansionary monetary policy since 1998–1999 to 2009–2010 and again contractionary monetary policy since 2010–2011 to 2014–2015. During these phases RBI initiated policy measures pursuant to the policy stance taken, but in only 10 years out of 24 years analyzed RBI was able to achieve its own target of M_3 growth.

Table 1 Monetary policy and industrial production, 1991–1992 to 2014–2015

Years	Monetary variable (growth)		mnf. IIP
	M_3 (%)	WALR (%)	Growth (%)
1991–1992	19.3	16.67	−0.77
1992–1993	15.7	16.95	2.18
1993–1994	18.4	16.5	6.07
1994–1995	22.3	16.0	9.10
1995–1996	13.7	17.13	14.12
1996–1997	16.2	17.0	7.31
1997–1998	17.6	17.48	6.66
1998–1999	18.4	15.53	4.42
1999–2000	14.6	14.92	7.12
2000–2001	16.2	14.29	5.33
2001–2002	14.2	13.81	2.86
2002–2003	12.8	13.53	6.02
2003–2004	16.4	12.75	7.37
2004–2005	12.2	12.75	13.17
2005–2006	20.4	12.15	10.24
2006–2007	20.8	12.05	14.96
2007–2008	20.7	12.51	18.38
2008–2009	19.0	11.44	2.47
2009–2010	16.8	10.52	4.88
2010–2011	15.9	11.34	8.93
2011–2012	13.0	12.58	3.02
2012–2013	13.8	12.13	1.27
2013–2014	13.2	12.10	−0.76
2014–2015	10.8	11.51	2.31

Compiled by the researcher from the reports of RBI and MOSPI. Data Retrieved from www.rbi.org.in/Scripts/AnnualReportMainDisplay.aspx and mospi.nic.in/mospi_new/upload/iip/IIP_main.htm

From the table, it becomes clear that out of 24 years, direction of IIP-manufacturing growth path has been positive for 13 years and negative for 11 years. The path of monetary policy stance (expansionary or tightening) and IIP-manufacturing growth path has been same in 12 years, while it is opposite in 12 years. On the other hand, if we look at the money supply growth path and IIP-manufacturing growth path then the direction has been same in only 8 years. This analysis suggests conflicting relationships; while on one hand it suggests (policy stance) strong relationship, on the other (money supply growth path) it suggests weak relationship. These findings warrant further empirical study to analyze the relationship between monetary variables and industrial production.

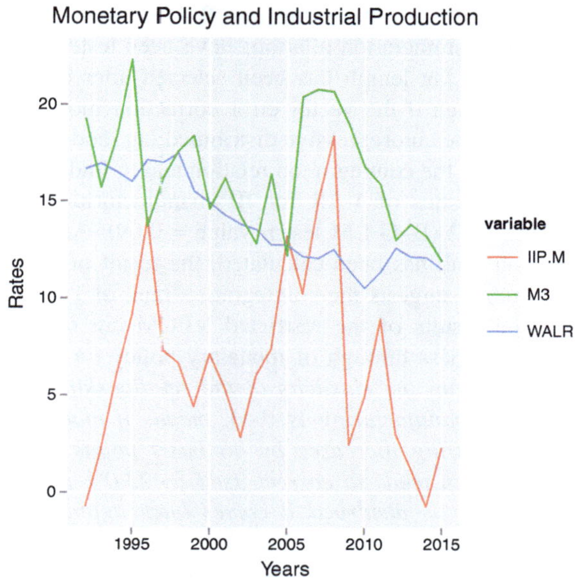

Fig. 1 Monetary policy changes and rate of IIP-manufacturing, 1991–1992 to 2014–2015

Table 2 Stationarity and integration of time series: ADF and KPSS test, April 1991–1992 to May 2015–2016

Variable	In level form		Stationarity	First difference		Stationarity
	ADF	KPSS	Result	ADF	KPSS	Result
$\ln M_3$	−0.68	5.26	Nonstationary	−5.38	0.19	Stationary
WALR	−2.93	1.92	Nonstationary	−6.45	0.05	Stationary
IIP-mnf.	−3.33	7.30	Nonstationary	−10.05	0.026	Stationary

ADF and KPSS critical values at 95% are −3.42 and 0.46 respectively

4 Empirical Results and Findings

Before testing the stationarity of the time series, logs of M_3 and IIP-manufacturing have been taken. Log of the weighted average lending rate (WALR) has not been taken as it is already in per cent. Stationarity of the time series variables has been tested using ADF and KPSS tests. Both of these tests indicate that all the time series variables are nonstationary in the level form, but stationary in first difference, i.e., they all are $I(1)$ (Table 2).

4.1 Relationship Between IIP-Manufacturing and M_3

For estimating the effect of monetary policy on production, two models have been estimated, one which includes IIP-manufacturing and M_3 and another which includes IIP-manufacturing and WALR. In modeling IIP-manufacturing and M_3, first the cointegration relations have been tested using Johansen cointegration test, for which lag length has been selected after diagnostics of the residual of VAR model. Then if the vector error correction model (VECM) suggests cointegration relation, the autoregressive distributed lag model (ARDL) bound test has been used to recheck the cointegration relation and to find out the best fitted regression model.

Diagnostics of VAR for IIP-manufacturing and M_3 has suggested using lag length of 2 (B–G LM test p value = 0.09). After selecting the lag length, cointegration rank has been calculated, the result of which has been shown in Table 3. The table suggests the cointegration rank of 1 at 5% level of significance.

The results of the restricted VECM are reported in Table 4. The table presents the pass through of monetary policy on IIP-manufacturing. It shows that *in the long run the elasticity of the relationship between the broad money supply and IIP-manufacturing is 0.46, means if money supply increases by 1.0% IIP-manufacturing increases by 46 basis points. Any deviation from the long-run relationship tends to correct itself by 23.0% points in a month period, i.e., once the system is disturbed it comes back again to the equilibrium at the rate of 23.0% every subsequent months.*

Orthogonal Impulse response function (IRF) has been used to explore the impulse response on a variable because of shock on another variable, by taking into account the impact on other variables simultaneously. The result has been depicted in Fig. 2. *The IRF shows that 100.0% increase in money supply will cause IIP-manufacturing to increase by 11.30% cumulatively in the next 5 years. The result also shows that once the money supply is given a shock it will have impact on the manufacturing even after 5 years.*

The variance decomposition analysis is shown in Table 5, which shows that M_3 explains 4.50% of the variation error in IIP-manufacturing 6 months ahead, while it explains 6.0% of the variation after 2 years.

Table 3 Cointegration rank (Johansen cointegration test for IIP-manufacturing and M_3 April 1991–1992 to May 2015–2016

Cointegration rank—eigenvalue statistics				
Cointegration rank	Test statistics	10%	5%	1%
$r \leq 1$	1.41	6.50	8.18	11.65
$r \leq 0$	48.84	12.91	14.90	19.19

Table 4 Long run and short run dynamic relationship-IIP-manufacturing and M_3, April 1991–1992 to May 2015–2016

Long run and short run dynamic relationship		
Variables	Long-run relation	Error correction term
lnIIP-mnf.		−0.23
lnM_3	0.46	

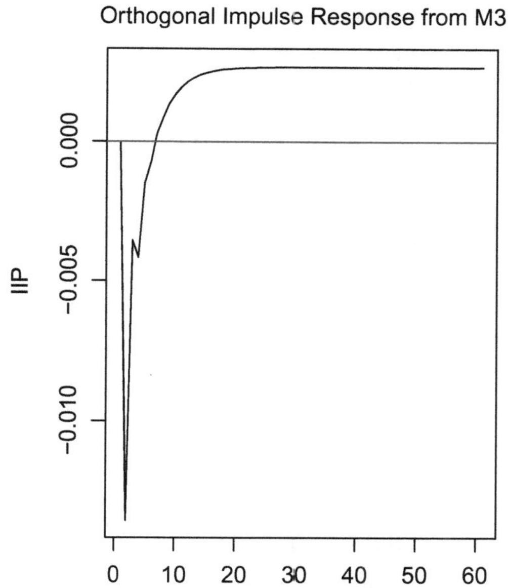

Fig. 2 Impulse response of IIP-manufacturing to a unit shock in M_3, April 1991–1992 to May 2015–2016

Table 5 Forecast error variance decomposition—IIP-manufacturing and M_3, April 1991–1992 to May 2015–2016

FEVD IIP-manufacturing				
Variable	Variance error in IIP-manufacturing explained— 6 months ahead (%)	Variance error in IIP-manufacturing explained— 12 months ahead (%)	Variance error in IIP-manufacturing explained— 18 months ahead (%)	Variance error in IIP-manufacturing explained— 24 months ahead (%)
IIP-mnf.	95.50	95.33	94.73	94.0
M_3	4.50	4.67	5.27	6.0

To check the validity of VECM results, ARDL-bound test has been applied, the results of which has been shown in the Table 6. From the table, it becomes clear that there is cointegration relationship between IIP-manufacturing and M_3 at lag 3. From the B–G serial correlation test it is clear that the errors of unrestricted error correction model (UECM) are serially not correlated. The error correction term (ECT) is −0.22 which is same as the result given by VECM model. The long-run multiplier between IIP-manufacturing and M_3 is 0.47, which means that in the long run 1.0% increase in M_3 will lead to 0.47 increase in IIP-manufacturing. This result is again same as given by the VECM model.

Table 6 ARDL bound test for IIP-manufacturing and M_3, April 1991–1992 to May 2015–2016

Bound test and restricted ECM results for ARDL(3, 3)		
Variables	Result value	Other relevant value
Bound test (Wald F statistic)	6.07	Pesaran and Shin critical values at 95% confidence level 4.94 for $I(0)$ and 5.73 for $I(1)$
$\ln \text{IIP}_{t-1}$ bound t statistic	−3.35	Pesaran and Shin critical t values at 95% confidence level −2.86 for $I(0)$ and −3.22 for $I(1)$
B–G serial correlation unrestricted ECM	p value = 0.47	
Error correction term	−0.22	p value = 0.00073
Long run effect	0.47	
B–G serial correlation restricted ECM	p value = 0.48	

Table 7 Cointegration rank (Johansen cointegration test for IIP-manufacturing and WALR), April 1991–1992 to May 2015–2016

Cointegration rank—eigenvalue statistics				
Cointegration rank	Test statistics	10%	5%	1%
$r \leq 1$	2.60	6.50	8.18	11.65
$r \leq 0$	10.15	12.91	14.90	19.19

Table 8 VAR (ΔIIP-manufacturing and ΔWALR), April 1991–1992 to May 2015–2016

Diagnostics analysis at lag 13		
Test	p value	Inference
Breusch–Godfrey LM test of correlation	0.43	No serial correlation
ARCH (multivariate)	0.42	No heteroscedasticity

4.2 Relationship Between IIP-Manufacturing and WALR

Diagnostics of VAR for IIP-manufacturing and WALR has suggested using lag length of 14 (B–G LM test p value = 0.096). After selecting the lag of 14, cointegration rank has been calculated, the result of which has been shown in Table 7. The table suggests that there is no cointegration relationship between IIP-manufacturing and WALR.

Since there is no cointegrating relationship between these two variables, in the next step first difference of the variables have been taken to make then stationary (Table 2) and then vector autoregression (VAR) model has been estimated. VAR lag length selection criteria have suggested using lag length of 24. Diagnostics of the model is reported in the Table 8 and Fig. 3. From the table and figure, it becomes clear that there is no serial correlation, heteroscedasticity, and structural

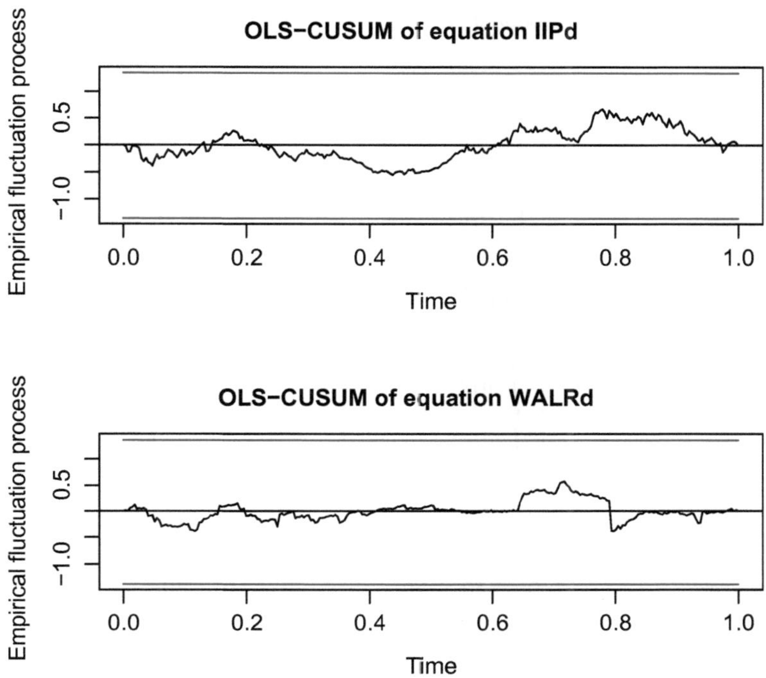

Fig. 3 VAR-structural stability plot (ΔIIP-manufacturing and ΔWALR)

Table 9 Granger causality result (VAR model for ΔIIP-manufacturing and ΔWALR), April 1991–1992 to May 2015–2016

Granger causality from ΔWALR to ΔIIP-manufacturing		
Test	*p* value	Inference
Granger causality	0.000	Null hypothesis of no Granger causality is rejected
Instant causality	0.013	Null hypothesis of no instantaneous causality is rejected

instability in the model. After the diagnostic tests, the model is used for further analysis. For this analytical purpose, Granger causality test, impulse response function (IRF), and forecast error variance decomposition (FEVD) is used.

The Granger causality result has been reported in Table 9. From the table, it is clear that *ΔWALR Granger causes ΔIIP-manufacturing, i.e., ΔWALR helps in predicting ΔIIP-manufacturing. Similarly, the hypothesis that there is no instantaneous causality is also rejected, which implies that ΔWALR has instantaneous impact on ΔIIP-manufacturing.*

Granger causality only tells about the direction of causality but does not quantify it. For the quantification of the relationship, impulse response function (IRF) and forecast error variance decomposition (FEVD) are used. IRF results have been

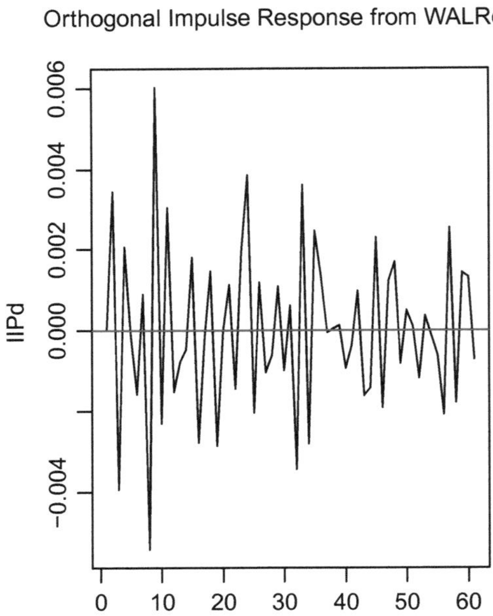

Fig. 4 Impulse response of ΔIIP-manufacturing in response of shock to ΔWALR, April 1991–1992 to May 2015–2016

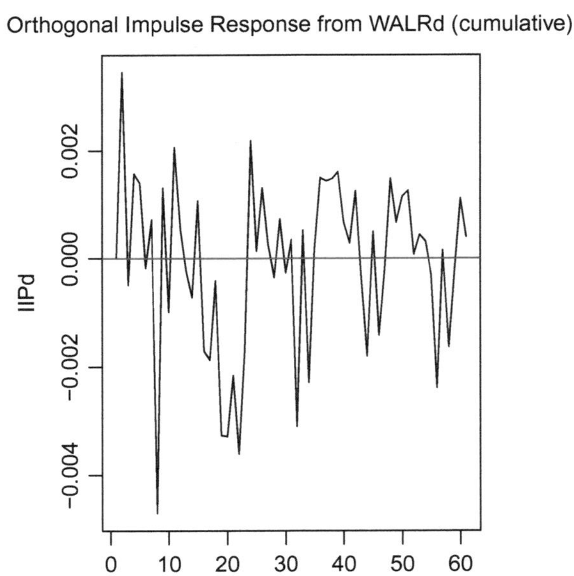

Fig. 5 Cumulative impulse response of ΔIIP-manufacturing in response of shock to ΔWALR, April 1991–1992 to May 2015–2016

Table 10 Forecast error variance decomposition—ΔIIP-manufacturing and ΔWALR, April 1991–1992 to May 2015–2016

FEVD IIP-manufacturing				
Variable	Variance error in ΔIIP-manufacturing explained—6 months ahead (%)	Variance error in ΔIIP-manufacturing explained—12 months ahead (%)	Variance error in ΔIIP-manufacturing explained—18 months ahead (%)	Variance error in ΔIIP-manufacturing explained—24 months ahead (%)
IIP-mnf.	96.16	90.0	89.0	88.95
WALR	3.83	10.0	11.0	11.05

shown in Figs. 4 and 5. Figure 4 depicts impulse response of ΔIIP-manufacturing in response of a unit shock to ΔWALR at time *t*, whereas Fig. 5 portrays the cumulative impact on ΔIIP-manufacturing of a unit shock to ΔWALR at time *t*. From the figures, it is clear that once the shock is given to ΔWALR, it will have impact on ΔIIP-manufacturing even after 5 years. *If 100.0% shock is given to ΔWALR (rate of growth) it will impact negatively to ΔIIP-manufacturing by 0.39% in the next 2 months, with cumulative 6-month impact being −0.47%.* To make comprehension easy let us imagine if ΔWALR (rate of growth) was 5.0% earlier and ΔIIP-manufacturing (rate of growth) was 8.0%, then due to shock in ΔWALR, ΔWALR will increase to 10.0% (100.0% shock), whereas ΔIIP-manufacturing (rate of growth) will decelerate to 7.97% (decrease by 0.39%) in the next 2 months.

Forecast error variance decomposition (FEVD) has been presented in Table 10. From the table, it becomes clear that at time $t + 24$, *11.0% variance error in ΔIIP-manufacturing is explained by shock in ΔWALR.*

5 Conclusion

This paper examines the empirical relationship between monetary variables and industrial production since the onset of economic reform. The study becomes important in the backdrop of recent changes in RBI's monetary policy stance to target inflation.

The study has found that there is long run relationship between the broad money supply (M_3) and IIP-manufacturing in the post liberalization period of India. This relationship is strong and any deviation from it is corrected by 23.0% in the subsequent months.

The IRF shows that if money supply is given a positive shock of 100.0% its cumulative impact in 5 years on IIP-manufacturing will be 11.5% and M_3 explains around 6.0% variance error in IIP-manufacturing.

Similarly, changes in weighted average lending rate (WALR) will have direct and immediate impact on IIP-manufacturing with approximately 11.0% of variance error in ΔIIP-manufacturing explained by ΔWALR.

Based on this empirical analysis, it is argued that monetary policy variables and production share a strong relationship and policy to control only inflation may impact adversely to production in the economy.

References

Alexius, A., & Holmlund, B. (2007). Monetary Policy and Swedish Unemployment Fluctuations. *Institute for the World Economy, 3*, 4.

Ball, L. (1997). *Disinflation and the NAIRU, Reducing Inflation: Motivation and Strategy*. Chicago: University of Chicago Press.

Bernanke, B. S., & Gertler, M. (1995). *Inside the black box: The credit channel of monetary policy transmission*. Technical report, National Bureau of Economic Research.

Bernanke, B. S., & Mihov, I. (1997). What does the bundesbank target? *European Economic Review, 41*(6), 1025–1053.

De Grauwe, P., & Costa Storti, C. (2008). *Monetary policy and the real economy*. Abingdon: Routledge.

Friedman, M., & Laidler, D. (2010). Trade-offs in monetary policy. In *David Laidler's contributions to economics* (pp. 114–127). UK: Palgrave Macmillan.

Johansen, S. (1988). Statistical analysis of cointegration vectors. *Journal of Economic Dynamics and Control, 12*(2–3), 231–254.

Johansen, S. (1991). Estimation and hypothesis testing of cointegration vectors in gaussian vector autoregressive models. *Econometrica: Journal of the Econometric Society* 1551–1580.

Johansen, S., & Juselius, K. (1990). Maximum likelihood estimation and inference on cointegration—With applications to the demand for money. *Oxford Bulletin of Economics and Statistics, 52*(2), 169–210.

Mallick, H., & Agarwal, S. (2007). Impact of real interest rates on real output growth in india: A long-run analysis in a liberalized financial regime. *The Singapore Economic Review, 52*(02), 215–231.

Palamalai, S., Mariappan, K., & Devakumar, C. (2014). On the temporal causal relationship between macroeconomic variables: Empirical evidence from india. *SAGE Open, 4*(1), 2158244014525419.

Pesaran, M. H., Shin, Y., & Smith, R. P. (1999). Pooled mean group estimation of dynamic heterogeneous panels. *Journal of the American Statistical Association, 94*(446), 621–634.

Pesaran, M. H., Shin, Y., & Smith, R. J. (2001). Bounds testing approaches to the analysis of level relationships. *Journal of Applied Econometrics, 16*(3), 289–326.

Ramachandran, M. (2004). Do broad money, output, and prices stand for a stable relationship in India? *Journal of Policy Modeling, 26*(8), 983–1001.

Roy, S. D., & Darbha, G. (2000). Dynamics of money, output and price interaction—Some indian evidence. *Economic Modelling, 17*(4), 559–588.

Schettkat, R., & Sun, R. (2009). Monetary policy and european unemployment. *Oxford Review of Economic Policy, 25*(1), 94–108.

Shams, N. (2012). Money, income, and prices in Bangladesh: A cointegration and causality analysis. *Journal of Economics and Sustainable Development, 3*(7), 82–88.

Sims, C. A. (1980). Macroeconomics and reality. *Econometrica: Journal of the Econometric Society* 1–48.

Taylor, J. B. (1980). Output and price stability: An international comparison. *Journal of Economic Dynamics and Control, 2*, 109–132.

Yadav, I. S., Lagesh, M., et al. (2011). Macroeconomic relationship in India: Ardl evidence on cointegration and causality. *Journal of Quantitative Economics, 9*(1), 156–168.

Co-movement Among Asian Forex Markets: Evidence from Wavelet Methods

Anoop S. Kumar and Bandi Kamaiah

Abstract In this article, we analyze the co-movements of nine Asian Forex markets China, India, Hong Kong, Malaysia, Indonesia, Singapore, Japan, Taiwan, Thailand, and South Korea using bilateral exchange rate against US Dollar from 03-01-2006 to 04-09-2015. We employ a wavelet-based methodology to analyze the extent to with the markets are correlated with each other across different timescales. It is found that the markets are moderately correlated at the intra-week scale and the extent of correlation increases with the increase in timescale. Near-perfect cointegration among the analyzed markets is found across annual–biannual timescale. The cross-correlation analysis shows that Singapore Forex market may lead the other Forex markets of the group across timescales from 16 to 64 days. Results indicate that there is a possibility of intervention as well as potential for portfolio diversification for the short term.

Keywords Forex · Asia · Wavelet · Cointegration

JEL Classification G1 · F3 · F4

1 Introduction

Forex markets are an important segment of any financial market. A stable currency is of paramount importance in economic growth. The increasing amount of financial and trade regulations have resulted in changing of Forex regimes of countries throughout the world, especially in the past two decades. Due to the increased level of integration and change in exchange rate regimes, Forex markets are now prone to

A.S. Kumar (✉)
Department of Economics, BITS Pilani KK Birla Goa Campus,
Vasco da Gama 403726, India
e-mail: anoopk@goa.bits-pilani.ac.in

B. Kamaiah
School of Economics, University of Hyderabad, Hyderabad 500046, India

B. Kamaiah et al. (eds.), *Current Issues in Economics and Finance*,
DOI 10.1007/978-981-10-5810-3_4

shocks compared to the fixed exchange rate regime era. It was evident in the 1997 East Asian currency crisis, the 2008 financial crisis, the 2010 Euro zone crisis and the recent market fluctuation due to the devaluation of Chinese Yuan. Analyzing the dynamics of co-movements among Forex markets are of great interest to the investors and the policy makers alike.

From the investors' point of view, it is about the diversification of risk while the policy makers will be interested in the usefulness of exchange rate as a macroeconomic policy tool. If the Forex market of a country is less affected by exogenous shocks, there is a scope for using exchange rate as a tool of monetary policy if the Forex market is impervious to external shocks to some extent.

Among the emerging foreign exchange markets of the world, Asian markets are of interest to researchers, especially after the 1997 East Asian crisis. Most of the Asian economies were liberalized in the late 1980s and 1990s. Some of these countries, the so-called East Asian tigers witness strong economic growth in the aftermath of liberalization, and the reason behind this growth was attributed towards market-oriented reforms, where at large the floating exchange rate was one of the main factors. East Asian Forex markets of that time have attracted many investors. However, the currency crisis of 1997 posed a serious question towards this model of economic growth, and towards the Forex regimes which are associated with it.

Asian Forex market has a mix of developing and developed economies, most of them following managed float exchange rate system with different degrees of intervention from the authorities. Table 1 presents an overview of the exchange rate regimes followed by major Asian economies as of 2014.

The 1997 crisis was a defining moment for many Asian economies, prompting them to reevaluate their exchange rate policies and initializing a research interest in the dynamics of Asian Forex markets.

Conventionally, the co-movements of Forex market were explained using cointegration and error correction models. A number of studies on developed Forex markets have been carried out by authors such as Baillie and Bollerslev (1989), Rapp and Sharma (1999), Jeon and Lee (2002), Aroskar et al. (2004), Phengpis and Nguyen (2009) and Bohadlova and Grigus (2014). There are a few studies on Asian

Table 1 Asian foreign exchange regimes

Markets	Exchange rate regime
Singapore	Stabilized arrangement
China	Crawl like arrangement
Malaysia	Managed float
South Korea	Managed float
India	Managed float
Japan	Free float
Thailand	Managed float
Taiwan	Managed float
Hong Kong	Currency board

Source IMF AREAER, 2014

Forex markets such as AuYong et al. (2004), Phengpis (2006), Ahmad et al. (2012), Chaudhry and Javid (2012) that employed same methods. In general, these results provide mixed results related to the co-movement structure of Forex markets. However, models based on cointegration and error correction have certain methodological limitations. These methods are designed to deal with just two time frames, i.e., the long-run co-movement and the short-run adjustment. However, given the heterogeneous nature of trading in Forex markets, we have participants operating at different frequencies or trade horizons. In other words, short-term investors would be interested in short-term fluctuations in the market, medium-term investors at medium fluctuations, and the long-term investors would be looking at the long-term fluctuations occurring in the market. Hence, it would be of practical importance to study the Forex market co-movements at multiple frequencies. Standard Frequency domain analysis such as Fourier-based method fails to provide information in this regard as well. Considering this limitations, researchers have resorted to wavelet analysis of financial markets.

Wavelets transforms are used to decompose a given time series into its high frequency and low frequency components without losing its timescale resolution. Wavelets are not affected by the nonstationary nature of the financial time series; hence it is preferred over other frequency domain methods such as Fourier transform.

Wavelets could be broadly classified into two categories: continuous wavelet transforms (CWT) and discreet wavelet transforms (DWT). In CWT, we decompose the given time series in continuous timescales, as suggested by the name. However, for many practical purposes, such detailing may not be required. DWT is applied in this context. The DWT carries out the decomposition only in dyadic scales. However, there were serious limitations associated with DWT. The given time series should be dyadic in nature. Further, the decomposed signal is subsampled at each level. This leads to the invention of Maximal Overlap Discreet Wavelet Transform (MODWT) that could address these issues. Here we employ MODWT-based methods namely wavelet multiple correlation and cross-correlation proposed by Fernandez-Macho (2012). This method is an improvement over bivariate wavelet analysis by the virtue of proposing two new statistics namely wavelet multiple correlation and wavelet multiple cross-correlation.

While the standard time series/frequency domain tests can provide information about the possible presence of cointegration among a multivariate time series, these tests have some serious limitations. First, even though these methods could identify the presence of cointegration and short-term adjustment, they fail to provide a statistic that could quantify the extent of co-movement. Considering the fact that there are agents with different trading time horizons operating in financial markets, it is possible that the nature of relationship between these markets vary across different timescales. The traditional time series measures can provide measures only at the given frequency. Further, it would be of interest to researchers and policy makers to see at what time scale the cointegration occurs.

Wavelet multiple correlation and cross-correlation measures can overcome these two shortcomings. The wavelet multiple correlation coefficient measure could provide the strength of co-movement among a multivariate time series across different timescales, so that one could distinguish between the short-run-, medium-run-, and long-run relationship.

Wavelet multiple cross-correlation provides a measure to identify a potential leader among the group, that could influence the other variables present in the group. Finally, these measures are better compared to the traditional wavelet correlation and cross-correlation measures. Imagine we have 10 markets, then we would have to calculate $n \times (n-1)/2$ wavelet correlation plots and J (order of wavelet decomposition) times wavelet cross-correlation plots, resulting in a cumbersome process. In such a context, a pairwise analysis could result into a spurious interpretation of the results. The proposed methodology estimates overall correlations and cross-correlation within the multivariate framework across different time scales making interpretation of the results easier and we will need to plot only two graphs compared to the traditional wavelet correlation measures.

This study analyzes the co-movement of Asian Forex markets using the methods mentioned above. A brief explanation about the data and methods employed is given in the forthcoming section.

2 Data and Methodology

We employ daily closing bilateral exchange rate series against US Dollar for major Asian economies viz. China, India, Hong Kong, Malaysia, Indonesia, Singapore, Japan, Taiwan, Thailand, and South Korea from 03-01-2006 to 04-09-2015. The data was collected from US Fed Reserve Database.

Let $\{X_t\}$ be a multivariate stochastic process and let $\{W_{jt}\}$ be the respective jth level wavelet coefficients obtained by the application of MODWT. The wavelet multiple correlation (WMC henceforth) $\phi x(\lambda_j)$ can be defined as one single set of multiscale correlations calculated from X_t as follows.

At each wavelet scale $\phi_X \lambda_j$ we calculate the square root of the regression coefficient of determination in that linear combination of variables w_{ijt}, $i = 1,2,\ldots n$, for which the coefficient of determination is a maximum. The coefficient of determination corresponding to the regression of a variable Z_i on a set of regressors $\{Z_k,\ k \neq i\}$, could be obtained as $R_i^2 = 1 - 1/\rho^{ii}$, where ρ^{ii} is the ith diagonal element of the inverse of the complete correlation matrix P.

The WMC $\phi x(\lambda_{j)})$ is obtained as

$$\phi_X(\lambda_j) = \sqrt{1 - \frac{1}{\max \operatorname{diag} P_j^{-1}}}, \tag{1}$$

where P is the $N \times N$ correlation matrix of W_{jt}, and the max diag(·) operator selects the largest element in the diagonal of the argument. Since the R_i^2 coefficient can be shown equal to the square of the correlation between the observed values of z_i and the fitted values z_i obtained from such a regression, $\phi x(\lambda_j)$ can also be expressed as

$$\begin{aligned}\phi_X(\lambda_j) &= \mathrm{Corr}(\omega_{ijt}, \hat{w}_{ijt}) \\ &= \frac{\mathrm{Cov}(\omega_{ijt}, \hat{w}_{ijt})}{\sqrt{\mathrm{Var}(\omega_{ijt})}\sqrt{\mathrm{Var}(\hat{w}_{ijt})}},\end{aligned} \tag{2}$$

where the wavelet variances and covariance are defined as follows:

$$\begin{aligned}\mathrm{Var}(w_{ijt}) &= \frac{1}{T_j}\sum_{t=j-1}^{T-1} w_{ijt}^2 \\ \mathrm{Var}(\hat{w}_{ijt}) &= \frac{1}{T_j}\sum_{t=j-1}^{T-1} \hat{w}_{ijt}^2 \\ \mathrm{Cov}(\omega_{ijt}, \hat{w}_{ijt}) &= \frac{1}{T_j}\sum_{t=L_j-1}^{T-1} \omega_{ijt}\hat{w}_{ijt},\end{aligned}$$

where w_{ij} on a set of regressors $\{w_{kj},\ k \neq i\}$, leads to the maximization of the coefficient of determination, $\hat{w}_{ij}$ represents the fitted values. The number of wavelet coefficients affected by boundary associated with a wavelet filter of length L and scale λ_j is calculated as $L_j = (2^j - 1)(L - 1) + 1$. Then the number of wavelet coefficients unaffected by the boundary conditions is obtained as $\tilde{T}_j = T - L_j - 1$.

Allowing a lag τ between observed and fitted values of the variables selected as the criterion variable at each scale λ_j, we may define the wavelet multiple cross-correlation (WMCC henceforth) as

$$\begin{aligned}\phi_{X,\tau}(\lambda_j) &= \mathrm{Corr}(\omega_{ijt}, \hat{w}_{ijt+\tau}) \\ &= \frac{\mathrm{Cov}(\omega_{ijt}, \hat{w}_{ijt+\tau})}{\sqrt{\mathrm{Var}(\omega_{ijt})}\sqrt{\mathrm{Var}(\hat{w}_{ijt+\tau})}}\end{aligned}$$

For $n = 2$ the WMC and WMCC are the same as the standard wavelet correlation and cross-correlation. Fernández-Macho (2012) constructs the confidence intervals using the Fisher's transform. Fisher's transformation is defined as arctanh(r); where arctanh $(\cdot)$ is the inverse hyperbolic tangent function, and it is used to construct confidence interval for a population correlation is based on the fact that if (X, Y) follows a bivariate normal distribution with $\rho = \mathrm{Corr}(X, Y)$, then the transformed sample correlation coefficient calculated from T independent pairs of observations can be shown to be approximately normally distributed with meanarctanh(r) and variance $(T-3)^{-1}$ (Fisher 1921; Johnson et al. 1995). This result is applied to the sample wavelet multiple correlation coefficient $\tilde{\phi}_X(\lambda_j)$ as follows.

Let $X = (X_{1t}, X_2, \ldots, X_T)$ be a realization of multivariate Gaussian stochastic process $X = (x_{1t}, x_2, \ldots, x_t)$ and let

$$\tilde{W}_j = \left(\tilde{W}_{j0}, \ldots, \tilde{W}_{j,T-1}\right) = \left\{\left(\tilde{w}_{1j0}, \ldots, \tilde{w}_{nj0}\right), \ldots, \left(\tilde{w}_{1j,T/2^j-1}\right)\right\}, j = 1, 2, \ldots J,$$

be vectors of wavelet coefficients obtained by applying a MODWT of order J to each of the univariate time series $(x_{i1}, x_{i2}, \ldots x_{iT})$ for $i = 1,2\ldots n$. If $\tilde{\phi}_X(\lambda_j)$ is the sample wavelet correlation obtained from Eq. (1), then $\tilde{z}_j \sim FN(z_j, (T/2^j - 3)^{-1})$, Where $z_j = \operatorname{arctan} h(\phi_X(\lambda_j))$, $\tilde{z}_j = \operatorname{arctan} h\left(\tilde{\phi}_X(\lambda_j)\right)$ and FN stands for Folded Normal Distribution. The $100(1-\alpha)\%$ confidence interval for the true value of $\phi_{X,\tau}(\lambda_j)$ is then obtained as $\mathrm{CI}_{1-\alpha}(\phi_{X,\tau}(\lambda_j)) = \tanh(\tilde{z}_j - c_2/\sqrt{T/2^j - 3};\ \tilde{z}_j + c_1/\sqrt{T/2^j - 3})$ where c_1 and c_2 are folded normal critical values.

3 Analysis

First, we present the summary statistic of the nine Forex markets under analysis. The results are shown in Table 2.

From the table, it could be seen that the Chinese market has the least deviation, something that is in line with China's tightly controlled Forex market. Among the group, South Korea registers the highest variance, followed by Japan and India. None of the series follow normal distribution, as the JB statistic rejects the null of normalcy.

Next we proceed towards the main part of the analysis. First, we present the result of wavelet multiple correlation. The wavelet multiple correlation values along with 95% upper and lower confidence intervals are displayed in Table 3 and the WMC plot is shown in Fig. 1.

Table 2 Summary statistics

Market	Min	Mean	Max	SD	JBS
China	−0.00433	−4.2636e−005	0.00788	0.000524	130.09 (0.000)
Hong Kong	−0.00107	−8.2865e−008	0.00109	0.000140	956.09 (0.000)
India	−0.01631	6.9667e−005	0.01710	0.002468	474.26 (0.000)
Japan	−0.02265	4.1086e−006	0.01451	0.002894	108.60 (0.000)
South Korea	−0.05742	3.1479e−005	0.04401	0.003578	69.76 (0.000)
Malaysia	−0.01178	2.1163e−005	0.01205	0.001859	111.56 (0.000)
Singapore	−0.009614	−2.6749e−005	0.01170	0.001564	26.48 (0.000)
Taiwan	−0.01486	4.4037e−007	0.01079	0.001354	93.09 (0.000)
Thailand	−0.0153	−2.2455e−005	0.01941	0.001845	167.60 (0.000)

Table 3 Wavelet multiple correlation results

Level	WMC	Lower CI	Upper CI
1 (2–4 days)	0.6656181	0.63305	0.695834
2 (4–8 days)	0.7247497	0.684622	0.760498
3 (8–16 days)	0.8072705	0.764096	0.843246
4 (16–32 days)	0.850749	0.799689	0.889592
5 (32–64 days)	0.8995558	0.845142	0.935518
6 (64–128 days)	0.9365296	0.879353	0.967084
7 (128–256 days)	0.9203176	0.79506	0.970286
8 (256–512 days)	0.9962693	0.981651	0.999246

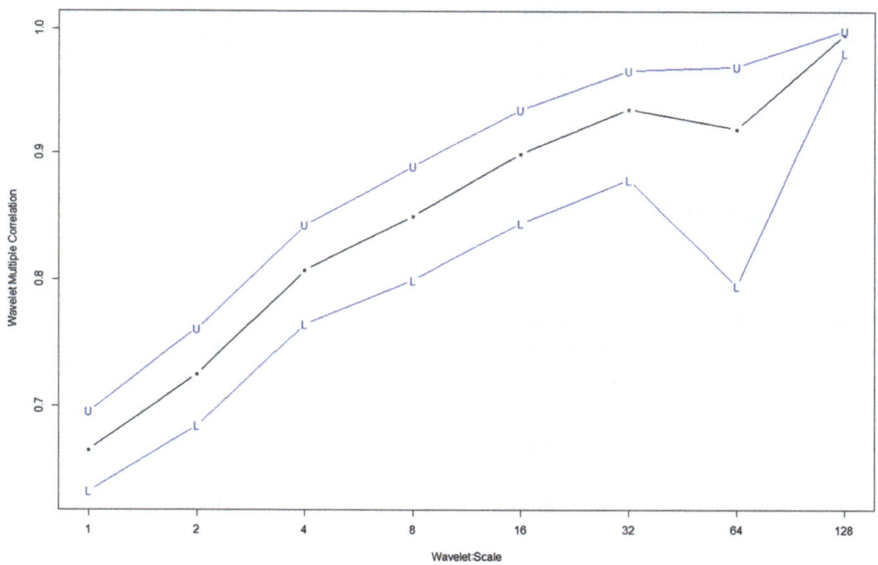

Fig. 1 Wavelet multiple correlation plot

It can be seen that the WMC values are lowest in the intra-week scale. Here, the WMC value 0.665. It implies that around 66.5% of return movement of one market could be explained by the performance of the other markets under analysis. From the perspective of investor, there exists possibility in the short run, up to monthly scales, as the WMC values are relatively low.

The correlation increases across scales and achieve the highest value at annual–biannual scale, indicating near-perfect cointegration, since return movement in one market could be explained by overall performance of other markets. The discrepancies among the Asian Forex market vanish over the long run. The wavelet multiple correlation plot is presented in Fig. 1.

The country that maximizes multiple correlations against others at each scale is selected as a potential leader/follower and wavelet multiple cross-correlation is estimated for positive and negative lags (leads). The country that maximizes WMC at various scales is shown in the top left corner of each plot. Here, Singapore maximizes WMC at each scale. From the plots, it could be seen that at low scales (1–3), the multiple correlation is moderate and become negligible after few lags. Here, the maximum value of multiple cross-correlation is found at the zero lag, hence, we could say the markets are synchronized at these scales. However, at scales 4 and 5, we can see that the maximum value of WMCC is obtained around a negative lag(Lead) of 1, implying that Singapore could possibility lead the other markets at these scales. Considering the fact that Singapore is one of the most developed Asian market economies and has the highest Per-capita GDP among the group, this behavior seems plausible. At scale 6 also, the maximum value of WMCC is obtained at lag zero, implying the lack of lead lag relationships. The WMCC values are depicted in Table 4 and the multiple cross-correlation plots are displayed in Fig. 2.

4 Concluding Remarks

The study employed a new methodology namely wavelet multiple correlation and wavelet multiple cross-correlation to analyze cointegration of nine Asian Forex markets. First, wavelet multiple correlation was estimated as the square root of the regression coefficient of determination in that linear combination of wavelet coefficients for which the coefficient of determination is maximum. At the shorter scales, the markets were moderately correlated and the value of correlation coefficient increases over scales. The results indicated that Asian Forex markets are co-integrated at the annual–biannual scale. Next, we estimated wavelet multiple cross-correlation, by considering 24 lags between the observed and fitted values from the same linear combination, as before, at six wavelet scales. It was found that Singapore is correlated against the linear combination of other Forex markets at all lags and frequencies. Multiple cross-correlation results showed that cross-correlation increases with the increase of scale. Singapore was identified as the potential leader at scales 4 and 5 (16–64 days).

The results could be interpreted both from the perspective of macroeconomic policy as well that of portfolio risk diversification. From a policy perspective, as the markets are moderately correlated at high frequencies, there is a chance of successful intervention by the monetary authority in the case of exogenous shocks for a short time. From the point of view of risk diversification, it could be seen that the Asian Forex markets offer the possibility of portfolio diversification opportunities for the investors with a short-term investment time horizon.

Table 4 Wavelet multiple cross-correlation results

Levels	Lags/Leads										
	−24	−18	−12	−6	−1	0	1	6	12	18	24
1	0.1044	0.0502	0.0979	0.0650	0.3406	0.6656	0.4706	0.0723	0.0818	0.0829	0.0675
2	0.0582	0.1401	0.0776	0.1209	0.4508	0.7247	0.2183	0.1617	0.1378	0.0827	0.0415
3	0.0983	0.1678	0.2046	0.4703	0.7535	0.8072	0.5439	0.3538	0.1549	0.1547	0.1165
4	0.1610	0.1656	0.4882	0.1828	0.8553	0.8507	0.7582	0.3725	0.4323	0.3191	0.2023
5	0.4807	0.5555	0.2246	0.6300	0.8942	0.8995	0.8480	0.3878	0.4114	0.6863	0.3239
6	0.3596	0.2958	0.5985	0.854	0.9344	0.9365	0.9236	0.7940	0.5017	0.2114	0.3493

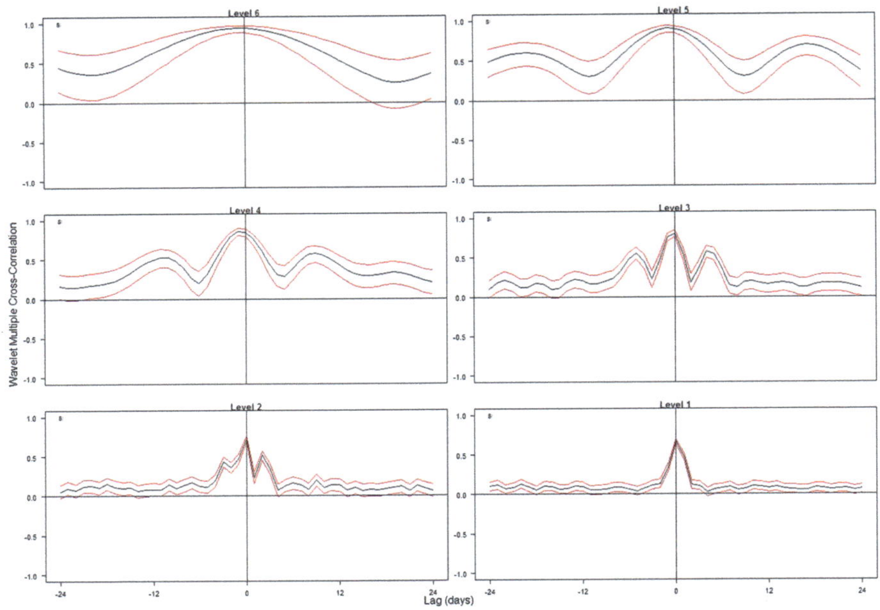

Fig. 2 Wavelet multiple cross-correlation plot

References

Ahmad, R., Rhee, S. G., & Wong, Y. M. (2012). Foreign exchange market efficiency under recent crises: Asia-Pacific focus. *Journal of International Money and Finance, 31*(6), 1574–1592. doi:10.1016/j.jimonfin.2012.02.016.

Aroskar, R., Sarkar, S. K., & Swanson, P. E. (2004). European foreign exchange market efficiency: Evidence based on crisis and non-crisis periods. *International Review of Financial Analysis, 13* (3), 333–347.

AuYong, H. H., Gan, C., & Treepongkaruna, S. (2004). Cointegration and causality in the Asian and emerging foreign exchange markets: Evidence from the 1990s financial crises. *International Review of Financial Analysis, 13,* 479–515. doi:10.1016/j.irfa.2004.02.024.

Baillie, R. T., & Bollerslev, T. (1989). Common stochastic trends in a system of exchange rates. *The Journal of Finance, 44*(1), 167–181.

Bohdalova, M., & Grigus, M. (2014). Cointegration analysis of the foreign exchange rate pairs. In *BTU conference on innovation, technology transfer and education* (pp. 147–153).

Chaudhry, S. A., & Javid, A. Y. (2012). *Efficiency of the foreign exchange markets of South Asian countries*. Pakistan Institute of Development Studies, Working Paper 82.

Fernández-Macho, J. (2012). Wavelet multiple correlation and cross-correlation: A multiscale analysis of Eurozone stock markets. *Physica A: Statistical Mechanics and its Applications, 391* (4), 1097–1104. doi:10.1016/j.physa.2011.11.002.

Fisher, E. A. (1921). On the "probable error" of a coefficient of correlation deduced from a small sample. *Metron, 11,* 3–32.

Jeon, B. N., & Lee, E. (2002). Foreign exchange market efficiency, cointegration, and policy coordination. *Applied Economics Letters, 9*(1), 61–68.

Johnson, N. L., Kotz, S., & Balakrishnan, N. (1995). *Continuous univariate distributions* (Vol. 2). New York: Wiley.

Phengpis, C. (2006). Market efficiency and cointegration of spot exchange rates during periods of economic turmoil: Another look at European and Asian currency crises. *Journal of Economics and Business, 58*(4), 323–342. doi:10.1016/j.jeconbus.2005.10.003.

Phengpis, C., & Nguyen, V. (2009). Policy coordination and risk premium in foreign exchange markets for major EU currencies. *Journal of International Financial Markets, Institutions and Money, 19*(1), 47–62.

Rapp, T. A., & Sharma, S. (1999). Exchange rate market efficiency: Across and within countries. *Journal of Economics and Business, 51*(5), 423–439.

Part II
International Trade and Economic Growth

Nexus Between International Trade and Economic Growth

Laila Memdani

Abstract Trade is considered by many economists as an engine of economic growth. Trade openness accelerates economic development is believed by many economists. The main objective of this paper is to study the link between economic growth and trade and also to study how the link varies according to the level of income of the countries. There are allegations by poor and middle income countries that trade is not promoting growth for them but it helps the rich countries to become richer. The data for all the countries of the world is collected from the official website of World Bank from 1990 to 2014. The countries are divided into high income countries, middle income countries and low income countries. VECM is used to study the long–run- and short-run causality between trade and growth.

Keywords Trade · Development · FDI · Exports · Imports · Panel data analysis

JEL Classification F2 · F14 · F15 · F63

1 Introduction

Trade is considered by many economists as an engine of economic growth. Many economists believe that trade openness accelerates economic development. The swift growth may be a transitional effect so that it is reasonable to consider trade openness to be accelerating economic growth, rather than just leading to a, one-time adjustment in real income (Dollar and Kraay 2004). When India slowly opened its economy, there were fears that imports will shoot up and there may also be capital flight. But many others are also skeptical about it. Competition will increase and domestic industries will be killed, i.e., the phenomenon of big fish eats the smaller

L. Memdani (✉)
Department of Economics, IBS Hyderabad (a Constituent of IFHE University), Hyderabad, India
e-mail: lailam@ibsindia.org

B. Kamaiah et al. (eds.), *Current Issues in Economics and Finance*,
DOI 10.1007/978-981-10-5810-3_5

fish. There are fears among the poor countries that trade may be an engine of growth for rich countries but same may not be true for poor countries.

2 Literature Review

The relationship between economic growth and international trade has attracted attention of many economists. Many researchers studied export-led growth hypothesis, since export is an important component of International trade (Lee and Huang 2002; Zhang et al. 2015, Gokmenoglu et al. 2015). Even though export-led growth is intensively researched, the direction of causality is ambiguous (Gokmenoglu et al. 2015; Katircioglu and Benar 2007). But they failed to produce conclusive results (Deme 2002). According to, Rivera-Batiz and Romer (1991) increase of international trade also increases growth by increasing the number of specialized production centers. According to them, economic integration can cause a permanent increase in the worldwide rate of growth. Starting from a position of no trade, closer integration is possible by increasing either trade in goods or by flows of ideas. Both the forms of integration increase the rate of growth if it leads to increasing returns to scale in the research and development sector.

Many empirical studies confirmed the trade-led growth hypothesis for some group of countries whereas others rejected it for some other group of countries (Deme 2002). Arkolakis et al. (2012), aimed to study the welfare gains of trade and came to conclusion that "So far, not much."

The link between trade and development has been examined via financial development by many researchers (Zhang et al. 2015, Gokmenoglu et al. 2015). They found that trade leads to economic development of the country concerned. Open trade will increase competition and force domestic producers to produce quality products which will increase exports, income levels and will have multiplier effects in the economy.

Batiz and Romer (1991) there are two main findings: first, market liberalization alone is not sufficient, and economic system reform and the liberalization are closely related and complement and promote each other. Second, experimentations via special economic zones (SEZs) and opening to foreign direct investment (FDI), which facilitated and supported cluster development and learning-by-doing, are needed for industrial upgrading and export competitiveness.

According to Arnim and Sundaram (2008) World Bank has developed a number of models to show large gains for developing countries through trade liberalization. They observe that actual gains are far less for developing countries and much more for the developed rich countries. These models ignore the risks of displacement, economic downturns, and rising debt (Table 1).

The aim of this paper is to study the link between trade and economic development in high income countries of Europe and America and low and middle income countries of Asia and Africa and study if there is any significant difference in the link between these two groups of countries.

Table 1 Literature review

Author	Methodology	Findings
Zhang et al. (2015)	Dynamic panel estimation for provinces of China	Both trade and financial openness are statistically significant determinants of but that openness has a negative impact on the size of financial development
Jawaid (2015)	Granger causality tests for Thailand	FDI and international trade have positively contributed to the economic growth of Thailand
Greenaway et al. (2011)	Dynamic panel framework	Liberalization positively impact on growth, with a lag
Gries et al. (2009)	Hsiao-Granger method for 16 sub-Saharan African countries	Trade openness has influenced economic development marginally. The Sub-Saharan African countries have failed to benefit from trade openness
Tekin (2012)	Granger causality testing for African Least developed countries over a period from 1970 to 2010	The paper finds no significant causality amongst foreign aid, openness to trade, and economic growth in a panel of African LDCs
Gokmenoglu et al. (2015)	Granger causality testing for Pakistan	The paper confirms for a long-run relationship among international trade, financial development and economic growth. The findings indicate that international trade and financial development drive economic growth in Pakistan
Katircioglu and Benar (2007)	Annual data over the period ranging from 1965 to 2004 was used to investigate cointegration and Granger causality tests between financial development, international trade, and growth	Results reveal that there is a long-run equilibrium relationship between financial development, international trade and real income growth in the case of India. Unidirectional causality was between real income to exports and imports, from exports to imports, M2 and domestic credits, from M2 to imports, from imports to domestic credits. Bidirectional causality was observed between real income and M2, and between real income and domestic credits. Finally, no causality was found between M2 and domestic credits
Katircioglu Kahyalar and Benar (2007)	Annual data from 1965 to 2004 has been used to examine the relationship between the variables. Co-integration and Granger causality tests were employed to find the relationship between financial development and growth	Results show that there exists a long-run relationship between financial development, trade and growth in the case of India
Dollar and Kraay (2004)	Panel data of over 100 countries	That changes in growth rates are highly correlated with changes in trade volumes

3 Methodology

Since most of the researchers studied the relation using Granger Causality and Dynamic Panel Data analysis, in this paper an attempt is made to study the relation using cointegration and Vector Error Correction Mechanism model. The data is for all the countries of the world are collected from World Bank's official website from 1990 to 2014 for Per capita Gross Domestic Product (PCGDP), Exports (EX), Imports (IMP) and Foreign Direct Investment (FDI). The countries are then divided into three categories viz., high income countries (HIC), middle income countries (MIC) and low income countries (LIC). The categorization is also as per the World Banks division.

In stage one, all the variables were transformed into their natural logarithms (which also avoids the problem of hetroscedasticity) and tested for the presence of unit roots in the variables.

In the second stage, if the variables are found to be I(1), i.e., is integrated of order one, then they are to be tested for the cointegration among the variables using Johansen Cointegration methods.

In stage three, since the variables are found to be cointegrated, then the linkages among the variables using the Vector Error Correction Mechanism (VECM) methodology is done. VECM gives both short-run- and long-run causality among the variables.

4 Results and Discussion

The results of Panel Unit root tests are summarized in Table 2. The results revealed that all the variables for all the three categories of countries had unit root at levels but they become stationary at first difference, i.e., all the variables are I(1).

In the second stage, cointegration test was performed and the results are summarized in Table 3. Cointegration test is used to find out the presence of long-run relationship between the set of variables. The absence of cointegration suggests that the variables have no long-run equilibrium relationship and they can wander randomly away from each other (Dickey et al. 1991).

Both the trace test and max-eigen tests show that the variables are cointegrated and when the variables are cointegrated the VECM methodology is most appropriate.

The VECM results for the three categories of countries are summarized in Table 4.

The VECM results give short-run- and long-run causality amongst the variables for the three groups of countries. The ECT coefficient for all the three group of countries is negative but for HIC it is not significant meaning that there is no significant long-run causality for HICs from trade to growth. It is highly significant for LICs and it is also significant for MICs. For HIC the LPCGDP terms are

Table 2 Unit root test results

Variable	Test	MIC				HIC				LIC			
		Level		First difference		Level		First difference		Level		First difference	
		Statistic	Prob	Statistic	Prob	Statistic	Prob	Statistic	Prob	Statistic	Prob	Statistic	Prob
LPCGDP	Levin, Lin and Chu t*	23.67	1	−26.1	0	13.68	1	−24	0	6.557	1	−51.81	0
	ADF -	8.86	1	1063	0	6.57	1	764.8	0	7.596	1	449.7	0
	PP -	8.28	1	1113	0	5.78	1	766.8	0	7.761	1	468.3	0
LIMP	Levin, Lin and Chu t*	22.63	1	−31.6	0	16.62	1	−27	0	9.375	1	−111	0
	ADF -	5.27	1	1227	0	5.29	1	857.2	0	8.989	1	375.2	0
	PP	5.17	1	1287	0	4.78	1	891.1	0	9.22	1	400.6	0
LEX	Levin, Lin and Chu t*	23.48	1	−28.9	0	1	57	−25	0	9.956	1	−106.5	0
	ADF	7.93	1	1131	0	1	57	809.8	0	9.417	1	393.9	0
	PP -	6.05	1	1263	0	1	57	895.5	0	9.27	1	418.7	0
LFDI	Levin, Lin and Chu t*	8.47	1	−48.9	0	3.23	1	−42.2	0	3.57	1	−29.1	0
	ADF -	37.19	1	1813	0	62.44	1	1407	0	22.61	1	507	0
	PP -	32.88	1	1943	0	71.22	1	1402	0	33.94	0.96	650.4	0

Table 3 Results of cointegration test

Cointegration test												
No. of CE (s)	MIC				HIC				LIC			
	Trace test	Prob	Max-eigen test	Prob	Trace test	Prob	Max-eigen test	Prob	Trace test	Prob	Max-eigen test	Prob
None	966.9	0.00	765.0	0.00	636.0	0.00	484.7	0.00	436.3	0.00	357.9	0.0
At most 1	428.3	0.00	335.5	0.00	262.2	0.00	212.0	0.00	126.0	0.00	96.16	0.0
At most 2	248.4	0.00	195.5	0.06	137.6	0.07	111.8	0.54	68.21	0.04	66.58	0.06
At most 3	255.1	0.00	255.1	0.00	168.9	0.00	168.9	0.00	48.66	0.53	48.66	0.53

Table 4 VECM results

	HIC	LIC	MIC
LPCGDP(−1)	1	1	1
LEX(−1)	−66.0367	−0.30935	10.85996
	−16.9114	−0.1147	−3.63718
	[−3.90486]	[−2.69711]	[2.98582]
LIMP(−1)	85.70099	0.380335	3.529008
	−17.9152	−0.11548	−4.04602
	[4.78371]	[3.29350]	[0.87222]
LFDI(−1)	−20.8824	−0.06225	−16.6803
	−1.37754	−0.01199	−1.02373
	[−15.1592]	[−5.19086]	[−16.2937]
C	−57.4512	−6.45558	−1.64621
Error correction:	D(LPCGDP)	D(LPCGDP)	D(LPCGDP)
CointEq1	−5.65E−05	−0.18832	−0.00048
	−5.80E−05	−0.01706	−0.00017
	[−0.96926]	[−11.0409]	[−2.79609]
D(LPCGDP(−1))	0.087644	0.007208	0.020698
	−0.03543	−0.04147	−0.03394
	[2.47345]	[0.17381]	[0.60983]
D(LPCGDP(−2))	−0.10354	0.04823	0.010225
	−0.03465	−0.03718	−0.03138
	[−2.98855]	[1.29717]	[0.32580]
D(LEX(−1))	0.006368	−0.03054	0.050915
	−0.03507	−0.04894	−0.02839
	[0.18157]	[−0.62409]	[1.79325]
D(LEX(−2))	0.094112	−0.01448	−0.01946
	−0.03233	−0.04853	−0.02739
	[2.91126]	[−0.29831]	[−0.71043]
D(LIMP(−1))	0.036875	0.028554	0.048857
	−0.03657	−0.04565	−0.02963
	[1.00830]	[0.62551]	[1.64869]
D(LIMP(−2))	−0.02064	0.007985	0.010184
	−0.03433	−0.04543	−0.02855
	[−0.60129]	[0.17574]	[0.35673]
D(LFDI(−1))	0.000445	−0.00071	−0.00241
	−0.00114	−0.00244	−0.00404
	[0.39191]	[−0.28950]	[−0.59813]
D(LFDI(−2))	0.000841	0.000951	−0.00125
	−0.00092	−0.00227	−0.0036
	[0.91414]	[0.41898]	[−0.34544]
C	0.037824	0.046727	0.054239

(continued)

Table 4 (continued)

	HIC	LIC	MIC
	−0.00465	−0.01104	−0.00431
	[8.13179]	[4.23315]	[12.5877]
R-squared	0.030709	0.204149	0.02659
Adj. *R*-squared	0.023623	0.190635	0.021066
F-statistic	4.333423	15.10599	4.81376

significant. D(LEX) with two lags is significant. LIMP and LFDI are also not significant. Coming to MICs D(LEX) is significant with a lag and D(LIMP) is also significant with one lag. FDI terms are not significant. For MIC we do not have any significant terms.

5 Conclusions

Trade has got long-term convergence with LPCGDP for LICs and MICs but not for HICs. There is short-run causality from trade to GDP for MIC and HIC but not for LIC. Thus the results disapprove the strong trade and development linkages which are being discussed in theory. Of course, we find long-run causality existing but very less short-run causality. The article also proves that low income countries are not much benefitted with trade. This result suggests that the governments of LICs rather than concentrating on external sector for development can focus on internal sector. They can focus on the development of infrastructural, education, and health facilities and on the development of its manufacturing and agricultural sector for the development. Development of these sectors will lead to the development of the external sector as well.

References

Arkolakis, C., Costinot, A., & Clare, A. (2012). New trade models, same old gains? *American Economic Review, 102*(1), 94–130.

Arnim, R., & Sundaram, J. K. (2008). Trade liberalization for development? Who gains? Who loses? *Economic and Political Weekly, 43*(48), 29.

Deme, M. (2002). An examination of the trade led growth hypothesis in Nigeria: A cointegration, causality and impulse response analysis. *Journal of Developing Areas, 36*(1), 1–15.

Dickey, D. A., Jansen, D. W., & Fuller, W. A. (1991). A primer on cointegration with an application tomoney andincome. *Review Federal Reserve Bank of St Louis, 73,* 58e78.

Dollar, D., & Kraay, A., (2004). Trade, Growth, and Poverty*. *The Economic Journal, 114,* F22–F49. doi:10.1111/j.0013-0133.2004.00186.x

Gokmenoglu, K. K., Amin, M. Y., & Taspinar, N. (2015). The relationship among international trade, financial development and economic growth: The case of Pakistan. *Proceedia Economics and Finance, 25,* 489–496.

Gries, T., Kraft, M., & Meierrieks, D. (2009). Linkages between financial deepening, trade openness, and economic development: Causality evidence from Sub-Saharan Africa. *World Development, 37*(12), 1849–1860.

Jawaid, S. T. (2015). Trade openness and economic growth: A lesson from Pakistan. *Foreign Trade Review, 49,* 193–217.

Katircioglu, S., & Benar, H. (2007). Financial development, trade and growth triangle: The case of India. *International Journal of Social Economics, 34,* 586–598.

Lee, C. H., & Huang, B. N. (2002). The relationship between exports and economic growth in East Asian countries: A multivariate threshold autoregressive approach. *Journal of Economic Development, 27*(2), 45–68.

Rivera-Batiz, L. A., & Romer, P. M. (1991). Economic integration and endogenous growth. *The Quarterly Journal of Economics, 106*(2), 531–555.

Tekin, R. B. (2012). Development aid, openness to trade and economic growth in least developed countries: Bootstrap panel granger causality analysis. *Procedia—Social and Behavioral Sciences, 82,* 716–721.

Zhang, C., Zhu, Y., & Lu, Z. (2015). Trade openness, financial openness, and financial development in China. *Journal of International Money and Finance, 59,* 287–309.

Causality Between Exports and GDP: An Empirical Evidence from BIMSTEC Region

Gurpreet Kaur, Vishal Sarin and Jasdeep Kaur Dhami

Abstract The purpose of this study is to assess the empirical relationship between Export and GDP for BIMSTEC nations by using time series data from the period 1997–2015. Economic integration within regional trading blocs adds the significant value to increase economic growth, trade, investment, etc. BIMSTEC was proposed with the object to merge the Thailand's "Look West" policy and ASEAN with the "Look East" policy of India and South Asia. To achieve the aim of study time series data had been used for testing econometric technique (Augmented Dickey-Fuller Test, Co integration and Granger Causality) to the assessment of hypothesis of GDP strategy led by exports and exports led by GDP. Granger Causality model is based on the following hypotheses for testing the causality and cointegration between GDP and export for BIMSTEC nations. (1) Whether there is bidirectional causality between GDP growth and export for BIMSTEC nations. (2) Whether there is unidirectional causality between the two variables, (3) Whether there is no causality between GDP and export for BIMSTEC nations. (4) Whether there exists a long-run relationship between GDP and EXPORT for BIMSTEC nations. The results explained the evidence of bidirectional causality between GDP and export among BIMSTEC bloc. The results support the exports led growth and growth-led export in case of BIMSTEC. For making BIMSTEC a "vibrant regional entity", there are needs to revitalize coastal shipping preparations and inter-modal transport, practices for easy flow of goods and services.

Keywords BIMSTEC · Export · GDP · Cointegration · Unit root
Granger causality

JEL Classification F15 · C13 · C12

G. Kaur · V. Sarin
School of Business, Lovely Professional University, Phagwara, India
e-mail: preeeti30@gmail.com

V. Sarin
e-mail: vishal.sarin09@gmail.com

J.K. Dhami (✉)
CT Institute of Management and Information Technology, Jalandhar, Punjab, India
e-mail: bawa_mangat@yahoo.com

B. Kamaiah et al. (eds.), *Current Issues in Economics and Finance*,
DOI 10.1007/978-981-10-5810-3_6

1 Introduction

In the present world, no nations survive into economic isolation. Each and every aspects of economy—its industries, service sector, employment and levels of income, and living standard are associated to the economies of its trading cohorts (Cherunilam 2006). The high level of economic interdependence between economies reflects the historical advancement of the world's economic and political regulation. International economics continues to flourish present world because the analytical and policy issues that brought it into being still demand attention (Carbaugh 2008). In Asia there are different regional trading blocs such as Association of Southeast Asian Nations (ASEAN), South Asia Association of Regional Cooperation (SAARC), Economic Cooperation Organization (ECO), Mekong–Ganga Cooperation (MGC), Bay of Bengal Initiative for Multi-Sectoral Technical and Economic Cooperation (BIMSTEC), Shanghai Cooperation Organization (SCO), Asia Cooperation Dialogue (ACD), Gulf Cooperation Council (GCC). These trade blocs plays significant role for the growth of Asian nations. BIMSTEC is an intercontinental organization linking a cluster of nations in South Asia and South East Asia including Bangladesh, Bhutan, India, Nepal, Myanmar India, Sri Lanka, and Thailand. In 1990s, these countries determined to get engaged in a regional corporation with a view to attain superior economies of scale in production, achieve specialism, boost competitiveness, expand export basket, and make utilization of their under-utilized economic impending in terms of human being, technological, and natural resources with lesser potential of back-sliding. In Bangkok, in June 1997 the new sub-regional alliance was created and specified the name BIST-EC, i.e., Bangladesh, India, Sri Lanka, and Thailand Economic Cooperation. Myanmar was present at the foundational gathering as a spectator and connected with group as a complete part at a special ministerial conference convened at Bangkok on December 1997, and the name has been altered to BIMSTEC. BIMSTEC took initiative with the objective to merge the Thailand's "Look West" policy and ASEAN with the "Look East" policy of India. BIMSTEC can explain as association among ASEAN and SARRC. The uniqueness of BIMSTEC is in multi-sectoral approach compared to other Asian blocs. Seven members of BIMSTEC cover up 14 main concern sectors escort through associate nations in a voluntary approach, i.e., Agriculture, Cultural Cooperation, Environment and Disaster Management, Public Health, People-to-People Contract, Poverty Alleviation, Trade and Investment, Technology, Energy, Transport and Communication, Tourism, Fisheries, Counter-Terrorism and intercontinental Crimes and Climate Change (BIMSTEC.org).

Historically, the Bay of Bengal has been an essential component of India's strategic, economic, and civilization areas of interest and consciousness. BIMSTEC was formed at the time when the process of globalization was sweeping the world. At the end of cold war, the nonaligned movement lost its relevance. China had emerged as a strong economy. WTO had been formed in 1995. SAARC, the South Asian regional organization, which was formed in 1985, was not making any headway due to mutual dissensions and mistrust of member countries. This was broadly the international and regional scenario when BIMSTEC was being conceived and formed in 1997. The creation of BIMSTEC can be accredited to two things—one is the breakdown of SAARC to form energetic regional environment for trade and economic cooperation and second is ongoing procedure of liberalization of South Asian economies frantic to find out latest markets in the ASEAN region as alternative of SAARC, whose scale is restricted due to non-economic aspect that is improbable to alter in the close future. One more aspect, which might be cited for the creation of this bloc, is Thailand's craving to set up strong grip on the Indian subcontinent as of escalating competition it has been facing in the ASEAN markets. Although BIMSTEC came into reality very recently, its creation can be traced back to mid-1960 s, when together India and Sri Lanka were invited to attach ASEAN but declined. In 1981, Sri Lanka made vain effort to join ASEAN, but it was mutually India and Pakistan which obtained Dialogue Partner status in 1993. The approach of South Asian nations to establish connection and enlarge economic cooperation shows their purpose to support economic associations with the ASEAN countries. BIMSTEC might be used as instrument for South Asian nations to set up and enlarge a good-quality relationship with the ASEAN nations (Devi 2007).

The main thing that makes BIMSTEC dissimilar as of other groups is that BIMSTEC represents one of the most varied region of the world in the sense of life style, religion, language, and culture. BIMSTEC has visibly renowned issues of development and scrutinizing into 14 main concern sectors which covers a diversity of facets of "development" and the issue of general concern like counterterrorism and intercontinental crime. The seven new sectors were discussed in the first BIMSTEC Summit. BIMSTEC links 1.5 billion people, more than 21% of world population and has a combined GDP of nearly US$2.5 trillion (BIMSTEC.org). BIMSTEC was to create economic and social affluence based on equality in order to enhance of common benefits in economics, social, and technological aspects, it also engross intra-regional aid in training, research and development as well as cooperation in industry, agriculture, expansion of trade and investment, upgradation in communication and transport, improving living standard and collaboration with other international organization (Chakraborty 2007). In Asia Pacific, BIMSTEC is playing important role to attract trade and investment. India played a significant role to integrate trade and investments for the promotion of economic cooperation in the region. The northeastern states of Mizoram, Nagaland, Assam, Arunachal Pradesh, Meghalaya, Sikkim, Tripura, and Manipur are enclosed by Bangladesh, Myanmar, and Bhutan, and are essential to the BIMSTEC proposal. These are essential to BIMSTEC in the sense its association consist of nations from South and Southeast Asian regions. BIMSTEC has a potential to enhance the trade between member countries by taking benefit of their geographical position in the region of the Bay of Bengal and the Eastern Coast of the Indian Ocean. A number of initiatives towards intra-regional trade liberalization among individual associate nations of BIMSTEC under bilateral and regional trade agreements have been undertaken in the earlier period.

Being lead country in the grouping, India draws attention in the BIMSTEC framework and its functioning in the backdrop of the fast changing global economic environment. India is the fast emerging global power and is both the factor for peace and stability as well as dynamic economic player in the region. India with its recent economic clout, capacity building measure and IT prowess, together with the gradual shift in the foreign policy outlook to suit to be rapid change in global geo-political issues, deserve a special status in the BIMSTEC region. The BIMSTEC nations contain both developing nations and Least Developed Countries (LDCs). Therefore, they are characterized by higher tariff barriers on their imports, vis-à-vis their developed counterparts. It was anticipated that while on one hand the special treatment would permit the nations to increase improved access in each other's market. Furthermore apart from the tariff barriers, it was predictable that the trade facilitation procedures would considerably lower the level of transaction costs, which presently put a downward pressure on the intra-regional trade dimensions (Devi 2007).

2 Rationale and Objective of Study

This study conducted with aim to evaluate the empirical analysis of causality between GDP and exports in case of BIMSTEC region. The existing literature focused on the issues such as trade, investment, economic cooperation, political diplomacy, etc., but there is lack of existence of studies on the exports and GDP relations in BIMSTEC region. Since issue is a vital one, the paper is conducted for intensive analysis on the topic "Causality between Exports and GDP: Empirical Evidence from BIMSTEC Region" to overcome the research gap. The study provides the policies formulation to gain from their mutual trade. The famous econometric model Granger Causality has been used to analyze the cause and effect relationship between GDP and Exports in case of BIMSTEC region.

3 Review of Literature

This section provides an overview of previous research on knowledge sharing and intranets. It introduces the framework for the research paper that comprises the main focus of the research methodology used for paper.

Stait (2005) studied the export-led growth pattern for Egypt from 1977 to 2003. The study employed cointegration analysis, Granger causality tests, and unit root tests, joined with Vector Auto Regression (VAR), and Impulse Response Function (IRF) analyses. After making analysis paper concluded that there was unidirectional relationship between exports and GDP, but no relationship between exports and investment. At last, the study depicted the effect of economic reforms that was undertaken in 1991 and still holds the Export-Led Growth hypothesis in Egypt economy.

Clarke and Ralhan (2005) derived the direct and indirect causality between exports and economic output for Bangladesh and Sri Lanka. The study revealed that Granger causality at longer horizons that usually used in multivariate system, leads to bidirectional causality between exports and output of economy, even when there was not one period causality. The longer horizon causality rises indirectly through one or more of the supplementary variables.

Dritsakis et al. (2006) developed the empirical causal relationship among exports, gross capital formation, foreign direct investments and economic growth using a multivariate autoregressive VAR model for Greece for the period 1960–2002. The results indicated that there was only one cointegrated vector between the observed variables, while Granger causality tests uncovered that there had been unidirectional causal relationship between exports and gross fixed capital formation and unidirectional causal relationship between foreign direct investments and economic growth.

Jordaan and Eita (2009) explained the causal relationship between export and economic growth for Botswana from 1996 to 2007. The study illustrated that there had been two-directional causality between export and economic growth. These variables complement each other indicated that the export-led growth hypothesis as well as reverse causality. The results recommended that in order to achieve high economic growth, policies meant for export expansion has to be encouraged and dedicated resources on the non-export goods and services production.

Mehrara and Firouzjaee (2011) revealed the Granger causality relationship between exports of non-oil and economic growth has been investigated based on panel cointegration analysis for 73 developing countries from 1970 to 2007. The results demonstrated that in both bi- and tri-variate models, there has been bidirectional long run causality between export and GDP growth. Moreover, in case of bivariate model, bidirectional short-run causality between export and GDP growth for non-oil developing countries. However, for oil exporting nations, there has been no short-run causality relationship between the variables.

Ray (2011) accessed empirical the relationship between export and economic growth in India using annual data during the period from 1972–1973 to 2010–2011. The cointegration test established the relationship between economic growth and exports and showed that both were cointegrated and indicated an existence of long-run equilibrium relationship between the two as confirmed. The Granger causality test depicted that the occurrence of bidirectional causality which runs from economic growth to export and vice versa. The error correction estimates provided evidence that in short-run export and GDP are commonly causal.

Mukherji and Pandey (2014) provided extensive examination on relationship between growth of exports and GPD of India by using data from 1969 to 2012 and follow the technique of three steps that demonstrated the relationship between the variable, i.e., Vector Auto Regression (VAR) analysis monitored by a Granger Causality Test and Impulse Response Function. Results explored that growth of exports depends positively on growth of GDP with a year lag. And Granger Causality Test determined that GDP Growth causes Export growth in India. Impulse Response Functions generated indicated that there are much higher responses of export through a change in GDP. Finally, concluded that India backs the theory of Growth-Led Exports.

Amiri (2012) introduced a new way of examined linear and nonlinear Granger causality between exports, imports, and economic growth in France during the period (from 1961 to 2006) using geo-statistical models. Considering the observations of linear and nonlinear using geo-statistical method causality analysis, results have given strong confirmation about causality running from GDP to trade.

Jarra (2013) found the causality between exports, domestic demand and economic growth in Ethiopia by using time series data from the period 1960–2011. The results of Johansen cointegration test revealed the existence of long-run relationship between the variables and the Granger causality test results expressed a dynamic relationship between export and economic growth. The study concluded that exports and domestic demand remained an important factor for economic growth and vice versa.

Kumari and Malhotra (2014) studied the export-led growth in India with cointegration and causality analysis with annual time series data on India for the variables exports and GDP per capita stemming from 1980 to 2012 for analysis. The tests on the long-run- and short-run relationship between exports and economic growth had conducted. The results concluded that there was no long-run equilibrium relationship exists between exports and GDP per capita. The Granger causality test showed bidirectional causality between exports and GDP per capita and vice versa.

Aydin and Sari (2014) explored the relationship between GDP and export for Turkey. The results exposed the series was not stationary for both variables. The obtained results concluded that there has unidirectional causal relationship from the GDP to the export. The study provided a better understanding of possible effects of the GDP in a country related to sustainable development in terms of the export. The study helped in targeting beginner groups in economical society for economical modelling.

Travkina (2015) opined the export and GDP growth in Lithuania with short-run- or middle-run causality. This paper discussed the relationship between international trades especially export and the economic growth, presented by GDP, in Lithuania during the period of 2000–2015. The study observed that the test based on Granger causality in the export–GDP system has been export-led growth hypothesis found in Lithuania only in the short run.

4 Research Methodology

This study uses an augmented granger causality model to analyze the cause-and-effect relationship between the two macroeconomic variables, i.e., GDP and Exports in BIMSTEC region combining seven nations of South Asia and South East Asia.

4.1 Data Source

To make the analysis, time series data has been used from 1997 to 2015. The study has been based on secondary data. The data has been compiled from a wide variety of sources such as yearbooks publishing statistical data with respect to trade, UNCTAD, UNCOMTRADE, IMF, Trade Map, and through diverse online data sources.

4.2 Model Specification

To find out the effect of macroeconomic indicators (GDP and Exports) on performance of BIMSTEC nations, the econometrics model Granger Causality has been used. And it is based on the following hypotheses for testing the causality and cointegration between GDP and Export for BIMSTEC nations. (1) Whether there is bidirectional causality between GDP growth and export for BIMSTEC nations. (2) Whether there is unidirectional causality between the two variables, (3) Whether there is no causality between GDP and export for BIMSTEC nations. (4) Whether there exists a long-run relationship between GDP and EXPORT for BIMSTEC nations. Model specification mention below as

$$\text{GDP} = f(\text{Export}),$$

where,

GDP	Gross Domestic Product of BIMSTEC nations
Export	Export of BIMSTEC nations.

The relationship between GDP and EXPORT for BIMSTEC nations is expressed with the help of following model:

$$\text{GDP}_t = a + b_t\,\text{Export} + \varepsilon_t$$

The model is based on the assumption that other variables except export remain constant. GDP is Gross Domestic Product of the BIMSTEC nations, Export is the for BIMSTEC nations for specific time period. While ε_t is the error term a and *b* represent the slope and coefficient of regression. The coefficient of regression, i.e., *b* postulate how a unit change in the independent variable affects the dependent variable. The error term (ε_t) is incorporated in the equation to accommodate for other factors that may affect GDP. The validity of the Ordinary Least Squares (OLS) method is determined by the accuracy of assumptions. The study used Gauss–Markov (GM) assumptions including that the dependent and independent variables (GDP and EXPORT) are linearly co-related, the estimators (*a*, *b*) are unbiased with an expected value of zero, i.e., $E\ (\varepsilon_t) = 0$, which indicates that on average the errors cancel out each other. The technique contains postulating the dependent and independent variables. This study used GDP as dependent variable, on the other hand Export as independent variable. In addition, whereas the Ordinary Least Squares regression analysis can establish the dependence of either GDP on EXPORT or not.

4.3 Unit Root Test: Augmented Dicky Fuller

In time series data realization is used to draw conclusion regarding the core stochastic procedure. To draw conclusion from the time series investigation, stationarity test becomes necessary. A stationarity test which has been generally accepted over the past years is unit root test. In this paper Augmented Dickey-Fuller (ADF) test was used to estimation of unit root. ADF consists of estimate the following regression equation:

$$\Delta Yt = \beta o + \omega Yt - 1 + \sum_{i-2}^{m} \Delta Yt - i + \varepsilon,$$

where ,

Y_t VA intellectual coefficient for a company
Δ a first difference operator
ε error term.

The null hypothesis for unit root is

H0: Real GDP has a unit root
H0: Real Exports has a unit root.

Macroeconomic time series data usually characterize through a stochastic trend which can be detached via differencing. A few variables are stationary on levels, others turn into stationary after one differentiation, and a few might turn into stationary through more than one differentiation. The ADF equation has been performed for two cases when it include intercept only and when it include both intercept and time trend (Ray 2011).

4.4 Johanson Cointegration Test

Cointegration, an econometric technique of time series variable, is a prerequisite for the extension of a long term or stability in economic association among two or more variables which has a unit roots. The Johansen technique can establish the number of cointegrated vectors for every certain number of nonstationary variables of the identical order. Two or more random variables are known as cointegrated if each time series have been themselves nonstationary. The test might be regard as a long-term symmetry association between the variables. The rationale of the cointegration tests is to establish whether a cluster of nonstationary series is cointegrated or not. Having recognized the time series characteristic of the data, the test for the presence of long-term association among the variables is done via the Johansen and Juselius (1992). The main approach which is used in this study is Johansen cointegration approach. The Johanson approach can establish the number of cointegrated vectors for any known number of nonstationary variables of the identical order (Ray 2011).

4.5 Granger Causality Test

Causality is a type of statistical reaction theory which is generally using in the construction of forecasting models. Previously, Granger (1969) and Sims (1972) have dignified the application of causality in economics. Granger causality test is a procedure for decisive whether one time series is important in forecasting or not (Granger 1969). The standard Granger causality test seek to establish whether historical values of a variable supports to forecast changes in another variable (Granger 1988).

The simple Granger causality test estimate the bivariate autoregressive processes for GDP and exports to examine the causality between GDP and exports on the one hand and exports and GDP on the other. The purpose is to test the Export-Led Growth (ELG) hypothesis for BIMSTEC (Mehrara and Firouzjaee 2011). To assess causation direction between exports and GDP, Granger test involves estimation of following regression equations:

If causality runs from EXPORT to GDP, the equation is

$$\mathrm{GDP} = \sum_{i=1}^{n} aiXt - i + \sum_{j=1}^{n} \beta j\,\mathrm{EXPORT}_t - j + \in 1_t$$

If causality runs from GDP to EXPORT, the equation is

$$\text{Exports} = \sum_{i=1}^{n} \gamma i X t - i + \sum_{j=1}^{n} \partial j \text{GDP}_t - j + \in 2_t,$$

where GDP_t and Export_t represent gross domestic product and export respectively, ε_{it} is uncorrelated stationary random process, and subscript t denotes the time period.

5 Overview of BIMSTEC Exports and GDP

India is the biggest economy in terms of its macroeconomic indicators while Bhutan is the smallest in the bloc among all the member nations. In between these two, only Thailand can be noticed as a dominant nation in the group. The member states collectively having a combined GDP of US$1.7 trillion in nominal terms and US $4.2 trillion in purchasing power parity (PPP) terms account for approximately one-fifth of the world's population and occupy 3.64% of surface area. The BIMSTEC is characterized by momentous heterogeneity of income among the member countries as all nations are at diverse levels of development (Batra 2010).

The integration of BIMSTEC is one of the most important regional integration process developed among developing countries. It consists of heterogeneous group of countries with wide socioeconomic development. The description provided by Table 1 gives some statistics on GDP growth rates, per capita incomes and demography for the BIMSTEC countries for the periods of 1997 and 2015.

Assessment of Table 1 clearly indicates, in 2015 growth rate has been in double digits for all the countries along with a two to three times increase in the per capita incomes. However, among BIMSTEC countries, India is biggest nation in terms of land area, and Bhutan is the smallest one. India having first rank in population among the BIMSTEC countries lowest population country is Bhutan. As shown in the above table, these countries have a fairly young population with only Thailand having 10% of its population above the age of 65. Almost all the member nations of BIMSTEC have been performing fairly well to make their population literate. Literacy rate in countries like Thailand, Myanmar, Sri Lanka, and Bhutan was more than 90%.

Table 2 depicts that percentage share of exports of BIMSTEC nations in total world exports of and India's share in BIMSTEC exports from 1997 (formation year of BIMSTEC) to 2015. During 1997, the share of BIMSTEC exports in world exports was 0.67% and it increased by 3.01% in 2015. India's share in BIMSTEC exports was 35.84% in 1997 and increased by 63.64% in 2015. The reason for less share in total world exports was BIMSTEC-restricted activities lead to some serious problems such as structural constraints on member states in the form of limited technological, lead-actor inertia, operational and financial capabilities.

Table 1 Demographic and Macroeconomic Indicators of BIMSTEC economies

Parameter/country	Year	India	Bangladesh	Bhutan	Myanmar	Nepal	Sri Lanka	Thailand
Land area (000 km^2)	2015	2,973,190	130,170	38,117	653,080	143,350	62,710	510,890
Population (thousand)	1997	202,853.85	123,574.11	520.92	45,895.99	22,395.25	18,323	60,544.94
	2015	257,563.82	160,995.64	774.83	53,897.15	28,513.70	20,966	67,959.36
% Share of above 65 pop to total pop.	2015	6	5	5	5	6	9	10
% share of population above 15–65 years	2015	66	66	68	67	62	66	72
GCI index ranking	2015	55	107	105	131	100	68	32
Life expectancy (years)	2015	61	63	58	61	60	70	70
Adult literacy (15–24)	2015	89.66	83.20	92.04	96.33	89.95	98.77	98.64
Compound growth rate of GDP in current prices (in %)	1997	4.0	4.5	5.4	5.7	5.0	6.4	−2.8
	2015	7.6	6.6	3.3	7.0	3.4	4.8	2.8
Per capita in current prices (in US$)	1997	47,477.48	325.4765	418,933.7	9332.566	5097.386	15,457.5	145,444.1
	2015	138,103.7	1770.005	1,856,518	59,441.95	18,202.31	58,258.3	370,693.7
HDI rank	2015	130	142	132	148	145	73	93
HDI values	2015	0.609	0.507	0.605	0.536	0.548	0.757	0.726
GDP (US$ billions)	2015	2090.71	205.71	2.21	66.98	21.35	82.09	395.28
Gini index	2015	33.9	32.1	38.1	N/A	32.8	36.4	39.4
Per capita GDP (US $)	1997	434.73	402.89	667.84	155.89	244.087	882.95	2475.10
	2015	1688.38	1265.71	2836.80	1268.68	751.12	3767.58	5426.30

Source World development Report (2015), International Monetary Fund, World Economic Outlook (2015), UNESCO, UNDP

Table 2 Percentage share of BIMSTEC members nations in total exports of BIMSTEC trading bloc

Year	BIMSTEC total exports (in US$ million)	India's total exports (in US$ million)	India share of exports (in BIMSTEC region)	Total world exports (in US$ million)	Share in world exports of BIMSTEC region (%)
1997	3479.375	9709.371	35.84	518,040	0.67
1998	3320.732	9236.492	35.95	515,675	0.64
1999	3691.998	10,045.1	36.75	534,740	0.69
2000	4235.810	12271.7	34.52	612,818	0.69
2001	4387.849	11,891	36.90	591,914	0.74
2002	5009.796	12,834.6	39.03	622,215	0.81
2003	5936.066	15,160.8	39.15	727,197	0.82
2004	7590.420	18,588.6	40.83	882,605	0.86
2005	10,035.264	22,621.3	44.36	996,056	1.01
2006	12,120.061	27,065.2	44.78	1,163,260	1.04
2007	14,589.805	32,094.8	45.46	1,327,590	1.10
2008	18,186.090	38,197.4	47.61	1,537,620	1.18
2009	17,676.504	35,332.4	50.03	1,196,750	1.48
2010	22,040.850	45,216.8	48.74	1,455,890	1.51
2011	30,148.325	56,599.3	53.27	1,738,000	1.73
2012	28,956.477	52,988.2	54.65	1,689,320	1.71
2013	33,661.139	57,600.6	58.44	1,614,760	2.08
2014	37,892.873	61,382.3	61.67	1,856,230	2.59
2015	41,432.672	63,782.5	63.64	1,985,320	3.01

Source UNCTAD and World Trade Organization (WTO)

6 Empirical Results

The model estimated with panel data for seven BIMSTEC countries. It includes Bangladesh, Bhutan, India, Myanmar, Nepal, Sri Lanka, and Thailand. To explore the dynamics of the association among export and economic growth between BIMSTEC with data for the period, 1997–2015 and this include the 17 observations. The two main variables are real GDP and real Export. Both the variables economic growth rate (GDP) and exports measured in US$ million. Study scrutinizes the long-time- and causal dynamic associations among the level of export and GDP. The methodology used in study is the Unit Root Analysis, Co-integration and Granger Causality technique.

If the value of Durbin Watson statistics is close to 2 then the test is reliable, which means no autocorrelation among residuals. If ADF is less (even more negative) than the negative critical value, then series is stationary. If the ADF statistic is greater than the negative critical value, the series is not stationary. Table 3 depicts the results of the unit root test. The outcome showed that variables,

Table 3 The results of the augmented Dickey-Fuller (ADF) test on Real Log_Exports with intercept only

Variables	ADF (0)	ADF(1)	ADF (2)
Intercept only			
Log_Exports	−0.805961	−3.529667	−5.506331
AIC	−2.854670	−2.811707	−2.570938
SB	−2.755740	−2.713682	−2.429328
DW	1.721993	1.824467	1.949881
Prob.[a]	0.432081	0.003033	0.000046
Test critical values			
1% levels	−3.857386		
5% levels	−3.040391		
10% levels	−2.660551		

H0: real GDP has a unit root
AIC Akaike info criterion, *SBC* Schwarz criterion, *DW* Durbin–Watson stat
[a]MacKinnon (1996) one-sided *p* values

Table 4 The results of the augmented Dickey-Fuller (ADF) Test for Log_GDP with intercept only

Variables	ADF (0)	ADF(1)	ADF (2)
Intercept only			
Log_GDP	−1.557235	−2.137017	−7.524975
AIC	−4.467625	−4.383834	−4.169919
SBC	−4.231608	−4.195021	−4.028309
DW	2.192021	1.727483	1.622686
Prob.[a]	0.044233	0.001910	0.000014
Test critical values			
1% levels	−3.959148		
5% levels	−3.081002		
10% levels	−2.681330		

H0: real exports has a unit root
AIC Akaike info criterion, *SBC* Schwarz criterion, *DW* Durbin–Watson stat
[a]MacKinnon (1996) one-sided *p* values

log_exports attained after stationarity at second differencing, using ADF test. The augmented Dickey-Fuller Test (ADF) provides result of stationary at second difference at all lag differences. At this level we reject the null hypothesis and concluded that series of log_exports has stationarity.

Table 4 depicts the outcome of the unit root test. The outcome demonstrate that variable Log_GDP attained stationarity at level using Augmented Dickey-Fuller Test. The augmented Dickey-Fuller Test provides stationary result at first difference at all lag differences. At this level we reject the null hypothesis and concluded that series of Log_GDP has stationarity.

Table 5 illustrates the cointegration rank test for trace and maximum eigen value. At 5% level of significance test statistic was greater than its *p* values. So we

Table 5 Unrestricted cointegration rank test (Trace) and unrestricted cointegration rank test (maximum eigenvalue)

Hypothesized No. of CE(s)	Eigenvalue	Trace statistic	0.05 critical value	Prob.[b]	Max-eigen statistic	0.05 critical value	Prob.[b]
None[a]	0.514117	19.64020	25.87211	0.2447	12.27037	19.38704	0.3904
At most 1	0.351776	7.369828	12.51798	0.3075	7.369828	12.51798	0.3075

Trace test and indicates 1 cointegrating eqn (s) at the 0.05 level Max-eigenvalue test indicates 1 cointegrating eqn (s) at the 0.05 level
H0: Log_Exports and Log_GDP are correlated
[a]Rejection of the hypothesis at the 0.05 level
[b]MacKinnon–Haug–Michelis (1999) *p* values

Table 6 Granger causality test between Log_Exports and Log_GDP

Null hypothesis	Obs	*F* statistic	Prob.
LOG_EXPORTS does not Granger Cause LOG_GDP	17	4.24555	0.0403
LOG_GDP does not Granger Cause LOG_EXPORTS		4.62955	0.0323

accept the null hypothesis at 5% level. Hence we can conclude that Log_exports and Log_GDP are correlated. There are long-run relationship existing between the Log_GDP and Log_Exports.

Table 6 explicates that that there is bidirectional causality between both the variables. Hypothesis was rejected in both the cases since the *F* statistic values greater than 4 and having lag length of 1–4. So reject the null hypothesis in both cases and concluded that LOG_EXPORTS Granger Cause LOG_GDP. In second case also reject the null hypothesis and concluded that Log_GDP Granger Cause to Log_Exports and long-run relationship exists between GDP and Exports. Both leads to economic developments of the region.

7 Policy Implications

Most of the countries in the world have realized that a speedy growth of their economies can be achieved only through integrating their respective economies with the global economy. For that it is necessary for governments of different countries will focus on their energies of liberalization and economic reforms. In order to achieve high level of economic cooperation among the BIMSTEC countries, it is very important to understand and appreciate the structures of individual economies as well as identify the potential areas of trade and economic cooperation.

The existing high tariff barrier among the BIMSTEC countries worked against their basic development objectives. The BIMSTEC accord aimed to form a Free Trade Zone (FTZ) where tariffs would be bring down to zero by 2014. The LDCs that are Bangladesh and Myanmar of the bloc has given additional time to drop their tariff rates to zero level by 2017. There will be need to softening and liberalizing of complex and extensive trade formalities to move towards the millennium goals.

The BIMSTEC was the initiative of creating free trade area among the member nations and expanding it to other nations and regional trade blocs also. The member nations together signed a Framework Agreement to set up a FTZ to create a favorable atmosphere for trade for the member nations without any barriers. The agreement Free Trade Agreement was signed between Bangladesh, India, Myanmar, Sri Lanka, and Thailand on February 8, 2004 at Phuket, (Thailand) but its implementation had been delayed. There is a need to take the necessary steps for implementation of FTZ for trade promotion.

The necessity of hour is interdependence between member nations to compete the fast globalized economy of the world. The member states had agreed in 2004 on creating the FTZ but ignore the two less developed countries Bhutan and Nepal. To create a free trade zone there is need to include these two nations also.

Another thing is to improve the technology for the promotion of trade. The need of hour is to adopt the cost effective technology and better technology so that the BIMSTEC increases their share in world exports. Research and development will be necessary from the promotion of exports in these nations.

There is need to improve R&D in BIMSTEC regions. Because major reason for the decrease in the percentage share of some member nations in world exports was that following the 19 rounds of Free Trade Agreements (FTA) negotiations, till agreement not able to sort out issues such as dispute-settlement mechanism or a. Another reason for the underperformance of some nations was the basic fundamentals of collaboration remaining unfinished. BIMSTEC-restricted activities lead to some serious problems such as structural constraints on member states in the form of limited technological, lead-actor inertia, operational and financial capabilities. More provision of export incentives cannot expand exports. There is need for coordination between production planning and trade policies with a specific orientation towards the market demand.

The comparative study of trade regimes and exports expansion and the growth among the BIMSTEC nations reveals that there seems to be a correlation between the intensity of market forces and rate of growth of GDP. The greater the scope of market forces, the larger seems to have been the growth in general. The study also support for growth-led export in case of BIMSTEC. So, the need of hour is to create the custom union for the development of these countries. A trade creating Custom Union helps to promote the welfare of member nations. Trade creation encourages the full utilization of the resources and further leads to greater specialization based on the comparative advantages. It also increases the welfare of member nations because of increase in real income.

So, the successful promotion of the mutually beneficial cooperation in the Bay of Bengal requires the speedy development of transport and communication linkages, exchange of information, relating the supply capabilities, progress in science and technology and enhanced technical cooperation, simplification and coordination of customs procedure and formalities and above all the establishment of institutional support for hastening the utilization of enhanced opportunities for multilateral regional cooperation.

8 Conclusion

BIMSTEC nations are prosperous in resources, but they remain underdeveloped and disengaged from Asia's development story. Although the member nations of BIMSTEC are linked by regional cooperative process, and remained on the margins of Asian market integration. The high potential of mutual trade with rest of the world has remained unexploited for various hurdles such as lack of shipping and road connectivity. For making BIMSTEC a "vibrant regional entity", there are needs to revitalize coastal shipping preparations and inter-modal transport, practices that had flourished in the past, for easy flow of goods and services. Now requirement of time is that member nations to stress on encouraging investment for operating actions for economic development and to build capability in the sectors of comparative advantage such as tourism, hydropower, agriculture and others to attain the greater goals and objectives. The econometrics technique was used to test the causality among Log_GDP and Log_Exports. To test for unit roots of the variables, Augmented Dickey-Fuller (ADF) tests had been utilized. The calculated critical values of this test reveal that result of stationary at level in case of GDP and result of stationarity at second difference at all lag differences in case of Exports. However, stationarity properties had been found in the level and second differencing level of the variables. To test the cointegration among variables, Johansen cointegration approach had been used. This study has examined the role of export in the GDP process among BIMSTEC nations using causality tests for data over the period 1997–2015. Granger causality was applied to test the causal association among Export and Economic Growth. The results explained the facts of bidirectional causality between GDP and export among BIMSTEC bloc. In nutshell, this study provided support for growth-led export and growth-led exports for BIMSTEC region. Conversation about BIMSTEC in the Indian strategic society has also been limited, brief and fairly periodic in nature. As a consequence, the cluster has stayed on marginal to integrative conversation in South and Southeast Asia. Another is structural constraints, in the form of limited state capabilities of the bulk of its member nations, have also foiled the development of the cluster. Most of the BIMSTEC nations are characterized by lack of technology and deficiency in the resources to invest in growth and infrastructure projects, with Bangladesh, Bhutan, Myanmar, and Nepal along with the world's least developed nations (LDCs).

9 The Way Forward

The scope of study is limited only to association between GDP and Export of BIMSTEC. India's possibility of emerging as a regional energy hub in South Asia depends on its likely setting up of bilateral grids in the coming years. Poor communication and transport facilities, lack of information regarding capabilities and resources across the countries are important stumbling blocks, along with tariff and non-tariff barriers to the evolution of the Bay of Bengal Economic community. In future, plan to work on role of geo-politics and investment for the promotion of trade among the BIMSTEC regions that would help the successful promotion of mutually beneficial cooperation in the Bay of Bengal region.

References

Amiri, A., & Gerdtham, U. G. (2012). Granger causality between exports, imports and GDP in France: Evidence from using geostatistical models. *Economic Research Guardian, 2*(1), 43–59.

Aydin, M., & Sari, M. (2014). Relationship between GDP and export in Turkey. *Annals-Economy Series*, 282–288.

Batra, A. (2010). Asian economic integration and sub-regionalism: A case study of the BIMSTEC. *International Studies, 47*(1), 1–25.

Carbaugh, R. J. (2008). *International economics*. New Delhi: Cengage Learning India Limited.

Chakraborty, D. (2007). *Trade performance and integration experience of BIMSTEC: A review of issues*. Centre for Studies in International Relations and Development, Discussion Paper No. 30, pp 1–50.

Cherunilam, F. (2006). *International economics*. New Delhi: Tata McGraw Hill Education Private Limited.

Clarke, J. A., & Ralhan, M. (2005). *Direct and indirect causality between exports and economic output for Bangladesh and Sri Lanka: Horizon matters*. Econometrica working paper EWP05012. University of Victoria, Victoria, BC, Canada.

Devi, T. N. (2007). Economic cooperation in BIMSTEC: Emerging trends and prospects. In T. NirmalaDevi (Ed.), *India and Bay of Bengal Community: The BIMSTEC experiment* (pp. 128–154). New Delhi: Gyan Publishing House.

Dritsakis, N., Varelas, E., & Adamopoulos, A. (2006). The main determinants of economic growth: An empirical investigation with Granger causality analysis for Greece. *European Research Studies Journal, 9*(3–4), 47–58.

Granger, C. W. (1969). Investigating causal relations by econometric models and cross-spectral methods. *Econometrica: Journal of the Econometric Society*, 424–438.

Granger, C. W. (1988). Some recent development in a concept of causality. *Journal of econometrics, 39*(1–2), 199–211.

Jarra, S. T. (2013). Exports, domestic demand and economic growth in Ethiopia: Granger causality analysis. *Journal of Economics and International Finance, 5*(9), 357–372.

Jordaan, A. C., & Eita, J. H. (2009). Testing the export-led growth hypothesis for Botswana: A causality analysis. *Botswana Journal of Economics, 6*(10), 2–14. Retrieved from http://www.ajol.info/index.php/boje/article/view/60205.

Kumari, D., & Malhotra, N. (2014). Export-led growth in India: Cointegration and causality analysis. *Journal of Economics and Development Studies, 2*(2), 297–310.

MacKinnon, J. G. (1996). Numerical distribution functions for unit root and cointegration tests. *Journal of applied econometrics*, 601–618.

MacKinnon, J. G., Haug, A. A., & Michelis, L. (1999). Numerical distribution functions of likelihood ratio tests for cointegration. *Journal of applied Econometrics*, 563–577.

Mehrara, M., & Firouzjaee, B. A. (2011). Granger causality relationship between export growth and GDP growth in developing countries: Panel cointegration approach. *International Journal of Humanities and Social Science, 1*(16), 223–231.

Mukherji, R., & Pandey, D. (2014). The relationship between the growth of exports and growth of gross domestic product of India. *International Journal of Business and Economics Research, 3* (3), 135–139. doi:10.11648/j.ijber.20140303.13.

Ray, S. (2011). A causality analysis on the empirical nexus between export and economic growth: Evidence from India. *International Affairs and Global Strategy, 1,* 24–38.

Sims, C. A. (1972). Money, income, and causality. *The American economic review, 62*(4), 540–552.

Stait, A. F. (2005). *Are exports the engine of economic growth? An application of cointegration and causality analysis for Egypt.* Working paper 76. Retrieved from https://ideas.repec.org/p/adb/adbwps/211.html.

Travkina, I. (2015). Export and GDP growth in Lithuania: Short-run or middle-run causality? *Entrepreneurship and Sustainability Issues, 3*(1), 74–84.

Part III
Productivity and Firm Performance

Intellectual Capital and Financial Performance: Evidences from Indian Business Process Outsourcing Industry

Mohd Anas Raushan and Ahmed Musa Khan

Abstract The purpose of this study is to empirically measure the impact of intellectual capital performance on the traditional financial performance measures of selected Indian Business Process Outsourcing (BPO) and Knowledge Process Outsourcing (KPO) companies. Data of 13 prominent Indian BPO/KPO companies listed on Bombay Stock Exchange is taken for study. The selected companies of BPO/KPO sector are heavily reliant on intellectual capital. Financial data of nine years i.e. from 2007 to 2015 is collected from financial database CMIE's Prowess. Literature available on intellectual capital and efficiency measurement is thoroughly reviewed. Value Added Intellectual Coefficient (VAIC™) method is used to measure the value based intellectual capital performance of the selected companies. The financial performance variables used in the study are return on assets, return on equity and operating income ratio for profitability and asset turnover ratio for productivity. VAIC™ and its components are calculated i.e. efficiency of capital employed and efficiency of intellectual capital. Empirical analysis is conducted using models of panel data i.e. fixed and random to analyse the impact of VAIC™ components on financial performance measures. Findings from the analysis suggest that intellectual capital efficiency has a significant impact on profitability but not on productivity. While capital employed efficiency has a significant impact on profitability and productivity both.

Keywords Intellectual capital · VAIC™ · Financial performance
Value added · Indian IT/BPO companies

M.A. Raushan (✉)
Indian Institute of Management Kashipur, Kashipur, Uttarakhand, India
e-mail: anas.raushan@gmail.com

A.M. Khan
Aligarh Muslim University, Aligarh, India
e-mail: musakhan.rs@amu.ac.in

B. Kamaiah et al. (eds.), *Current Issues in Economics and Finance*,
DOI 10.1007/978-981-10-5810-3_7

1 Introduction

The intangible assets are the key driver of all the tangible resources of a firm. In this knowledge based economy the intangible assets have become the most valuable assets for a company and they have replaced the traditional factor of production like land, labor and physical capital (Hsu, 2001; Drucker, 1988). Some of the most successful companies of the world like Apple, Microsoft, Infosys, TATA have successfully managed their knowledge and intellectual capital resources. These companies used the knowledge, skills and expertise of their employees to create products which were class apart from their competitors. It has been consensually agreed upon by the social scientist that 'knowledge is the new basis of competition and the most important factor in the creation of economic value and maintaining the competitive advantage' (e.g. Drucker, 1993; Sveiby, 2008; Stewart, 1997). When this knowledge is reported from the perspective of value creation it is known as intellectual capital (Kianto, Ritala, Inkinen & Vanhala., 2013). In his landmark article in *Fortune* magazine Stewart (1997) defines intellectual capital as "*the intellectual material—knowledge, information, intellectual property, experience—that can be put to use to create wealth*". Intellectual capital is the documented knowledge which is available in the form of research papers, reports, books, articles, manuscripts, patents and software (Joshi, Ubha & Sidhu, 2012). Itami (1991) in his landmark book *'Moving Intangible Assets'* recognized the information based resources such as consumer trust, brand image, corporate culture, control of distribution and management skill more important than the visible corporate resources (people, goods and capital). He called these information based resources as *invisible assets*. According to the Organization for Economic Co-operation and Development (OECD, 1999), intellectual capital is the economic value of two categories of intangible assets of a company: organizational capital and human capital.

Firms in this knowledge economy face a real challenge of measuring and reporting of these intangible resources. The major focus of these firms is mainly on measuring and accounting the financial performance of the organization. Benefits of intellectual capital such as management efficiency, customer relation, R&D, innovations etc. are difficult to measure and quantify (Svieby, 1997). Considering this, Pulic (1998), has suggested a measure named Value Added Intellectual Coefficient^{TM} (VAIC). Following his proposition of VAIC, Firer and Stainbank (2003); Firer and Williams (2003) have used this measure to examine the intellectual capital efficiency and its impact on financial performance measure in the context of South Africa. The present study also measures the impact of intellectual capital on the firm's financial performance in Indian context.

The remaining parts of this paper include a brief summary of the relevant literature on intellectual capital and brief profile of Indian BPO/KPO industry (Sect. 2), an explanation of development of hypotheses (Sect. 3), the research methodology used is described in (Sect. 4), sample, descriptive statistics and multiple regression analysis (Sects. 5 and 6), discussion of the results (Sect. 7) and conclusions and managerial implications (Sects. 8 and 9).

2 Literature Review

Defining Intellectual Capital Intellectual capital is defined and interpreted by different researchers in their own understanding but the underlying theory remains the same that the intellectual capital is in the form of the human resource, reputation, goodwill, structural capital etc.

> "The possession of knowledge, applied experience, organizational technology, customer relationships and professional skills" which has been simplified to human capital plus structural capital which equals to intellectual capital. (Edvinsson, 1997).

Svieby (1997) is attributed with the founder of intellectual capital movement in Sweden. He emphasised that the invisible and intangible assets of knowledge are in fact more important than the companies tangible and financial assets. As for the fact the stock markets around the world are recognising and rewarding the companies for years upon their knowledge and intangible assets in the company. The new wealth of the companies is the invisible assets like employee competence, internal structure and external structure; the internal structure is the management practices, patents, concepts, models research and development capability while the external structure is the brand, reputation, supplier and customer relation (Marquardt, 1999).

Stewart (2001) describe the essential elements or assets that contribute to the development of intellectual capital: Structural capital, representing "the codified bodies of semi-permanent knowledge that can be transferred" and "the tools that augment the body of knowledge by bringing relevant data or expertise to people" Human capital, or "the capabilities of the individuals required to provide solutions to customers" Customer capital, or "the value of an organization's relationships with the people with whom it does business—shared knowledge".

Intellectual capital management: Since the last two decades the IC research has undergone tremendous change by developing measures and models to measure IC. The traditional measure of performance measurement ignores the contribution of IC. The substantial number of IC measurement models proposed by IC managers and scholars have proved the worth of IC as a serious issue for research (Chatzkel, 2004) but measuring and reporting of IC is not an easy but a highly complicated one (Cuganesan, 2005; Bueno, 2006). Some of the commonly used models to measure partially or specifically the elements of intellectual capital are given below in chronological order:

(1) The Balanced Scorecard (Kaplan and Norton, 1992).
(2) Skandia's IC Navigator (Edvinsson and Malone, 1997).
(3) The Intangible Asset Monitor (Sveiby, 1997).
(4) Intellectual Capital Services' IC-Index^{TM} (Roos and Roos, 1997).
(5) Value Added Intellectual Coefficient, VAIC^{TM} (Pulic, 1998).

Since the evolution of this intellectual capital concept there have been large number of studies validating the relationship and impact of intellectual capital on organizational performance (including financial) in different geographical settings. Some of the prominent international and Indian studies are reviewed for reference.

International Studies: Chen, Cheng & Hwang (2005) empirically investigated the relation between the value creation efficiency of firm's and their market value and financial performance. Using the data drawn from Taiwanese listed companies from 1992 to 2002 and analysing it through Pulic's Value Added Intellectual Coefficient (VAIC™) by constructing regression models, the results are in confirmation of hypothesis that intellectual capital has an impact on the firm's financial performance and market value. They also deducted that R&D expenditure captures additional information on structural capital and has a positive impact on firm's profitability and firm value.

Dzenopoljac, Janosevic & Bontis (2016) in their large scale study on 13,989 Serbian Information Communication Technology companies explored whether the Intellectual components of these companies created value and up to which extent the IC and is components impact the financial performance of these companies. They used the VAIC™ method to measure the value created through IC and its impact on financial performance measures such as ROA, ROE, ROIC, profitability and asset turnover ratio. The results were indicative of capital employed efficiency having significant impact on financial performance when firm size and leverage were used as control variables. Social scientists such e.g. Ghosh and Mondal (2009), Chen et al. (2005), Gan and Saleh (2008), Young, Su, Fang & Fang (2009), Janosevic, Dzenopoljac, & Bontis (2013), Maditinos, Chatzoudes, Tsairidis, & Theriou (2011), Mehri, Umar, Saeidi, Hekmat, & Naslmosavi (2013) all have used VAIC™ method to measure the value based performance and its impact on different financial performance such as return on asset, asset turnover ratio and market to book value ratio with varying results.

Indian Studies There has been also significant number of studies on Indian companies to test the relationship of intellectual capital and firm performance as in case of pharmaceutical companies (Kamath, 2008; Vishnu and Gupta, 2014), pharmaceutical and software companies (Ghosh and Mondal, 2009), banks (Mondal and Ghosh, 2012), Information technology companies (Kavida and Sivakoumar, 2010); pharmaceutical and textile companies (Pal and Soriya, 2012); CNX Nifty index companies including IT, banking and pharmaceuticals (Tandon, Purohit & Tandon, 2016).

The Indian BPO/KPO segment faces a stiff competition with other destinations such as China, Indonesia, Philippines, and Argentina etc. Moreover, this segment has an inherent problem of employee retention, health hazards, gender issues, work life balance, and cultural differences with the customers. Hence, it becomes very essential to manage the human resource efficiently in order to achieve sustained competitive advantage in the market. The measurement of intellectual capital is an efficient way to manage the intellectual capital of a firm.

Indian IT-BPM Industry profile: NASSCOM (National Association of Software and Services Companies) is the leading association of IT and BPO companies. NASSCOM names this sector as Information technology—Business Process Management (IT-BPM) sector. Information technology has contribution to almost all the sectors of the economy. It is contributing to different sectors such as health-hospitality, communication, banking, travel, research and development etc. The IT-BPM industry has achieved astonishing growth since its inception in 1960s and its growth got accelerated after the economic reforms of 1991. This sector is growing sustainably and in fact India is world leader in this sector since two decades (Malik and Velan, 2016). The contribution of IT-BPM sector in the growth is prominent almost in all the developed economies. Its impact is so strong that the US was compelled to change its visa policies in order to prevent landing of IT jobs to Indians (Arun, 2015). India has indeed became the back office of the world. The Indian IT-BPM industry is a USD 180 billion industry, it exported for around USD 98 billion in 2014. The contribution of the IT-BPM sector to the GDP has significantly increased from 1.2% in FY 1998 to record high 9.5% in FY 2015. It is the largest private sector employer in the country employing directly 3 million professionals. The IT-BPM sector is fuelled by a huge network of public and private educational institutions (NASSCOM, 2015).

The Indian IT-BPM industry is heavily reliant on intellectual resources such as human resources, software's, programmes, knowledge, experience, intellectual property, research and development etc. The Indian IT-BPM industry is human capital intensive and physical capital requirements are only related to computer hardware, servers and office space. The productivity depends on skills, knowledge and the innovation of employees (Patibandla and Petersen, 2002). It is evident that not many Indian companies have a practice of recording and reporting intellectual capital (Joshi et al., 2012; Kamath 2008). There is no established financial reporting framework for disclosing the intellectual capital information. Researchers have done content analysis of the companies annual reports and came out with the same conclusion of a minimal disclosure of intellectual capital information (Joshi et al., 2012; Kamath, 2008).

3 Development of Hypothesis

As the companies selected for the study are those mainly from BPO/KPO so as their major product is to offer IT enabled services, thus it is one of the highly intellectual capital intensive sector. So it becomes all the more compelling to know the impact of the intellectual capital on their financial performance This study explores empirically the relationship between the Intellectual capital efficiency and the financial performance of the selected IT/BPO companies. The impact of the components of VAIC™ is analysed on the commonly used financial performance measures of profitability and productivity.

H1: *The components of VAIC™ has a significant impact on the profitability of the selected Indian BPO/KPO firms*

H2: *The components of VAIC™ has a significant impact on the productivity of the selected Indian BPO/KPO firms*

These two hypothesis translate into 4 sub-hypothesis for profitability.

H1a: *the components of VAIC have a significant impact on return on assets (ROA).*

H1b: *The component of VAIC has a significant impact on return on equity (ROE).*

H1c: *the components of VAIC has a significant impact on operating income ratio (OIR).*

H2a: *the components of VAIC has a significant impact on asset turnover ratio (ATO).*

4 Research Methodology

The first part of this section describes the dependent variables, followed by independent variables and control variables. The multiple regression equations are outlined in the last part of this section.

Measures of dependant variable For the analysis three dependent variables of profitability are selected and one for productivity. These are represented as follows:

(1) Return on assets (ROA) (Net income/Total assets).
(2) Return on Equity (ROE) (Net Income/Shareholder's Equity).
(3) Operating Income ratio (OIR) (Operating Income/Net sales).
(4) Asset Turnover Ratio (ATR) (Net Sales/Avg. Total Assets).

Return on Assets, Return on Equity and Operating income ratio are measures of profitability and Asset turnover ratio is used to measure productivity as these variables are also used in other studies (Ghosh and Mondal, 2009; Dzenopoljac et al., 2016; Vishnu and Gupta, 2014).

Independent variables The VAIC^{TM} method was developed by Pulic (1998, 2004). It is the main methodology used in this study. VAIC ^{TM} enables to find the value added by the important resources of the firm. VAIC^{TM} is the sum of three component. These are:

(1) Capital employed efficiency (CEE)—Value added efficiency by capital employed;
(2) Human capital efficiency (HCE)—Value added efficiency by of human capital; and
(3) Structural capital efficiency (SCE)—Value added efficiency by structural capital.

The equation given below gives the relationship among the three components of VAIC:

$$\mathrm{VAIC} = \mathrm{CEE} + \mathrm{HCE} + \mathrm{SCE}$$

where:

VAIC VA intellectual coefficient for a company
CEE Capital employed efficiency coefficient for a company
HCE Human capital efficiency coefficient for a company; and
SCE Structural capital efficiency for a company.

Higher will be the efficiency of the value added by the different components of VAIC higher will be the VAIC coefficient The first step in calculating CEE, HCE and SCE is to determine a firm's total VA.

Value added can be calculated by using the company's accounts as follows (Pulic 2004):

$$\mathrm{VA} = \mathrm{OP} + \mathrm{EC} + \mathrm{D} + \mathrm{A}$$

where

OP operating profit;
EC Employees Cost;
D Depreciation;
A Amortisation.

According to Pulic (1998, 2004), Value added is an indicator which shows the ability of a company to create value. Value added is the difference between a company's sales and its input. After calculating Value added it becomes easier to calculate all the components of VAIC.

Efficiency of Human capital is calculated by using formula:

$$\mathrm{HCE} = \mathrm{VA/HC}$$

HCE Human Capital Efficiency;
HC Total salaries and wages paid by the company;
VA Value added.

In this study the researchers have used "total salary and wage costs" as the indicator of a firm's human capital (HC) which are consistent with other leading Intellectual capital researchers (Pulic, 1998, 2004). HCE, is calculated as the ratio of total VA divided by the total salary and wages spent by the firm on its employees

Structural Capital as the second component is calculated by

$$\mathrm{SC} = \mathrm{VA} - \mathrm{HC}$$

SC Structural capital of the company;
VA Value added;

HC Total salaries and wages paid by the company, thus after calculating structural capital its efficiency can be calculated by using formula SCE = SC/VA.

where

SCE Structural capital efficiency;
SC Structural Capital;
VA Value Added.

Intellectual capital efficiency can also be calculated by adding up these two efficiencies of Structural and Human capital:

$$\mathrm{ICE} = \mathrm{HCE} + \mathrm{SCE}$$

ICE Intellectual Capital Efficiency;
HCE Human Capital Efficiency;
SCE Structural Capital.

Since intellectual capital cannot create value on its own so we also need to take into account the efficiency of the capital employed which can be calculate by using this formula(Vishnu and Gupta 2014):-

$$\mathrm{CEE} = \mathrm{VA}/\mathrm{CE}$$

CEE Capital employed efficiency;
VA Value added;
CE Capital employed.

The capital invested in the company in the past is shown as capital employed (CE). CE is also known as companies net assets. Thus CEE is the efficiency of the financial capital employed in a company.

Control Variables there are two control variables used in the empirical analysis:

i. Firm Size (LS): Firm size is measured through total assets, natural logarithm of total assets is taken of the selected companies
ii. Physical Capital Intensity (CI): the physical capital intensity is taken as the ratio of fixed assets to total assets of the company (Firer and Stainbank, 2003; Firer and Williams, 2003).

5 Sample Selection and Descriptive Statistics

This section first presents the sample selection criteria and then the descriptive statistics of the variables which have been in the study. The sample of this study consists of 13 Indian Business Processing Outsourcing companies which were listed on BSE (as on 24th May 2015). Financial data was collected from the reputed database Prowess. Data of nine years was taken into consideration i.e. from 2007–2015. E-views 8 was used to analyse the data.

Table 1 presents the value of minimum, maximum, mean and standard deviation of the dependent, independent and control variables used in the study. The mean value of ICE was found 2.52 which means that sampled companies of Indian BPO/KPO sector are quiet efficient in generating value out of their intellectual capital. This means that it has created value of 2.52 rupees for every one rupee invested. The mean values of CEE is 0.56, thus it is clear that ICE is generating more value than CEE. It is clear that these companies heavily invest in their intellectual capital assets. The mean value of the financial performance measures also indicates that the selected companies are financially sound. If we take profitability in terms of ROA, ROE and OIR it has a mean value of 14%, 10% and 26%. The productivity is also good as the mean value of ATR is 62%.

Table 2 reveals the normality test results. Jarque–Bera test was applied in E-views, it shows that the analysed variables have normal distribution of data ($p < 0.05$). The null hypothesis states that the data is normal and in this case all the variables are significant at 1% level of significance.

The results of the implemented pair wise correlation analysis are presented in Table 3 which shows that a positive correlation between CEE and ATR while there is also a positive correlation between ROA and ROE. There is no multicollinearity among the independent variables.

Table 1 Descriptive statistics

	n statistic	Minimum statistic	Maximum statistic	Mean statistic	SD statistic
ROA	117	−0.589802	1.116207	0.105494	0.164476
ROE	117	−0.927477	1.351618	0.141871	0.224870
ATR	117	0.012814	2.783298	0.629292	0.478322
OIR	117	−0.2978339	1.390805	0.2678281	0.2581687
CEE	117	0.005512	2.334923	0.566207	0.428757
ICE	117	0.386189	8.987823	2.529277	1.276553
LA	117	3.949319	13.36228	7.792762	2.312653
CI	117	1.299975	82.71375	28.51176	17.02477

Table 2 Normality Test

	Jarque–Bera	Significance
ROA	4968.94	0.0000
ROE	8042.85	0.0000
OIR	358.68	0.0000
ATR	52.592	0.0000

Table 3 Correlation analysis

	CEE	ICE	OIR	ROA	ROE	ATR
CEE	1.000000					
ICE	−0.135071	1.000000				
OIR	0.067824	0.683189	1.000000			
ROA	0.687543	0.230341	0.397333	1.000000		
ROE	0.678506	0.211595	0.377381	0.986843	1.000000	
ATR	0.961682	−0.146741	0.007012	0.716306	0.711360	1.000000

6 Multiple Regression Analysis

Multiple regression analysis is used to assess the impact of the elements of VAIC on the selected dependant variables of financial performance. This will help us in finding the value drivers in the Indian BPO industry. Since there are four dependant variables, so four multiple regression models were constructed. Each multiple regression model was analysed with all three models i.e. pooled regression, fixed effect and random effect. After performing the multiple regression analysis with random effect the Hausman test is applied to know which model suits best for the analysed panel data. Formally the model of multiple regression gives '*n*' observation, is

$$Y_i = \beta_\circ + \beta_1 x_1 + \beta_2 x_2 + \cdots \beta_n x_n + e_n$$

In the present model of multiple linear regression Y is a dependant variable,

Table 4 presents the regression result of first multiple regression model in which ROA is used as the dependant variable. The Hausman test result states that the random effect model is best for analysing the panel data. It has a good explanatory power of 46%. Both the independent variables have a positive significant impact on ROA. Among the control variables CI has a negatively significant impact, while LA has insignificant impact on ROA. It indicates that increasing ICE and CEE improves the ROA. So the hypothesis $H1a$ is accepted. The coefficients explain that 1% increase in the value of ICE increases the value of ROA by 0.02% holding other variable constant. And the 1% increase in the value of CEE increases the value of ROA by 0.30%.

Table 4 Relationship between VAIC and ROA

Dependant variable ROA	Pooled regression		Fixed effect		Random effect	
R-squared	0.6089		0.7316		0.4689	
Adjusted R square	0.5949		0.6886		0.4499	
	P-value	Coefficient	P-value	Coefficient	P-value	Coefficient
Constant	0.5551	−0.0330	0.0325	0.2939	0.6588	0.0364
LA	0.0356	−0.0118	0.0281	−0.0443	0.2472	−0.0161
CI	0.0073	−0.0017	0.0107	−0.0016	0.0000*	−0.0017
ICE	0.0000	0.0414	0.0000	0.0196	0.0000*	0.0274
CEE	0.0000	0.3110	0.0125	0.2736	0.0008*	0.3076

Note: *Significant at $\alpha = 0.99$

Table 5 Relationship between VAIC and ROE

Dependant variable ROE	Pooled regression		Fixed effect		Random effect	
R-squared	0.5799		0.6915		0.4421	
Adjusted R square	0.5649		0.6422		0.4221	
	P-value	Coefficient	P-value	Coefficient	P-value	Coefficient
Constant	0.4633	−0.0581	0.0319	0.3654	0.7777	0.0271
LA	0.0926	−0.0132	0.0316	−0.0538	0.2467	−0.0182
CI	0.0120	−0.0023	0.0077	−0.0029	0.0028*	−0.0025
ICE	0.0000	0.0540	0.0000	0.0279	0.0000*	0.0389
CEE	0.0000	0.4113	0.0081	0.3686	0.0001*	0.4068

Note: *Significant at $\alpha = 0.99$

Table 5 presents the regression result of second multiple regression model in which ROE is used as the dependant variable. The Hausman test result states that the random effect model is best for analysing the panel data. It has a good explanatory power of 44%. Both the independent variables have a positive significant impact on ROE. Among the control variables CI has a negatively significant impact; while LA has insignificant impact on ROA. So the hypothesis *H1b* is accepted. The coefficients explain that 1% increase in the value of ICE increases the value of ROE by 0.03% holding the other variable constant. And 1% increase in the value of CEE increases the value of ROE by 0.40% holding other variable constant.

Table 6 presents the regression result of third multiple regression model in which OIR is used as the dependant variable. The Hausman test result states that the random effect model is best for analysing the panel data. It has a good explanatory power of 47%. Both the independent variables have a positive significant impact on OIR. Among the control variables CI has a negatively significant impact, while LA has insignificant impact on ROA. So the hypothesis *H1c* is accepted. The coefficients explain that 1% increase in the value of ICE increases the value of OIR by 0.106% holding other variable constant. And the 1% increase in the value of CEE increases the value of OIR by 0.11% holding other variable constant.

Table 6 Relationship between VAIC and OIR

Dependant variable OIR	Pooled regression		Fixed effect		Random effect	
R-squared	0.5874		0.7595		0.4755	
Adjusted *R* square	0.5727		0.7210		0.4568	
S.E. of regression	0.1556		0.1257		0.1312	
	P-value	Coefficient	*P*-value	Coefficient	*P*-value	Coefficient
Constant	0.0806	0.1462	0.8718	−0.0280	0.1499	0.2539
LA	0.0182	−0.0199	0.1175	0.0254	0.866	−0.0185
CI	0.0000	−0.0048	0.0000	−0.0080	0.0000*	−0.0061
ICE	0.0000	0.1335	0.0168	0.0881	0.0037*	0.1067
CEE	0.0007	0.1404	0.0001	0.1880	0.0001*	0.1178

Note: *Significant at $\alpha = 0.99$

Table 7 Relationship between VAIC and ATR

Dependant variable ATR	Pooled regression		Fixed effect		Random effect	
R-squared	0.9278		0.9517		0.8701	
Adjusted *R* square	0.9252		0.9440		0.8655	
S.E. of regression	0.1307		0.1131		0.1128	
	P-value	Coefficient	*P*-value	Coefficient	*P*-value	Coefficient
Constant	0.1250	0.1077	0.3122	0.4010	0.0748	0.1273
LA	0.1236	−0.0108	0.2683	−0.0512	0.0054	−0.0163
CI	0.6066	0.0004	0.4355	0.0005	0.6476	0.0003
ICE	0.2644	−0.0110	0.4075	0.0036	0.5396	−0.0028
CEE	0.0000	1.0986	0.000	1.0644	0.0000*	1.1077

Note: *Significant at $\alpha = 0.99$

Table 7 presents the regression result of third multiple regression model in which ATR is used as the dependant variable. The Hausman test result states that the random effect model is best for analysing the panel data. It has a good explanatory power of 87%. Out of the two components of VAIC only CEE has a significant impact on the operating income ratio while the impact of ICE is insignificant and has a negative relationship with ATR. The capital intensity in this case does not play any significant role as in the earlier regression equations. So the hypothesis *H2a* is rejected. The coefficients explain that 1% increase in the value of ICE decreases the value of ATR by 0.002% holding other variable constant. And the 1% increase in the value of CEE increases the value of ATR by 1.10% holding other variable constant.

7 Discussion

Only ICE component of VAIC™ had a significant impact on ROA, ROE and OIR. While CEE has a significant impact on all the financial performance measures taken in the study namely ROA, ROE, OIR and ATR. The results are in confirmation with the earlier studies which have given similar result e.g.: Firer and Stainbank (2003), Chen et al. (2005), Kamath (2008), Gan and Saleh (2008) and Ghosh and Mondal (2009). In all the regression equations the CEE is having a significant impact on all the dependant variables used. It is evident from the analysis that the companies which efficiently utilise the financial capital employed have higher financial performance in terms of profitability as well as productivity. The significant impact of CEE can also be interpreted in a way, that in this rapidly innovating era it is imperative to invest in latest technology, machines, software's scientifically designed offices, etc. otherwise the technologically ill-equipped companies will not be able to keep pace with the market. Although intuitive assumptions in the beginning of research were that ICE should have impact on productivity, as the BPO/KPO companies are intellectual capital intensive firms. But findings showed that the ICE has an insignificant impact but CEE has a significant impact on productivity. This can also mean that the tangible assets are essentially required by the human resource to produce quality business services, which is needed in this technologically advanced era. Intellectual capital efficiency also have a significant impact on all the three dimensions of profitability but it was found insignificant in case of productivity when measured through ATO. The results have approved three out of four sub hypothesis formed.

8 Conclusion

The prime focus of this study is to measure the impact of intellectual capital performance on the financial performance measures of BPO/KPO companies. Intellectual capital performance is measured through Pulic's (1998, 2004) VAIC™ method and the financial performance measures has been captured through return on assets (ROA), return on equity (ROE) and operating income ratio (OIR) for profitability and asset turnover ratio (ATO) for productivity. Present empirical analysis is conducted on 13 Indian BPO/KPO specific companies listed on Bombay Stock Exchange. The companies are knowledge intensive and rely heavily on intellectual capital for generating high quality services as their main product. Also it can be deducted that in an emerging country like India a lot of emphasis is being given to the physical capital and even in the core services sector like BPO/KPO physical infrastructure, such as computers, machines, office space, modern office amenities etc. are important and required by the human resource to provide better services to their clients. The empirical findings clearly indicate that intellectual capital is a strong driver for profitability and productivity. The profitability and productivity of the companies can be raised significantly by managing intellectual capital efficiently and wisely. Managing the intellectual capital is the new 'mantra' for success in this twenty-first century. However a fairly large sample of BPO/KPO companies can be taken to validate the results.

9 Managerial Implications

The managers of these BPO/KPO companies by now are aware that IC is a valuable resource rather than a liability, which creates economic value (Edvinsson and Malone, 1997; Guthrie, 2001; Bontis, 2001). The managers of these companies should start measuring and reporting intellectual capital of their companies for a more robust evaluation of organizational performance and aptly managing the intellectual capital resources of the company. The managers can use any of the available methods for measuring and managing the IC resources. Specifically VAIC^{TM} can be used to measure the IC efficiency and comparative analysis can be done to know the IC strength of the competitors in the industry. The analysis provide information that how efficient are their own IC resources in creating the economic value, so that appropriate improvement decisions would be taken.

References

Arun, S. (2015, December 28). IT sector worried; India to take up visa fee with U.S. The Hindu.

Bontis, N., Janošević, S., & Dženopoljac, V. (2013). Intellectual capital in Serbia's hotel industry. *International Journal of Contemporary Hospitality Management, 27*(6), 1365–1384. doi:10.1108/IJCHM-12-2013-0541.

Bontis, N., & Nikitopoulos, D. (2001). Thought leadership on intellectual capital. *Journal of Intellectual Capital, 2*(3), 183–191. doi:10.1108/14691930110400182.

Bueno, E., Salmador, M. P., Rodríguez, Ó., & Martín De Castro, G. (2006). Internal logic of intellectual capital: A biological approach. *Journal of Intellectual Capital, 7*(3), 394–405. doi:10.1108/14691930610681474.

Chatzkel, J. (2004). Moving through the crossroads. *Journal of Intellectual Capital, 5*(2), 337–339. doi:10.1108/14691930410533740.

Cuganesan, S. (2005). Intellectual capital-in-action and value creation. *Journal of Intellectual Capital, 6*(3), 357–373. doi:10.1108/14691930510611102.

Chen, M. C., Cheng S. J., & Hwang, Y. (2005). An empirical investigation of the relationship between intellectual capital and firms' market value and financial performance. *Journal of Intellectual Capital, 6*(2), 159–176.

Drucker, P. F. (1988). The coming of the new organization. *Harvard Business Review, 66*(1), 45–53.

Drucker, P. F. (1993). Postcapitalist Society. Herper Collins Publishers. New York

Dženopoljac, V., Janoševic, S., & Bontis, N. (2016). Intellectual capital and financial performance in the Serbian ICT industry. *Journal of Intellectual Capital, 17*(2), 373–396. doi:10.1108/JIC-07-2015-0068.

Edvinsson, L. (1997). Developing intellectual capital at Skandia. *Long Range Planning, 30*(3), 320–373.

Edvinsson, L., & Malone, M. S. (1997). *Intellectual capital: The proven way to establish your company's real value by measuring its hidden brainpower*. London: Piatkus Books.

Firer, S., & Mitchell Williams, S. (2003). Intellectual capital and traditional measures of corporate performance. *Journal of Intellectual Capital, 4*(3), 348–360. doi:10.1108/14691930310487806.

Firer, S., & Stainbank, L. (2003). Testing the relationship between intellectual capital and a company's performance: Evidence from South Africa. *Meditari Accountancy Research, 11*(1), 25–44.

Gan, K., & Saleh, Z. (2008). Intellectual capital and corporate performance of technology-intensive companies: Malaysia evidence. *Asian Journal of Business and Accounting, 1*(1), 113–130. doi:10.1108/14691930010324188.

Ghosh, S., & Mondal, A. (2009). Indian software and pharmaceutical sector IC and financial performance. *Journal of Intellectual Capital, 10*(3), 369–388. doi:10.1108/14691930910977798.

Guthrie, J. (2001). The management, measurement and the reporting of intellectual capital. *Journal of Intellectual Capital, 2*(1), 27–41. doi:10.1108/14691930110380473.

Hsu, G. H. Y. (2001). Knowledge-based economies and competition policy: Developmental strategy concerning the liberalization and internationalization of Taiwan's business. *Fair Trade Quaterly, 4*(9), 123–136.

Itami, H. (1991). *Mobilizing invisible assets*. Massachusetts: Harvard University Press.

Janosevic, S., Dzenopoljac, V., & Bontis, N. (2013). Intellectual capital and financial performance in Serbia. Knowledge and Process Management. *20*(1), 1–11.

Joshi, M., Ubha, D. S., & Sidhu, J. (2012). Intellectual capital disclosures by Indian and Australian information technology companies. *Journal of Intellectual Capital, 13*(4), 582–598. doi: 10.1108/14691931211276142 .

Kamath, G. B. (2008). Intellectual capital and corporate performance in Indian pharmaceutical industry. *Journal of Intellectual Capital, 9*(4), 684–704. doi: 10.1108/14691930810913221 .

Kianto, A., Ritala, P., Inkinen H., & Vanhala, M. (2013). The interaction of intellectual capital stocks and knowledge management practices in organizational value creation, *Paper presented at 8th International Forum on Knowledge Asset Dynamics* Zagreb.

Kaplan, R. S., & Norton, D. P. (1992). The balanced scorecard—Measures that drive performance. *Harvard Business Review, 70*(1), 71–79.

Kavida, V., & Sivakumar, N. (2010). The Relevance of Intellectual Capital in the Indian Information Technology Industry. *The IUP Journal of Knowledge Management, 8*(4).

Maditinos, D., Chatzoudes, D., Tsairidis, C., & Theriou, G. (2011). The impact of intellectual capital on firms' market value and financial performance. *Journal of Intellectual Capital, 12*(1), 132–151. doi:10.1108/14691931111097944.

Malik, M., & Velan, N. (2016). Trends and determinants of IT-BPM exports in India. *Journal of Science and Technology Policy Management, 7*(2).

Mehri, M., Umar, M., Saeidi, P., Hekmat, R., & Naslmosavi, S. (2013). Intellectual Capital and Firm Performance of High Intangible Intensive Industries: Malaysia Evidence. *Asian Social Science, 9*(9).

Marquardt, M. J. (1999). *Action Learning in Action: Transforming Problems and People for World-class Organizational Learning. Palo Alto: Davies-Black Publishing*.

Mondal, A., & Ghosh, S. K. (2012). Intellectual capital and financial performance of Indian banks. *Journal of Intellectual Capital, 13*(4), 515–530. doi:10.1108/14691931211276115.

NASSCOM. (2015). *The IT-BPM sector in India*. New Delhi: Strategic Review.

OECD. (1999). Measuring and reporting intellectual capital: experience, issues and prospects; an international symposium. *Organisation for Economic Co-operation and Development*, Amsterdam.

Pal, K., & Soriya, S. (2012). IC performance of Indian pharmaceutical and textile industry. *Journal of Intellectual Capital, 13*(1), 120–137. doi:10.1108/14691931211196240.

Patibandla, M., & Petersen, B. (2002). Role of transnational corporations in the evolution of a high-tech industry: The case of India's software industry. *World Development, 30*(9), 1561–1577.

Pulic, A. (2004). Intellectual capital—Does it create or destroy value? *Measuring Business Excellence, 8*(1), 62–68.
Pulic, A. (1998). Measuring the performance of intellectual potential in knowledge economy. Presented at the *2nd McMaster World Congress on Measuring and Managing Intellectual Capital by the Austrian Team for Intellectual Potential.*
Roos, G., & Roos, J. (1997). Measuring your company's intellectual performance. *Long Range Planning, 30*(3), 413–426.
Stewart, T. (1997). *Intellectual capital: The new wealth of organizations.* New York, NY: Doubleday.
Stewart, T. A. (2001) *The Wealth of Knowledge: Intellectual Capital and the Twenty-first Century Organization,* Currency, New York.
Sveiby, K. (1997). The intangible assets monitor. *Journal of Human Resource Costing & Accounting, 2*(1), 73–97.
Sveiby, K.-E. (2008). East and West do meet—That is the real issue! *Journal of Intellectual Capital, 9*(2). doi:10.1108/jic.2008.25009baf.001.
Tandon, K., Purohit, H., & Tandon, D. (2016) Measuring Intellectual Capital and Its Impact on Financial Performance: Empirical Evidence from CNX Nifty Companies. *Global Business Review, 17*(4), 980–997.
Vishnu, S., & Kumar Gupta, V. (2014). Intellectual capital and performance of pharmaceutical firms in India. *Journal of Intellectual Capital, 15*(1), 83–99. doi:10.1108/JIC-04-2013-0049.
Young, C.-S., Su, H.-Y., Fang, S.-C., & Fang, S.-R. (2009). Cross-country comparison of intellectual capital performance of commercial banks in Asian economies. *The Service Industries Journal, 29*(11), 1565–1579. doi:10.1080/02642060902793284.

CSR as Investment: An Analysis of Ownership Structure and Firm Performance

Vasiq Nuvaid, Sucheta Sardar and Sujoy Chakravarty

Abstract CSR can be considered as an investment which is decided by the owners of the firm, and it can affect the performance of the firm. In this paper, we try to analyse how spending in CSR is related to the ownership pattern and firm performance in India. First, we analyse the CSR expenditure of Bombay Stock Exchange (BSE)-listed Indian firms and try to look at the changes in the number of firms actually spending on CSR over the years 2010–2015 due to the mandate on CSR spending in the Companies Act of 2013. Second, we analyse how the ownership structure, firm size and leverage of a firm affect its CSR expenditure. Finally, we look at the relationship between the performance of a firm and the CSR spending in these years. We use 176 listed firms in the BSE sourced from Centre for Monitoring Indian Economy's (CMIE) PROWESS database. We find that CSR spending and institutional ownership share have a positive relationship while the leverage of the firm has a negative relationship with CSR spending. We also find that CSR spending has a circular causation with firm performance. It has a significant and positive influence on the firm value while the firm value affects CSR spending positively.

Keywords Corporate social responsibility · Ownership structure
Size · Firm performance · Leverage

JEL Classification G32 · L25 · M14

V. Nuvaid (✉) · S. Sardar · S. Chakravarty
Centre for Economic Studies and Planning (CESP), Jawaharlal Nehru University, New Delhi, India
e-mail: vasiqnuvaid@gmail.com

S. Sardar
e-mail: sucheta.sardar@gmail.com

S. Chakravarty
e-mail: sujoyc@gmail.com

B. Kamaiah et al. (eds.), *Current Issues in Economics and Finance*,
DOI 10.1007/978-981-10-5810-3_8

1 Introduction

Corporate Social Responsibility is a worldwide phenomenon widespread in the developed nations. A number of Universities, healthcare institutes and NGOs are sponsored as a part of the program of CSR activities by large multinational corporations. Many emerging economies have also started putting emphasis on CSR activities of large companies which help in the development of these nations. India, with the passage of the Companies Act 2013, formally started the mandate for Corporate social responsibility. Clause 135 of the Act defines:

> Every company having net worth of rupees five hundred crore or more, or turnover of rupees one thousand crore or more or a net profit of rupees five crore or more during any financial year shall constitute a Corporate Social Responsibility Committee of the Board consisting of three or more directors, out of which at least one director shall be an independent director

Though Indian firms have been informally into the CSR activities by making voluntary donations on community development and environment-related issues with philanthropic motives, the enactment of the law has made them allocate funds for CSR activities specifically. In fact, more companies have started to participate in the corporate social responsibility expenditure program leading to an increase in the total CSR spending of companies. This leads us to the question as to what impact does the CSR expenditure of a company have on its performance and its ownership structure?

CSR can be considered as an investment which is decided by the owners of the firm, and it can affect the performance of the firm as well in this way. However, the return on CSR is usually reflected in the long run value of the firm. This will cause short-term investors to vote against CSR while long-term investors may favour a higher social spending. Owners can affect the decision of a firm to invest in different areas through a number of means. The managers act as agents of other shareholders and take decisions on their behalf which may not fully affect the managers themselves (Jensen and Meckling 1976). In the Indian case, we can use the promoters' share as a proxy for the managers' share in the shareholding pattern of the company. A group of shareholders holding a large percentage of shares can influence the firm's decision making by appointing their own directors (Boyd 1994). A few studies have found a positive relation between top management equity and social performance (Johnson and Greening 1999). Institutional ownership can influence the decisions of the firm significantly. Since CSR spending can influence the long-term value of the firm, institutional investors are more likely to support a higher CSR spending as evident from a few studies (Graves and Waddock 1994).

According to the theory, there are two competing views on how the CSR spending affects the ownership structure, one having a positive relation between CSR spending and ownership structure and the other having a negative relation between the two. A positive relation between CSR spending and shareholder value maximisation relates to 'doing well by doing good' (Freeman 1984). That is, the firm's self-interested focus on shareholders' value increase, increases shareholders' willingness to support the CSR spending (Manchiraju and Rajgopal 2015). A negative relationship between the CSR spending and the ownership structure speaks about two views: (i) the CSR spending at the cost of shareholders' money leading to a moral hazard problem. (ii) Even if moral hazard is absent, CSR spending is the sacrifice of a firm's profit in the interest of society. Friedman (1970) was of the view that CSR involves managers spending shareholders' money and 'in effect imposing taxes on one hand, and deciding how the tax proceeds shall be spent, on the other'. It is the drain of firm's value that should have been utilised for maximising shareholders value. While a few studies like Waddock and Graves (1997), Mishra and Suar (2010) and Li and Forster (2010) find a positive relation between CSR performance and firm performance, there are some other studies like Aupperle et al. (1985) and Iqbal et al. (2012) which finds a negative relation between corporate social performance and firm value.

In this paper, we try to look at the relation between CSR expenditure in India and the factors influencing it. First, we analyse the CSR expenditure of a sample of firms and try to look how many firms were actually spending on CSR over the years from 2010 to 2015. Second, we analyse how the ownership structure, firm size and leverage of a firm affect its CSR expenditure. Finally, we look at the relation between the performance of a firm and the CSR spending in these years. We use 176 listed firms in the Bombay Stock Exchange sourced from Centre for Monitoring Indian Economy's (CMIE) PROWESS database.

This paper is organised as follows. The following section reviews some literature on the subject. Next section describes the data and specifies the model used in this study. Section 4 reports and analyse the results and the last section summarises and concludes the paper.

2 Review of Literature

2.1 Related Studies

Graves and Waddock (1994) use 430 US firms to analyse the relation between the number of institutional shareholders and the corporate social performance and finds a positive relation between corporate social performance and the number of institutions holding the shares of a company and a positive, but insignificant relationship between social performance and the percentage of shares held by institutions. Zahra (1996) using 127 US Fortune 500 firms find that corporate entrepreneurship is positively related with executive stock ownership and long-term institutional ownership, but finds a negative relation with short-term institutional ownership. They use a factor analysis and regression model. In another paper, Waddock and Graves (1997) uses S&P 500 US firms for the years 1989–1991 to analyse the relation between corporate social performance and financial performance and find that social performance is positively related to prior financial performance. In addition to the social performance and financial performance variables, they used control variables such as total assets and total sales as a proxy for size, debt to asset ratio as a proxy for riskiness in the model. Li and Zhang (2010) use a multivariate regression to analyse the relation between Corporate Social Responsibility, ownership structure and political interference for more than 1000 Chinese firms in the year 2008. They find that for non-state owned Chinese firms, corporate ownership dispersion is positively related to CSR. Iqbal et al. (2012) uses 156 listed Pakistani firms and find a negative impact of Corporate Social Responsibility on the financial performance of firms using a regression model for the years 2010 and 2011. Li and Forster (2010) also uses S&P 500 firms in the US but for the post-crisis years 2009–2014 to analyse the relation between CSR and financial performance using a similar model as Waddock and Graves (1997) and find a positive relationship between corporate social responsibility and financial performance.

2.2 Unrelated Studies

Aupperle et al. (1985) send out a survey to 818 CEOs in the US and use a forced choice instrument to analyse the relation between the social responsibility and profitability of the firm. They find a negative relation between economic and non-economic components using a factor analysis of four components viz., economic, legal, ethical and discretionary responsibilities. Manchiraju and Rajgopal (2015) use 2120 Indian firms for the year 2012 making a comparison between treatment and a control group which are spending and nonspending firms in CSR. They use several identification strategies, including an event study, regression discontinuity design, difference-in-difference tests, and the instrumental variable approach, and find that those companies which are forced to spend money on CSR because of the new CSR law in India saw a drop in the stock prices.

3 Research Methodology

3.1 Data Source

For this analysis, we use 176 listed firms in the Bombay Stock Exchange sourced from Centre for Monitoring Indian Economy's (CMIE) PROWESS database for the years 2009–2010 to 2014–2015. This database covers financial data for over 27,000 companies in India. It provides financial statements, ratio analysis, fund flows, product profiles, returns and risks on the stock market, etc. It covers listed companies, large and medium public limited companies, government owned companies, some privately held companies, some cooperatives and even some business entities that are not companies. The companies covered include many sectors of the economy including manufacturing companies, service providing companies, financial companies, etc. The firms are shortlisted on two criteria viz. those firms coming under the purview of the new law and those with data availability over these years. Firms with missing data of CSR spending are dropped.

CSR expenditure in this paper is calculated as the sum of donations, social and community expenses and environment-related expenses as mentioned in the annual financial statement of the firm. Although the CSR expenditure head in the financial statement is included as social and community expenses, we include donations and environmental expenses as CSR expenditure assuming they serve the same social purpose since many firms do not provide CSR expenditure details. In fact, a few firms that were showing the CSR expenditure under the donations and environmental expenditure head, are now showing it under the social and community expenses over the past 2 years. In addition to CSR expenditure, we take variables such as ownership structure, total assets, size, age and total debt of the firm from PROWESS.

3.2 Model Specification

First, we analyse the trend of CSR spending in India for the years 2009–2010 to 2014–2015. This gives us the idea about the participation of the firms in CSR before and after the enforcement of law. Then to analyse how ownership structure of a firm affect the CSR spending of each firm, we use the following econometric model.

$$\begin{aligned} \text{CSR\_INR} = \alpha_{\text{it}} + \beta 1_{\text{it}}\text{PROM} + \beta 2_{\text{it}}\text{FORN} + \beta 3_{\text{it}}\text{INST} \\ + \beta 4_{\text{it}}\text{size} + \beta 5_{\text{it}}\text{age} + \beta 6_{\text{it}}\text{LEV} + u_{\text{it}} \end{aligned} \tag{3.1}$$

PROM, FORN and INST represent the promoters', foreign promoters' and institutional investors' share in the total equity shareholding of a company. Size, leverage and age of the firms are taken as the control variables. Age is calculated as the difference between the observation year and the incorporation year of the firm. LEV represents the leverage of the firm which is calculated as debt divided by the total assets of the firm. Size is included as control variable assuming larger firms tend to spend more on CSR expense than smaller firms as evident in many previous studies (Udayasankar 2008). Age is also assumed to affect the CSR spending as does the leverage of the firm.

Finally, we analyse the relation between the firm performance and CSR expenditure. For this, we use two different models. In the first model, we regress the firm performance indicator with the CSR expenditure intensity value and other control variables. In the second model, the CSR expenditure intensity is regressed on the firm value indicator in order to find out the direction of the causal relation we used these two models. For the firm performance value, we use one market value indicator and one accounting value indicator namely, Tobin's q and Return on Asset (RoA) respectively.

The first model is given in Eq. 3.2.

$$\begin{aligned} \text{PERF} = \alpha_{\text{it}} + \beta 1_{\text{it}}\text{CSR\_INT} + \beta 2_{\text{it}}\text{PROM} + \beta 3_{\text{it}}\text{FORN} \\ + \beta 4_{\text{it}}\text{INST} + \beta 5_{\text{it}}\text{size} + \beta 6_{\text{it}}\text{age} + \beta 7_{\text{it}}\text{LEV} + u_{\text{it}} \end{aligned} \tag{3.2}$$

where PERF is the firm performance measure captured by Tobin's Q and Return on Assets (RoA) in different models.

Firm performance here is the dependent variable measured by Tobin's Q and Return on Asset. Tobin's Q provides the market value of the firm while RoA provides with the accounting value of the firm. Tobin's Q is measured by the ratio of the market value of equity and debt to the replacement cost of assets. In this paper, as a proxy for the market value of equity, we have taken the market value of the equity shares and the preference capital. The market value of debt is proxied by borrowings of the firm. That is, it is the outstanding shares of the firms multiplied by its corresponding price plus the preference capital and the borrowings whole divided by the total asset of the firm. Return on Asset is calculated as the ratio of profitability to the total asset of the firm. CSR_INT spending of the firm and other control variables like size and age are included as the independent variables. This regression would tell us the effect of the CSR spending on the firm performance.

The second model is as in Eq. 3.3.

$$\text{CSR\_INT} = \alpha_{\text{it}} + \beta 1_{\text{it}}\text{PERF} + \beta 2_{\text{it}}\text{size} + \beta 3_{\text{it}}\text{age} + \beta 4_{\text{it}}\text{LEV} + u_{\text{it}} \tag{3.3}$$

This model tries to analyse how the impact of the performance of the firm in the CSR expenditure of the firm.

4 Results and Findings

4.1 Trend Analysis

Here, we took a sample of 812 firms coming under the purview of the new law and have data availability over these years. After analysing the CSR spending of these firms for the years 2010–2015, we found that the number of firms spending on CSR activities has considerably increased over the years especially for the past 2 years after the introduction of the new CSR law in the parliament (Table 1). This shows that the amendments in the 60-year-old company law to incorporate Corporate Social Responsibility has a positive impact on the CSR spending of firms in India. Many firms which were not spending anything on social responsibility have been forced to constitute a CSR committee and spend 2% of their average profit. Even

Table 1 Firms with a positive CSR spending out of 812 firms

Years	No. of firms having a positive CSR spending out of 812 firms
2009–2010	373
2010–2011	345
2011–2012	366
2012–2013	376
2013–2014	411
2014–2015	620

Source Prowess Database, Annual financial statement of companies

those companies which were already incurring social expenditure are doing so in a more organised fashion in the later years by forming mandatory CSR committees.

4.2 CSR Expenditure and Ownership Structure

In this section, we analyse how ownership structure of a firm affect the CSR spending of each firm.

After running the Hausman specification test for Eq. (3.1), we found the fixed effect model to be more appropriate than the random effect. Also, we used the variance inflation factor analysis to check the multicollinearity between the variables.

The result for the fixed effect-balanced regression in STATA is shown in Table 2.

From the results in Table 2, we see that institutional shareholders, the age of the firm and the leverage of the firm affect the CSR spending significantly although the coefficients are minuscule. An increase in the percentage share of institutional investors in the total shareholding structure of the firm has a positive effect on the CSR expenditure of the firm. The age of the firm also has a positive effect on the CSR spending. On the other hand, as expected, the leverage has a negative effect on the CSR expenditure. We see that the share of ownership of promoters and foreign promoters are not affecting the level of CSR spending of a company. However,

Table 2 Regression results for Eq. 3.1

Variable	CSR_INT
PROM	−9.90E−06
FORN	0.00001251
INST	0.00003053*
size	5.50E−10
age	0.00005687*
LEV	−0.00323456***
_cons	0.00034533

$^{*}p < 0.05$; $^{**}p < 0.01$; $^{***}p < 0.001$

institutional investors' share in the ownership affects the level of CSR spending of the firm. This is in congruence with the theory suggested by Graves and Waddock (1994) which contents that good management practices can improve the firm's performance in the long run and institutional investors will support a decision to that effect. The negative effect of leverage to the CSR spending can be interpreted as the debt disciplining the managers (Moussu and Ohana 2016).

4.3 CSR Expenditure and Firm Performance

The regression result for the Eq. (3.2) is tabled n Table 3. The result shows a significant increase in the performance of the firm as the CSR_INT spending rises of the firm. This indicates that the firm with high CSR spending signals a good reputation in the market which in turn increases the value of the firm. With the increase in reputation and the value of the firm, managers might be intended to further spend on social performance. Other variables are also significant. The promoters share and the institutional holding has a positive relation with the firm performance. The leverage of the firm has a negative effect on both the market value and accounting value of the firm. Interestingly, while the age of the firm has a positive influence on Tobin's Q, it has a negative influence on the return on assets. The size gives a negative coefficient for both the measures, but it is significant for Tobin's Q only.

The regression result for Eq. 3.3 is presented in Table 4.

Here we have taken just the opposite of the previous regression, CSR_INT as our dependent variable and firm performance as the independent variable taking size, age and leverage as control similar to the above regression. In both the measures, we find a positive significant relationship between the performance of the firm and the CSR spending intensity. This indicates that better the performance of the firm higher is the CSR spending of that firm. Firms with higher turnover and profits choose to spend more on the social activities that are 'doing good by doing well'. Leverage of the firm has a significant negative coefficient for both the measures. Size and ownership structure show no significant relationship in any of

Table 3 Regression results for Eq. 3.2

Variable	TobinsQ	RoA
CSR_INT	53.432524***	3.2227695***
PROM	0.0154013**	0.00095722**
FORN	0.00519929	−0.00035694
INST	0.04615049***	0.00111847***
Size	−8.785e−07*	−1.48E−09
Age	0.06034734***	−0.00540736***
LEV	−1.4892597***	−0.14955792***
_cons	−1.9614174***	0.3147437***

*$p < 0.05$; **$p < 0.01$; ***$p < 0.001$

Table 4 Regression results for Eq. 3.3

Variable	CSR_INT	CSR_INT
TobinsQ	0.00026941***	
PROM	−0.00001408	−0.00001411
FORN	0.00001099	0.00001395
INST	0.00001736	0.00002499*
Size	7.724e−10	5.488e−10
Age	0.00004078	0.00008065**
LEV	−0.00280832***	−0.00250618***
RoA		0.00455292***
_cons	0.00084455	−0.00109274

*$p < 0.05$; **$p < 0.01$; ***$p < 0.001$

the models except that of the institutional holding of the firms. Institutional holding and age are only significant in the model taken RoA as the independent variable. It does not show any significance in Tobin's Q model.

Thus, we find a two-way relationship between the CSR spending and the firm value although CSR spending has a higher influence on the firm value than the other way round.

5 Summary and Conclusion

This study tries to address an important question related to the causation between Corporate Social Responsibility, ownership structure and firm performance in the Indian scenario by assuming that CSR takes the form of investment which is decided by firm owners and can affect the firm performance. The passage of the changes in the Companies Act in 2013 to include CSR spending in it has brought more companies participating in CSR activities over the next 2 years in our study period.

With regard to the relationship between ownership structure and CSR spending, we could only find a small and significant positive relationship between CSR and the share of institutional investors among company owners. This can mean that with a higher share in the ownership of the company, institutional investors would like the company to spend more on the social responsibility front so that the firm has good long-term value. The average share of institutional ownership in India is very low at less than 10%. Therefore, as a policy implication, this calls for an improvement in the institutional quality and investments in the Indian equity markets which can further increase the CSR spending and the welfare of the society.

Most of the studies have contributed to the unidirectional causation of the CSR and firm performance with the latter increasing with higher CSR spending. We find a both-way positive relationship between the CSR spending intensity and the performance of Indian firms using the Prowess database. With higher spending in CSR, firm performance increases and with a rise in firm performance CSR spending increases. Thus, a 'doing well by doing good' strategy may actually be seen to be working where firms which are spending available resources for the development of society and the environment through education can generate long-term profits for themselves. If continued in a proper manner, this would create a win-win situation for both firms and the society as a whole. The firms would continue raising their value by spending on social activities, and society can gain from the firms' available resources leading to further development in the long run. Therefore, CSR spending improves the welfare of the society. Thus a higher spending on CSR could have a considerable improvement in the development of the economy. The two per cent mandate of the firms has been a successful move of the government where both companies and society benefit. However, the two per cent contribution from the profits is uniform across all those firms earning more than five crore profits annually. This is somewhat regressive in nature. Therefore as a policy measure, there need different rates for different slabs of profit earnings. This would add to the progressiveness of the mandate allowing the smaller firms to contribute proportionally less compared to the firms with relatively higher annual profits or turnover.

References

Aupperle, K. E., Carroll, A. B., & Hatfield, J. D. (1985). An empirical examination of the relationship between Corporate Social Responsibility and profitability. *Academy of Management Journal, 28*(2), 446–463.

Boyd, B. K. (1994). Board control and CEO compensation. *Strategic Management Journal, 75,* 335–344.

Freeman, R. (1984). *Strategic management: A stakeholder approach.* Boston, MA: Pitman.

Friedman, M. (1970). *Social responsibility of business.* New York Times Magazine.

Graves, S. B., & Waddock, S. A. (1994). Institutional owners and corporate social performance. *The Academy of Management Journal, 37*(4).

Iqbal, N., Ahmad, N., Basheer, N. A., & Nadeem, M. (2012). Impact of corporate social responsibility on financial performance of corporations: Evidence from Pakistan. *International Journal of Learning & Development.*

Jensen, M. C., & Meckling, W. H. (1976). Theory of the firm: Managerial behavior, agency costs and ownership structure. *Journal of Financial Economics, 3*(4), 305–360.

Johnson, R. A., & Greening, D. W. (1999). The effects of corporate governance and institutional ownership types on corporate social performance. *Academy of Management Journal, 42,* 564–576.

Li, F., & Forster, T. (2010). *Corporate social responsibility and financial performance following the global financial crisis.* Available at SSRN: http://ssrn.com/abstract=2700970; http://dx.doi.org/10.2139/ssrn.2700970.

Li, W., & Zhang, R. (2010). Corporate social responsibility, ownership structure, and political interference: Evidence from China. *Journal of Business Ethics, 96,* 631–645.

Manchiraju, H., & Rajgopal, S. (2015). *Does corporate social responsibility (CSR) create shareholder value? Exogenous shock-based evidence from the Indian Companies Act 2013.* Available at: http://ssrn.com/abstract=2602960.

Mishra, S., & Suar, D. (2010). Does corporate social responsibility influence firm performance of Indian companies? Journal of Business Ethics, 95(4).

Moussu, C., & Ohana, S. (2016). Do leveraged firms underinvest in corporate social responsibility? Evidence from health and safety programs in U.S. firms. *Journal of Business Ethics*.

Udayasankar, K. (2008). Corporate social responsibility and firm size. *Journal of Business Ethics, 83*(2), 167–175.

Waddock, S. A., & Graves, S. B. (1997). The corporate social performance-financial performance link. *Strategic Management Journal*.

Zahra, S. A. (1996). Governance, ownership, and corporate entrepreneurship: The moderating impact of industry technological opportunities. *Academy of Management Journal, 39,* 1713–1735.

Productivity Performance of Indian Banks with FDI Contents

Jayashree Patil-Dake

Abstract Indian banking has undergone a sea change after liberalization and reforms. Liberalization and reforms paved the way to foreign direct investment into Indian Banking Sector. It is more than a decade now that have we have received Foreign Direct Investment (FDI) in Banking and hence it is important to see its impact on the Indian Banking. The present paper is dedicated to analyze and evaluate the productivity performance of Indian banks in the post liberalization era with FDI contents.

Keywords FDI · Banks · Productivity · Performance · BPE · PPE
ROA · R

1 Introduction

Indian banking has undergone a sea change after liberalization and reforms. Liberalization and reforms paved the way to foreign direct investment into Indian Banking Sector. It is more than a decade now that have we have received Foreign Direct Investment (FDI) in Banking and hence it is important to see the impact on the Indian Banking. The present study is dedicated to analyze and evaluate the performance of Indian FDI and Non-FDI banks in the post liberalization era.

FDI is considered as an important source of financing the growth of Less Developed Countries (LDCs). It was advised by policy makers in India to throw wide open the doors to FDI which is supposed to bring "huge advantages with little or no downside". FDI flows significantly influences the growth of Gross Domestic Product (GDP) and its impact is relatively higher in India. FDI has promoted exports and there are no significant inter-country differences in the propensity of FDI to export and import increase with FDI but less than proportionately for which there are no inter-country differences.

J. Patil-Dake (✉)
Economics Department, K.P.B. Hinduja College of Commerce, Mumbai, India
e-mail: js_patil2001@rediffmail.com; jayashree.patil@gmail.com

B. Kamaiah et al. (eds.), *Current Issues in Economics and Finance*,
DOI 10.1007/978-981-10-5810-3_9

FDI is considered to be an important contributor to the performance of firms. Also that the performance of FDI is companies are better than that of non-FDI companies and however FDI companies' contribution to exports is not great and their import propensity is quite high.

It was discussed and now allowed to deregulate FDI restrictions further, e.g. by allowing FDI in retail trade, etc. Policymakers in India, as well as external observers, attach high expectations to FDI. "FDI worked wonders in China and can do so in India" (Indian Express, November 11, 2005).

The Deputy Secretary if OECD reckoned at the OECD India Investment Roundtable in 2004 that the improved investment climate has not only resulted in more FDI inflows but also in higher GDP growth (OECD India Investment Roundtable 1999). The implicit assumption seems to be that higher FDI has caused higher growth.

2 Need for the Study

In the contemporary literature review, it is believed that the FDI firms are better performers than that of Non-FDI firm in international economics (Jeromi 2002). It is more than two decades that FDI is introduced in the Indian banking industry as a bundle of reforms. Therefore, the impact of FDI on productivity, profitability and efficiency of Indian banking needs to be studied. There is a liberalization of FDI policy from 49 to 74% in 2005, so it becomes necessary to check if there was an impact of FDI and liberalized FDI policy on the Indian banking industry.

The present paper is undertaken to study the performance of FDI and Non-FDI banks, and the specific areas of economic performance in terms of Productivity, i.e., Business Per Employee (BPE) and Profit Per Employee (PPE).

3 Operational Definition for FDI and Non-FDI Banks

The present study undertakes FDI and Non-FDI Indian Commercial Banks' performance evaluation. The FDI definition includes FDI and FII both as FDI to show the impact of Foreign Investment as an impact of FDI Policy.

FDI Banks are Indian Commercial Banks that have significant level of total foreign investment in the form of FDI and FII. The significant level of FDI taken as more than that of the 50% of total allowed FDI limits in each private sector (37%, i.e., 50% of 74%) and for each public sector banks (10%, i.e., 50% of 20%). Therefore, for the present study, Public sector FDI banks are those banks which have more than 10% of FDI and are called as FDI banks. Private sector FDI banks are those banks, which have, more than 37% of FDI.

Non-FDI Banks are the Indian Commercial Banks having non-significant level of total foreign investment including FDI and FII. Indian Private sector Banks are allowed to have up to 74% of foreign investment according to the Indian FDI Policy.

For Public sector Non-FDI banks are those banks which have less than 10% of FDI.

For Private sector Non-FDI banks are those banks which have less than 37% of FDI.

3.1 Objectives of the Study

To study the productivity of FDI and Non-FDI banks in India post liberalization.

3.2 Hypothesis

Indian FDI banks have statistically significant productivity performance than the Indian Non-FDI Banks.

4 Research Methodology

4.1 The Data Sources

The study has extensively used secondary sources of data. Data used is yearly data for a financial year from April 2000–March 2001 to April 2011–March 2012.

Data pertaining to the banking sector is collected from Reserve Bank of India's published data. Data pertaining to the individual bank is collected from Indian Bank's Association, Mumbai. Also, important data related to foreign investment in individual banks is sought by query by the scholar with the help of Right to Information Act.

4.2 Tools

The Impact of FDI on Indian Banking which is measured using Panel Multiple Regression Approach using R software.

4.3 The Model Specifications, Data and Description of Variables

The model used is in testing for the presence of FDI effects on banking sector is following:

$$(\text{Performance})_{it} = \mu + \alpha' D + \beta' X_{it} + V_{it} \quad (1)$$

here

$(\text{Performance})_{it}$	is the performance measure for the ith bank during the tth period.
D	is a vector of dummy variable that characterizes FDI.
X_{it}	is a vector of other control variables that might affect performance and
V_{it}	is a random error term.
α and β	the column vectors of the coefficient to be estimated and the elements that characterize the FDI effects.

Regression analysis helps to measure the impact and relation of the different variables under study. The available data is a panel data, i.e., a combination of time series and cross section. Hence Panel Data Multiple Regression is used to see the impact of FDI on the entire banking sector. It includes 49 banks both from the public and private sector and six variables sought after factor analysis. The dummy variable is used to see the policy liberalization impact, i.e., by time dummy putting $2005 \geq 1$ and $2005 \leq 0$.

To measure the performance of FDI and Non-FDI banks, FDI content dummy is used. Accordingly, to government of India's definition (internationally accepted and accepted in India by P. Chidambaram in his budget speech of Feb 2013) more than 10% of direct or indirect foreign investment will be called as FDI firm.[56]

For public sector 20% FDI is upper limit of FDI ceiling. As already mentioned, the study takes 50% of that ceiling which is 10% FDI as non-significant FDI and hence dummy is written as

FDI > 10% = 1 and FDI < 10% = 0 for public sector banks.

For Private sector 74% FDI is the upper limit of FDI ceiling. So we are taking 50% of that ceiling which is 37% FDI as non-significant FDI and hence dummy is written as

FDI > 37% = 1 and FDI < 37% = 0 for private sector banks.

Total No. of banks under study	= 49
Public Sector Banks	= 27
Private Sector Banks	= 22

There is no single and uniform definition of the performance and efficiency. However, to measure productivity, the present study is measuring productivity as Profit per Employee (PPE) and Business per Employee (BPE).

4.4 Scope and Limitation of the Study

The scope of the study is limited to the Indian public sector and private sector banks. The study is limited to yearly data available from 2000 to 2012 from RBI and IBA, purely secondary sources of data. The study is hence limited to the time, data availability and reliability of data and sources. The study is further limited to the analysis of Indian banking industry in the advent of FDI policy.

4.5 Time Period of the Study

The data requirements of the study are from 1991 to 2012. The data from 2005 onwards (FDI data) can be availed from shareholding patterns published in the Appendix of Trends and Banking published by RBI but data before 2005 is not available with IBA or could not be reached from RBI. RBI is apex the body in banking and is having data of FDI since 2005–2012 on the website. And data from 2000–2001 to 2004–2005 was only made available by RBI under RTI. Data used is yearly data for a financial year from April 2000–March 2001 to April 2011–March 2012. Thus the study period is from 2000–2001 to 2011–2012.

5 The Study

As per our objectives the study analyzes the impact of FDI on the performance of Indian banking industry with respect to productivity. This paper deals with the testing of the hypothesis of the study: there is no significant impact of FDI on the productivity of the banks.

FDI was introduced in 1991 with the liberalization of Indian economy and financial sector reforms in Indian banking industry. Any policy takes some time period to show significant results and impact. So it was almost about 1995 when we first see FDI in the Indian banks with the new private sector banks getting formed such as ICICI, etc.

The bank wise FDI data that is available with RBI is from 2000–2001 to 2011–2012. So, the time period for the study is also chosen from 2000–2001 to 2011–2012. The effect of FDI on the performance of banks is studied by panel data regression method using dummy variable as year 2005 = 1 as that was the year of enhancement of FDI from 49 to 74% in Banks in the post-FDI liberalization period.

5.1 *FDI in Indian Banks*

These following sections will analyze the presence and role of FDI in public and private banks separately as they were subject to different conditions of FDI.

As per our objectives, the study analyzes the impact of FDI on the performance of Indian banking industry with respect to productivity. This paper analyzes productivity analysis of Indian public and private sector banks with different FDI contents. It is to see if the FDI content has an impact on the performance of these banks. The objective of the study is to analyze the productivity of Indian banks during post-FDI liberalization.

6 Productivity Analysis with Content Dummy

Here we are analyzing the productivity of Indian banks in the public and private sector in the post-FDI policy liberalization, and it is analyzed by the use of content dummy.

6.1 *Indian FDI and Non-FDI Banks: Public and Private*

Table 1 depicting results of time dummy for the productivity of all banks.

Profit per Employee

i. FDI is having a positive impact on the Profit per employee for all banks though it is not statistically significant for the period under study.

Table 1 Indian FDI and non-FDI banks' productivity: public and private

Sr. No	Dependent	Independent	Estimate	Pr (>|t|)	Adjst R^2	Significant
1	PPE	FDI	1.51E−03	0.92285†	0.13	No
		Expen	2.57E−04	1.121E−12***		Yes
		Staff	−1.35E−04	1.955E−05***		Yes
		Dummy	7.48E−01	0.02909*		Yes
2	BPE	FDI	−35.556	0.68087†	0.02	No
		Expen	0.36151	0.06464***		Yes*
		Staff	0.18238	0.29492***		No
		Dummy	2453.68959	0.19658*		No

Signif. codes: 0 '***' 0.001 '**' 0.01 '*' 0.05 '.' 0.1 '†' 1, Yes* = Significant at 0.1 and No = Not significant

All Banks = Public Sector: Old and New + Private Sector: Old and New Banks

Source Scholar's calculations on software R

ii. Expenditure is showing a positive impact on the Profit per employee for all banks and it is showing as statistically significant for the study period.
iii. The staff has a positive impact on Profit per employee for all banks. It has been observed to be statistically significant in the study period.
iv. Profit per employee for all banks is rising in the post-FDI liberalization period and is statistically significant in the study period.

Business per Employee

i. FDI is negative and has not shown statistical significance in the study period on Business per Employee of all banks.
ii. Expenditure also shows a positive impact on Business per Employee of all banks. And it is statistically significant in the study period.
iii. The staff is having a positive impact on Business per Employee for all banks and is statistically significant in the study period.
iv. Business per Employee is increasing for all banks and is statistically significant in the study period.

The empirical results reveal that in the case of all banks, FDI does not show any statistically significant impact on Profit per employee and Business per Employee in the study period. However, post-FDI liberalization dummy period shows the statistically significant impact of FDI on Profit per Employee and on the Business per Employee in the study period. Hence, the productivity of all FDI banks has gone up significantly in the study period.

6.2 Public Sector FDI and Non-FDI Banks

Table 2 depicts productivity results of Indian Public Sector banks with and without FDI as per operational definition of the present study.

Profit per Employee

i. FDI is having a positive impact on the Profit per employee for Public Sector Banks and it is showing as statistically significant for the study period.
ii. Expenditure is having a positive impact on the Profit per employee for Public Sector Banks and it is showing statistically significant impact during the study period.
iii. The staff has a negative impact on Profit per employee for Public Sector Banks. It has been observed to be statistically significant only at 10% level of significance.
iv. Profit per employee of Public Sector Banks is increasing in the study period. And it is showing the statistically significant impact of the time dummy.

Table 2 Public sector FDI and Non-FDI banks' productivity

Sr. No	Dependent	Independent	Estimate	Pr (>|t|)	Adjst R^2	Significant
1	PPE	FDI	6.81E−02	0.0007025***	0.43	Yes
		Expen	1.92E−04	<2.2E−16***		Yes
		Staff	−5.87E−05	0.0722263.		Yes*
		Dummy	1.18E+00	1.999E−06***		Yes
2	BPE	FDI	198.89096	0.46947†	0.07	No
		Expen	0.32836	0.245305†		No
		Staff	1.71364	0.000166***		Yes
		Dummy	4572.42506	0.173973†		No

Signif. codes: 0 '***' 0.001 '**' 0.01 '*' 0.05 '.' 0.1 '†' 1, Yes* = Significant at 0.1 and No = Not significant
Source Scholar's calculations on software R

Business per Employee

i. FDI is found to have a positive impact on Business per Employee of Public Sector Banks but has not shown statistical significance in the study period.
ii. Expenditure also shows positive impact on Business per Employee of Public Sector Banks and is not statistically significant in the study period.
iii. The staff is having a positive impact on Business per Employee of Public Sector Banks and is showing the statistically significant impact on BPE.
iv. Business per Employee is increasing in Public Sector Banks FDI banks but it is not statistically significant in the study period.

The empirical results reveal that in the case of public sector FDI banks, FDI is showing the statistically significant impact on PPE and not on BPE in the study period. Similarly, post-FDI liberalization dummy period results show a statistically significant impact of FDI on PPE and do not show statistically significant impact on BPE.

6.3 *Public Sector FDI and Non-banks: Old and New*

Table 3 depicts results of time dummy for the productivity of old and new public sector banks as under.

6.3.1 Old Public Sector Banks

Profit per Employee

i. FDI is having a positive impact on the Profit per employee for Old Public Sector Banks, and it is showing as statistically significant for the study period.

Table 3 Public sector FDI and non-FDI Banks: old and new

Sr. No	Dependent	Independent	Estimate	Pr (>|*t*|)	Adjst R^2	Significant
Old public sector FDI banks						
1	PPE	FDI	3.42E−01	0.01302*	0.24	Yes
		Expen	1.50E−04	9.947E−06***		Yes
		Staff	−1.99E−05	0.001533**		Yes
		Dummy	1.60E−01	0.61325†		No
2	BPE	FDI	9.38E+01	0.0002587***	0.34	Yes
		Expen	2.58E−02	2.763E−05***		Yes
		Staff	6.72E−03	0.3499714†		No
		Dummy	1.92E+02	0.0033616**		Yes
New public sector FDI banks						
1	PPE	FDI	5.22E−02	0.027270*	0.55	Yes
		Expen	3.56E−04	<2.2E−16***		Yes
		Staff	−1.58E−04	0.001533**		Yes
		Dummy	4.81E−01	0.11705†		No
2	BPE	FDI	281.54573	0.48174†	0.17	No
		Expen	0.97286	0.05018.		Yes*
		Staff	4.74852	4.667E−08***		Yes
		Dummy	3556.94854	0.49502†		No

Signif. codes: 0 '***' 0.001 '**' 0.01 '*' 0.05 '.' 0.1 '†' 1, Yes* = Significant at 0.1 and No = Not significant

Source Scholar's calculations on software R

ii. Expenditure is having a positive impact on the Profit per employee for Old Public Sector Banks and it is showing statistically significant impact during the study period.
iii. The staff has a negative impact on Profit per employee for Old Public Sector Banks. It has been observed to be statistically significant in the study period.
iv. Profit per employee of Old Public Sector Banks is increasing in the study period. However, it is not statistically significant.

Business per Employee

i. FDI is found to have a positive impact on Business per Employee of Old Public Sector Banks and has not shown statistical significance in the study period.
ii. Expenditure also shows a positive impact on Business per Employee of Old Public Sector Banks and is not statistically significant in the study period.
iii. The staff is having a positive impact on Business per Employee of Old Public Sector Banks and is statistically significant in the study period.
iv. Business per Employee is increasing in Old Public Sector Banks and it is statistically significant in the study period.

The empirical results reveal that in the case of old public sector banks; FDI is showing statistically significant impact on Business per Employee and Profit per Employee in the study period. However, post-FDI liberalization dummy period does not show any statistically significant impact of FDI on Profit per Employee but does show a statistically significant impact on Business per Employee in the study period.

6.3.2 New Public Sector Banks

Profit per Employee

i. FDI is having a positive impact on the Profit per employee for New Public Sector Banks, and it is statistically significant for the study period.
ii. Expenditure is showing a positive impact on the Profit per Employee for New Public Sector Banks and it is statistically significant for the study period.
iii. The staff has a negative impact on Profit per Employee for New Public Sector Banks. It has been observed to be statistically significant in the study period.
iv. Profit per Employee for New Public Sector Banks is rising in the study period. However, it is not statistically significant.

Business per Employee

i. FDI is found to have a positive impact on Business per Employee of New Public Sector Banks although it is not statistically significant in the study period.
ii. Expenditure also shows a positive impact on Business per Employee of New Public Sector Banks and is it also not statistically significant in the study period.
iii. The staff is having a positive impact on Business per Employee in New Public Sector Banks. It is statistically significant in the study period.
iv. Business per Employee is increasing in New Public Sector Banks. However, it is not statistically significant in the study period.

The empirical results reveal that in the case of new public sector banks; FDI is showing statistically significant impact on Profit per Employee, though it is not having statistically significant impact on Business per Employee in the study period. Profits per employee of these old public sector banks (i.e., SBI and group) has gone up significantly in dummy period but business per employee though positive does not show significant change. However, post-FDI liberalization dummy period does not show any statistically significant impact of FDI either on Profit per Employee or on Business per Employee in the study period.

6.4 SB Group's Productivity (Without SBI)

The State Bank group have total seven banks (Annexure-I); out of which SBI alone has consistently higher FDI for years and State bank of Indore had FDI levels pre-FDI liberalization but does not show the same consistency of FDI inflows in the post reform period. It is observed from the literature that SBI alone commands a major volume of banking business in India. Hence SBI is excluded from SB group to see the impact of FDI on State Bank Group. The following Table 4 depicts time dummy results for the entire SB group excluding SBI.

Profit per Employee

i. FDI is having a negative impact on the Profit per employee for SB group excluding SBI, and it is not statistically significant for the study period.
ii. Expenditure is showing a positive impact on the Profit per employee for SB group excluding SBI and the impact is statistically significant for the study period.
iii. The staff has a positive impact on Profit per employee for SB group excluding SBI, however, it is not statistically significant in the study period.
iv. Profit per employee for SB group excluding SBI is rising in the study period. However, it is not statistically significant.

Business per Employee

i. FDI is found to have a negative impact on Business per Employee of SB group excluding SB and it is not statistically significant in the study period.
ii. Expenditure also shows a positive impact on Business per Employee of SB group and is statistically significant in the study period.

Table 4 SB group's productivity (without SBI)

Sr. No.	Dependent	Independent	Estimate	Pr (>|t|)	Adjst R^2	Significant
1	PPE	FI	−3.55E−02	0.8082†	0.55	No
		Expen	8.14E−04	1.436E−08***		Yes
		Staff	2.63E−05	0.921†		No
		Dummy	3.44E−02	0.9287†		No
2	BPE	FI	−16.903414	0.342687†	0.75	No
		Expen	0.151985	1.279E−14***		Yes
		Staff	−0.032458	0.315317†		No
		Dummy	180.562382	0.000246***		Yes

Signif. codes: 0 '***' 0.001 '**' 0.01 '*' 0.05 '.' 0.1 '†' 1, Yes* = Significant at 0.1 and No = Not significant

Source Scholar's calculations on software R

iii. The staff is having a negative impact on Business per Employee of SB group excluding SBI. It is not showing statistically significant results in the study period.
iv. Business per Employee is increasing in the SB group during the post-FDI liberalization period, as shown by the time dummy, and the results are statistically significant.

The empirical results reveal that in the case of SB group (without SBI), FDI is showing no statistically significant impact on either Profit per employee or Business per Employee in the study period. PPE and BPE both have gone up in dummy period but only BPE has gone up with statistical significance in the study period. Business has gone up more than profits per employee in the case of SB group in the study period.

6.5 *Private Sector FDI and Non-FDI Banks*

Table 5 depicting the results of time dummy of productivity of private sector FDI and Non-FDI banks is shown as under.

Profit per Employee

i. FDI is having a positive impact on the Profit per employee for Private Sector Banks, but it is not statistically significant for the study period.
ii. Expenditure is showing a positive impact on the Profit per employee for Private Sector Banks. It is showing statistically significant impact on PPE for the study period.
iii. Staff has negative impact on Profit per employee for Private Sector Banks. It has been observed to be statistically not significant in the study period.

Table 5 Private sector FDI and non-FDI banks' productivity

Sr. No.	Dependent	Independent	Estimate	Pr (>|*t*|)	Adjst R^2	Significant
1	PPE	FDI	1.51E−03	0.92285†	0.13	No
		Expen	2.57E−04	1.121E−12***		Yes
		Staff	−1.35E−04	1.955E−05***		Yes
		Dummy	7.48E−01	0.02909*		Yes
2	BPE	FDI	−35.556	0.68087†	0.02	No
		Expen	0.36151	0.06464.		Yes*
		Staff	0.18238	0.29492†		No
		Dummy	2453.68959	0.19658†		No

Signif. codes: 0 '***' 0.001 '**' 0.01 '*' 0.05 '.' 0.1 '†' 1, Yes* = Significant at 0.1 and No = Not significant

All Banks = Public Sector: Old and New + Private Sector: Old and New Banks

Source Scholar's calculations on software R

iv. Profit per employee is increasing significantly in case of Private sector FDI banks in the post liberalization period as shown by a dummy variable.

Business per Employee

i. FDI is found to have a negative impact on Business per Employee of Private Sector Banks and not showing any statistically significant impact.
ii. Expenditure shows positive impact on Business per Employee of Private Sector Banks and is showing statistically significant impact on BPE only at 10% level of significance.
iii. The staff is having a positive impact on Business per Employee of Private Sector Banks. It is not statistically significant in the study period.
iv. Business per Employee is increasing in Private Sector Banks during the post-FDI liberalization period (as shown by the time dummy), however, it is not statistically significant.

The empirical results reveal that in the case of private sector banks; FDI is not showing statistically significant impact on PPE and BPE in the study period. The post-FDI liberalization dummy period notices that the Profits per Employee are increasing significantly and Business per Employee of these private sector banks has gone up; however, it is not statistically significantly. Private sector banks faced steep competition from existing large public sector banks which have had their existing market bases and wide network of branches, huge and experienced manpower, large number of years of experience in banking business, trust from government and public as they are in nationalized banks, etc. However, private sector banks have shown deepening in profits as PPE is significantly growing than the widening of Business. Private sector bank employees have given more profits than business per employee, which is also a good indicator of productivity.

6.6 Private Sector FDI and Non-banks: Old and New

Table 6 depicting the results of time dummy of productivity of FDI and Non-FDI Banks in old and new private sector banks is shown as under.

6.6.1 Old Private Sector Banks

Profit per Employee

i. FDI is having positive impact on the Profit per employee for Old Private Sector Banks, and it is not statistically significant for the study period.
ii. Expenditure is showing positive impact on the Profit per employee for Old Private Sector Banks. It is showing statistically significant impact on PPE for the study period.

Table 6 Private sector FDI and non-FDI banks' productivity: old and new

Sr. No.	Dependent	Independent	Estimate	Pr (>|t|)	Adjst R^2	Significant
Old private sector FDI banks						
1	PPE	FDI	2.13E−02	0.44073†	0.09	No
		Expen	2.14E−03	0.03103*		Yes
		Staff	−7.60E−05	0.91406†		No
		Dummy	−8.62E−01	0.23052†		No
2	BPE	FDI	−9.12E+00	0.562237†	0.06	No
		Expen	−1.54E−01	0.784606†		No
		Staff	2.54E−03	0.994957†		No
		Dummy	1.32E+03	0.001561**		Yes
New private sector FDI banks						
1	PPE	FDI	−4.58E−02	0.293798†	0.21	No
		Expen	7.27E−04	3.234E−05***		Yes
		Staff	−2.69E−04	0.003282**		Yes
		Dummy	−2.54E+00	0.113992†		No
2	BPE	FDI	−4.015934	0.1676688†	0.18	No
		Expen	0.046	7.164E−05***		Yes
		Staff	−0.020985	0.0006408***		Yes
		Dummy	−35.431322	0.0006408***		Yes

Signif. codes: 0 '***' 0.001 '**' 0.01 '*' 0.05 '.' 0.1 '†' 1, Yes* = Significant at 0.1 and No = Not significant

Source Scholar's calculations on software R

iii. Staff has negative impact on Profit per employee for Old Private Sector Banks. It has been observed to be statistically not significant in the study period.
iv. Profit per employee for Old Private Sector Banks is falling in the study period. However, it is not statistically significant.

Business per Employee

i. FDI is found to have positive impact on Business per Employee of Old Private Sector Banks and the impact is statistically significance in the study period.
ii. Expenditure also shows negative impact on Business per Employee of Old Private Sector Banks but it is not showing statistically significant impact on BPE in the study period.
iii. Staff is having a positive impact on Business per Employee of Old Private Sector Banks. It is statistically significant in the study period.
iv. Business per Employee is increasing in Old Private Sector Banks during the post-FDI liberalization period (as shown by the time dummy) and it is statistically significant in the study period.

The empirical results reveal that in the case of old private sector banks; FDI is not showing statistically significant impact on Profit per employee and Business per

Employee in the study period. The post-FDI liberalization dummy period notices that the Profits per employee are falling; however, Business per Employee of these old private sector banks has gone up and is statistically significantly. Old private sector banks faced steep competition from new private sector banks with new technology and aggressive marketing and that might have led to profits declining for them. However, their staff tried to expand business significantly in the study period.

6.6.2 New Private Sector Banks

Profit per Employee

i. FDI is having a negative impact on the Profit per employee for New Private Sector Banks, and it does not show statistically significant impact for the study period.
ii. Expenditure is showing a positive impact on the Profit per employee for New Private Sector Banks and it has a statistically significant impact on PPE for the study period.
iii. Staff has a negative impact on Profit per employee of New Private Sector Banks. It has been observed to be statistically significant in the study period.
iv. Profit per employee for New Private Sector Banks is falling in the post-FDI liberalization period as shown by the time dummy coefficient though it is not statistically significant.

Business per Employee

i. FDI is found to have a negative impact on Business per Employee of New Private Sector Banks; however, it is not shown to be statistically significant significance in the study period.
ii. Expenditure shows a positive impact on Business per Employee of New Private Sector Banks but is not statistically significant in the study period.
iii. Staff is having a negative impact on Business per Employee in New Private Sector Banks and it is statistically significant in the study period.
iv. Business per Employee is falling in New Private Sector Banks in the post-FDI liberalization period (as shown by time dummy) and it is statistically significant in the study period.

The empirical results reveal that in the case of New private sector banks, FDI is not showing no statistically significant impact on Profit per employee and Business per Employee in the study period. The post-FDI liberalization dummy period reveals that the Profits per employee and Business per Employee of these new private sector banks are falling and Business per Employee shows statistically significant impact of time dummy. It is to be noted that these New private sector banks are new entrants and faced tough competition from existing public sector giants and old private sector banks.

So between FDI and Non-FDI comparison in old and new private sector banks, FDI has not shown any significant difference in their performance. By and large, their performance in the dummy period has been growing with FDI liberalization. However, for New private sector banks expanding BPE and PPE, both have proved to be a challenge as both are negative and BPE is statistically significant.

6.7 Indian FDI and Non-FDI Banks (at 10% FDI)

Table 7 indicates results of content dummy for all the public and private sector banks together. The results of FDI more than 10% in all the banks from the year 2000–2001 to 2011–2012 are as follows:

Profit per Employee

i. FDI does not show statistically significant impact on the Profit per Employee performance of all banks with FDI content.
ii. Expenditure shows statistically significant impact on the Profit per Employee performance of all banks with FDI content.
iii. The Staff is showing a negative and statistically significant impact on the Profit per Employee performance of all banks with FDI Content.
iv. Profit Per Employee is positively growing for all banks with FDI content; however, content dummy does not show any significant impact on PPE.

Business per Employee

i. FDI is showing a positive but not statistically significant impact on the Business per Employee performance of all banks with FDI Content.
ii. Expenditure is positive and shows a statistically significant impact on the Profit per Business performance of all banks with FDI Content.

Table 7 Indian FDI and non-FDI banks at 10% FDI

Sr. No.	Dependent	Independent	Estimate	Pr (>|*t*|)	Adjst R^2	Significant
1	PPE	FDI	1.45E−02	0.29189†	0.12	No
		Expen	2.78E−04	8.063E−16***		Yes
		Staff	−1.35E−04	1.965E−05***		Yes
		Dummy	6.85E−01	0.06661.		Yes*
2	BPE	FDI	30.45173	0.686961†	0.02	No
		Expen	0.49319	0.007411**		Yes
		Staff	0.16448	0.33999†		No
		Dummy	−2840.56953	0.165511†		No

Signif. codes: 0 '***' 0.001 '**' 0.01 '*' 0.05 '.' 0.1 '†' 1, Yes* = Significant at 0.1 and No = Not significant
All Banks = Public Sector Old and New + Private Sector Old and New Banks: with 10% FDI Content
Source Scholar's calculations on software R

iii. The Staff is showing a negative but not statistically significant impact on the Business per Employee performance of all banks with FDI content.
iv. Business per Employee is falling for all banks with FDI content but content dummy does not show any significant impact.

It is observed that there is no statistically significant impact of content dummy (more than 10% FDI) on the Profit per Employee and Business per Employee in all the banks under in the study period.

6.8 Public Sector FDI and Non-banks

Table 8 depicts Productivity results for Public Sector FDI and Non-FDI Banks.

Profit per Employee

i. FDI shows positive and statistically significant impact on the Profit per Employee performance of public sector banks.
ii. Expenditure shows positive and statistically significant impact on the Profit per Employee performance of public sector banks.
iii. The Staff has a negative and not statistically significant impact on the Profit per Employee performance public sector banks.
iv. The FDI Liberalization (as shown by content dummy) has a negative impact on Profit per Employee of public sector FDI banks and it is statistically significant for banks.

Business per Employee

i. FDI shows a positive and statistically significant impact on the Business per Employee performance of all public sector banks.
ii. Expenditure shows a positive and significant impact on the Profit per Business performance of all public sector banks.

Table 8 Public sector FDI and non-FDI banks

Sr. No.	Dependent	Independent	Estimate	Pr (>|t|)	Adjst R^2	Significant
1	PPE	FDI	1.43E−01	9.595E−10***	0.43	Yes
		Expen	2.49E−04	<2.2E−16***		Yes
		Staff	−1.02E−04	0.001924**		Yes
		Dummy	−6.34E−01	0.042065*		Yes
2	BPE	FDI	−100.79267	0.7522128†	0.11	No
		Expen	0.32218	0.2227659†		No
		Staff	1.64017	0.0004597***		Yes
		Dummy	16176.57604	0.0002776***		Yes

Signif. codes: 0 '***' 0.001 '**' 0.01 '*' 0.05 '.' 0.1 '†' 1, Yes* = Significant at 0.1 and No = Not significant

Source Scholar's calculations on software R

iii. The Staff has positive impact on Business per Employee and is statistically significant on the performance of all public sector banks.
iv. Business per Employee is positive for public sector banks with FDI and the FDI Liberalization as shown by the content dummy shows it is statistically significant for public sector FDI banks.

The empirical results of content dummy for public sector banks therefore, shows that BPE is significantly increasing for FDI Public banks, however, PPE is falling significantly for public sector FDI banks in the study period.

6.9 Public Sector FDI and Non-banks: Old and New

Table 9 depicts Productivity results for Old and New Public Sector Banks with a minimum of 10% FDI henceforth called FDI banks.

- **Old Public Sector Banks**

Profit per Employee

i. FDI shows positive and statistically significant impact on the Profit per Employee performance of Old public sector banks with FDI.
ii. Expenditure shows positive and statistically significant impact on the Profit per Employee performance of all Old public sector banks with FDI.
iii. The Staff has a negative and not statistically significant impact on the Profit per Employee performance Old public sector bank with FDI.
iv. The FDI Liberalization (as shown by content dummy) has a negative impact on Profit per Employee although it is not statistically significant for banks with FDI in old public sector banks in the study period.

Business per Employee

i. FDI shows a positive and statistically significant impact on the Business per Employee performance of all Old public sector banks with FDI.
ii. Expenditure shows a positive and significant impact on the Profit per Business performance of all Old public sector banks with FDI.
iii. The Staff has positive impact on Business per Employee and is statistically significant on the performance of all Old public sector banks with FDI.
iv. Business per Employee is negative for all Old public sector banks (having 10% or more FDI) with FDI Liberalization as shown by the content dummy although it is not statistically significant.

The empirical results of content dummy with 10% or more FDI for old public sector banks therefore, shows positive and statistically significant impact on the Profit per Employee and Business per Employee in the study period. Thus it can be concluded that the productivity of old private sector banks has been positively impacted by FDI

Table 9 Public sector FDI and non-FDI banks: old and new

Sr. No.	Dependent	Independent	Estimate	Pr (>|t|)	Adjst R^2	Significant
Old public sector FDI banks						
1	PPE	FDI	2.76E−01	0.04754*	0.27	Yes
		Expen	1.43E−04	1.138E−05***		Yes
		Staff	−2.51E−05	0.51108†		No
		Dummy	−1.86E+00	0.09696.		No
2	BPE	FDI	9.87E+01	0.0004611***	0.28	Yes
		Expen	3.00E−02	3.085E−06***		Yes
		Staff	2.40E−03	0.7484319†		No
		Dummy	−2.14E+02	0.3253002†		No
New public sector FDI banks						
1	PPE	FDI	9.90E−02	1.023E−05***	0.55	Yes
		Expen	3.88E−04	<2.2E−16***		Yes
		Staff	−1.53E−04	0.00199**		Yes
		Dummy	−7.34E−01	0.01327*		Yes
2	BPE	FDI	−74.92368	0.83909†	0.19	No
		Expen	0.95597	0.025684*		Yes
		Staff	4.52887	1.07E−07***		Yes
		Dummy	14397.32738	0.004037**		Yes

Signif. codes: 0 '***' 0.001 '**' 0.01 '*' 0.05 '.' 0.1 '†' 1, Yes* = Significant at 0.1 and No = Not significant

Source Scholar's calculations on software R

- **New Public Sector Banks**

Profit per Employee

i. FDI shows a positive and statistically significant impact on the Profit per Employee performance of New public sector banks with FDI.
ii. Expenditure shows positive and statistically significant impact on the Profit per Employee performance of all New public sector banks with FDI.
iii. The Staff is negative and shows statistically significant impact on the Profit per Employee performance of New public sector banks with FDI.
iv. Profit per Employee is falling for banks with 10% and more FDI in New public sector banks in the study period and the content dummy results show statistically significant impact on PPE.

Business per Employee

i. FDI impact is negative but not statistically significant on the Business per Employee performance of all New public sector banks with FDI.
ii. Expenditure is positive and shows significant impact on the Profit per Business performance of all New public sector banks with FDI.

iii. The Staff is showing positive impact, which is statistically significant on the Business per Employee performance of all New public sector banks with FDI.
iv. Business per Employee is growing for all New public sector banks with FDI and the content dummy results show the impact to be statistically significant.

Therefore, the empirical results of content dummy with 10% or more FDI in New public sector banks shows positive and statistically significant impact on both-Profit per Employee and Business per Employee in the study period.

6.10 SBI's Productivity

Table 10 depicts results of Productivity of SBI with a minimum of 10% FDI, as other old public sector banks do not have up to 10% FDI in post-FDI liberalization period.

Profit per Employee

i. FDI shows positive and statistically significant impact on the Profit per Employee performance of SBI with FDI.
ii. Expenditure shows positive and statistically significant impact on the Profit per Employee performance of SBI with FDI.
iii. The Staff shows negative though not statistically significant impact on the Profit per Employee performance SBI with FDI.
iv. The content dummy results also show negative but are statistically significant impact only at 10% level of significance on the Profit per Employee in the dummy period in the case of SBI with FDI.

Business per Employee

i. FDI shows positive and statistically significant impact on the Business per Employee performance of SBI with FDI.

Table 10 SBI productivity (at 10% FDI) results

Sr. No.	Dependent	Independent	Estimate	Pr (>|t|)	Adjst R^2	Significant
1	PPE	FDI	2.76E−01	0.04754*	0.27	Yes
		Expen	1.43E−04	1.138E−05***		Yes
		Staff	−2.51E−05	0.51108†		No
		Dummy	−1.86E+00	0.09696.		Yes*
2	BPE	FDI	9.93E+01	0.000413***	0.28	Yes
		Expen	3.01E−02	2.667E−06***		Yes
		Staff	2.72E−03	0.71509†		No
		Dummy	−2.13E+02	0.327529†		No

Signif. codes: 0 '***' 0.001 '**' 0.01 '*' 0.05 '.' 0.1 '†' 1, Yes* = Significant at 0.1 and No = Not significant

Source Scholar's calculations on software R

ii. Expenditure shows positive and statistically significant impact on the Profit per Business performance of SBI with FDI.
iii. The Staff shows positive but not statistically significant impact on the Business per Employee performance of SBI with FDI.
iv. The content dummy results also show negative but do not show statistically significant impact on Business per Employee in the dummy period in the case of SBI with FDI.

The empirical results of FDI content dummy show negative but statistically not significant impact, on the Profit per Employee and Business per Employee, in the dummy period in the case of SBI with 10% FDI.

6.11 Private Sector FDI and Non-banks

Table 11 depicts results of Productivity of Private Sector FDI Banks with a minimum FDI content of 37% henceforth called FDI banks.

Profit per Employee

i. FDI shows negative but not statistically significant impact on the Profit per Employee performance of Private Sector Banks with FDI.
ii. Expenditure shows positive and statistically significant impact on the Profit per Employee performance of all Private Sector Banks with FDI.
iii. The Staff shows negative and shows statistically significant impact on the Profit per Employee performance of all Private Sector Banks with FDI.
iv. The content dummy results also show positive but not statistically significant impact on the Profit per Employee in the dummy period in the case of Private Sector Banks with FDI.

Table 11 Private sector FDI and non-FDI banks

Sr. No.	Dependent	Independent	Estimate	Pr (>|t|)	Adjst R^2	Significant
1	PPE	FDI	−0.00892228	0.6642†	0.08	No
		Expen	0.00073793	2.375E−06***		Yes
		Staff	−0.00034869	3.336E−05***		Yes
		Dummy	1.06104412	0.2857†		No
2	BPE	FDI	5.232705	0.5545†	0.01	No
		Expen	0.052653	0.4235†		No
		Staff	−0.031729	0.3721†		No
		Dummy	323.190672	0.4499†		No

Signif. codes: 0 '***' 0.001 '**' 0.01 '*' 0.05 '.' 0.1 '†' 1, Yes* = Significant at 0.1 and No = Not significant

Source Scholar's calculations on software R

Business per Employee

i. FDI shows positive but not statistically significant impact on the Business per Employee performance of Private Sector Banks with FDI.
ii. Expenditure shows positive but not statistically significant impact on the Profit per Business performance of Private Sector Banks with FDI.
iii. The Staff shows negative but not statistically significant impact on the Business per Employee performance of Private Sector Banks with FDI.
iv. The content dummy results also show positive but does not shows statistically significant impact on Business per Employee in the dummy period in the case of Private Sector Banks with FDI.

Our results of FDI content dummy shows statistically insignificant impact on the Profit per Employee and Business per Employee in the dummy period in the case of Private Sector Banks with FDI.

6.12 Private Sector FDI and Non-banks: Old and New

Table 12 depicts results of Productivity of Old and New Private Sector Banks with a minimum FDI content of 37%.

6.12.1 Old Private Sector Banks

Profit per Employee

i. FDI shows positive but not statistically significant impact on the Profit per Employee performance of Old Private Sector Banks with FDI.
ii. Expenditure shows positive but not statistically significant impact on the Profit per Employee performance of all Old Private Sector Banks with FDI.
iii. The Staff shows positive but not statistically significant impact on the Profit per Employee performance Old Private Sector Banks with FDI.
iv. The content dummy results also show positive but not statistically significant impact on the Profit per Employee in the dummy period in the case of Old Private Sector Banks with FDI.

Business per Employee

i. FDI shows positive but not statistically significant impact on the Business per Employee performance of all Old Private Sector Banks with FDI.
ii. Expenditure shows positive but not statistically significant impact on the Profit per Business performance of all Old Private Sector Banks with FDI.
iii. The Staff shows negative but not statistically significant impact on the Business per Employee performance of all Old Private Sector Banks with FDI.

Table 12 Private sector FDI and non-FDI banks: old and new

Sr. No.	Dependent	Independent	Estimate	Pr (>|t|)	Adjst R^2	Significant
Old private sector FDI banks						
1	PPE	FDI	0.00983347	0.7016†	0.09	No
		Expen	0.00145562	0.164†		No
		Staff	0.00013198	0.8538†		No
		Dummy	1.39187533	0.2364†		No
2	BPE	FDI	9.8151	0.516†	0.01	No
		Expen	0.11631	0.8497†		No
		Staff	−0.04173	0.9211†		No
		Dummy	232.18277	0.7367†		No
New private sector FDI banks						
1	PPE	FDI	−1.17E−01	0.0441707*	0.22	Yes
		Expen	7.10E−04	.0001265***		Yes
		Staff	−2.91E−04	.0023337**		Yes
		Dummy	−7.50E−01	0.7491119†		No
2	BPE	FDI	−2.61E+00	0.4512429†	0.28	No
		Expen	4.62E−02	4.452E−05***		Yes
		Staff	−1.95E−02	.0008447***		Yes
		Dummy	−3.41E+02	0.0187639*		Yes

Signif. codes: 0 '***' 0.001 '**' 0.01 '*' 0.05 '.' 0.1 '†' 1, Yes* = Significant at 0.1 and No = Not significant

Source Scholar's calculations on software R

iv. The content dummy results also show positive but does not shows statistically significant impact on Business per Employee in the dummy period in the case of Old Private Sector Banks with FDI.

Our results of FDI content dummy shows positive impact but statistically not significant, on the Profit per Employee and Business per Employee in the dummy period in the case of Old Private Sector Banks with 37% FDI.

6.12.2 New Private Sector Banks

Profit per Employee

i. FDI shows negative but statistically no significant impact on the Profit per Employee performance of New Private Sector Banks with FDI.
ii. Expenditure shows positive and statistically significant impact on the Profit per Employee performance of all New Private Sector Banks with FDI.
iii. The Staff has negative impact, which is statistically significant, on the Profit per Employee performance of New Private Sector Banks with FDI.

iv. Profit per Employee is falling for the New Private Sector Banks with FDI and the content dummy results show negative but not statistically significant impact, on PPE.

Business per Employee

i. FDI shows negative but not statistically significant impact on the Business per Employee performance of all New Private Sector Banks with FDI.
ii. Expenditure shows positive and statistically significant impact on the Profit per Business performance of all New Private Sector Banks with FDI.
iii. The Staff has negative impact and is statistically significant on the Business per Employee performance of all New Private Sector Banks with FDI.
iv. Business per Employee is declining for New Private Sector Banks with FDI and the content dummy results show statistically significant impact on BPE.

Our results of content dummy show negative but statistically significant impact on the Profit per Employee, and show no statistically significant impact on Business per Employee in the dummy period in the case of New Private Sector Banks with FDI.

6.13 New Private Sector FDI and Non-FDI Banks (Excluding ICICI)

Table 13 depicting the results of Productivity for private sector banks excluding ICICI banks with 37% FDI contents is shown below.

Profit per Employee

i. FDI is negative (and small) and shows statistically significant impact on the Profit per Employee performance of all New Private Sector Banks excluding ICICI with FDI.

Table 13 New private sector FDI banks excluding ICICI

Sr. No.	Dependent	Independent	Estimate	Pr (>|t|)	Adjst R^2	Significant
1	PPE	FDI	−0.1471782	0.0109887*	0.29	Yes
		Expen	0.00172238	0.0001370***		Yes
		Staff	−0.00061168	0.0002352***		Yes
		Dummy	−1.16833887	0.6149573†		No
2	BPE	FDI	−2.928708	0.3894417†	0.34	No
		Expen	0.093034	0.0005486***		Yes
		Staff	−0.034436	0.0005457***		Yes
		Dummy	−436.100696	0.0027576**		Yes

Signif. codes: 0 '***' 0.001 '**' 0.01 '*' 0.05 '.' 0.1 '†' 1, Yes* = Significant at 0.1 and No = Not significant

Source Scholar's calculations on software R

ii. Expenditure is positive and shows statistically significant impact on the Profit per Employee performance of all New Private Sector Banks excluding ICICI with FDI.
iii. The Staff is negative and it shows statistically significant impact on the Profit per Employee performance of New Private Sector Banks excluding ICICI with FDI.
iv. Profit per Employee is falling for all New Private Sector Banks in this category and the content dummy results do not show positive statistically significance on PPE.

Business per Employee

i. FDI is negative and does not show statistically significant impact on the Business per Employee performance of all New Private Sector Banks excluding ICICI with FDI.
ii. Expenditure shows a statistically significant impact on the Profit per Business performance of all New Private Sector Banks excluding ICICI with FDI.
iii. The Staff has a positive impact, which is statistically significant on the Business per Employee performance of all New Private Sector Banks excluding ICICI with FDI.
iv. The content dummy shows a statistically significant impact on the Business per Employee of New Private Sector Banks excluding ICICI with FDI.

7 Main Findings

The results of time and content dummy of productivity analysis of Indian public sector and private sector banks are as under.

7.1 Productivity Time Dummy Results

Table 14 depicts summary results of productivity of time dummy of all the banks as under.

7.1.1 Profit Per Employee

Profit per Employees is growing in the dummy period of FDI liberalization and it is showing a positive and statistically significant impact. However, for different groups categorized for our study the dummy period does not show similar levels of statistically significant impact on PPE. The dummy period shows growing PPE for all groups of FDI banks except that of private sector banks. It is interesting to note

Table 14 Productivity results: time dummy

Impact	PPE		BPE	
Banks	Estimate	Dummy	Estimate	Dummy
allbank	0.748	0.02909*	2453.690	0.19658*
public	1.179	1.999E−06***	4572.425	0.174
opub	0.160	0.613	191.580	0.0033616**
npub	0.481	0.117	3556.949	0.495
nsb	0.034	0.929	180.562	0.000246***
pvt	0.748	0.02909*	2453.690	0.197
opvt	−0.862	0.231	1316.000	0.001561**
npvt	−2.545	0.114	−35.431	0.0006408***

Signif. codes: 0 '***' 0.001 '**' 0.01 '*' 0.05 '.' 0.1 '†' 1, Yes* = Significant at 0.1 and No = Not significant
Source Consolidation of results

that PPE is falling in dummy period for old and new private sector FDI banks. When public sector banks were opting for no new recruitments and voluntary retirement options, etc., private sector banks were recruiting in the study period (Joshi 2001). The PPE is negative mainly because of the growing staff component that was being added in Private sector banks.

Based on our time dummy results we can conclude that hypothesis: *Indian FDI banks have a statistically significant productivity performance than the Indian Non-FDI Banks in terms of PPE* may be accepted for (1) all FDI banks (public and private sector together), (2) All Public sector FDI banks, and (3) All Private sector FDI Banks.

7.1.2 Business Per Employee

Business per Employee is growing for all the different categories of banks under study except that of new private sector banks where it is seen falling. BPE is growing and is statistically significant for All FDI Banks together, old public sector FDI Banks, non-SB group FDI Banks and also in case of old and new private sector FDI bank. However, it is interesting to note that BPE is falling and is not showing statistically significant impact on new private sector banks. It is mainly because of the staff element, which is growing in new private sector banks thereby reducing the business per employee.

Based on our time dummy results we can conclude that hypothesis: *Indian FDI banks have statistically significant productivity performance than the Indian Non-FDI Banks in terms of BPE* may be accepted for (1) all FDI banks (public and private sector together) and also (2) Old Public sector FDI banks, (3) Old Public sector FDI Banks excluding SBI and for (4) Old Private sector banks.

7.2 Productivity Content Dummy Results

Table 15 depicts the summary results of productivity of content dummy for ten different groups of banks under study and is shown as follows.

7.2.1 Profit Per Employee

PPE is showing mixed results for the Content Dummy for banks under study. We see that PPE is falling for Old Public sector FDI banks, new private sector FDI banks, for SBI and its group, and for all public sector FDI banks (here old public sector banks are pushing it down as it mainly comprises of SBI and its groups). In private banks, non-ICICI group of new private sector FDI banks are showing a declining impact on PPE though it is not significant. Overall, though PPE is falling it is showing statistically significant impact of FDI component only in case of New public sector banks and All public sector banks. So we can see that PPE is falling in case of pub 10% FDI, opub 10%, npvt at 10%, sbi at 10%, npvt and nicici at 10%

Based on our content dummy results we can conclude that hypothesis: *Indian FDI banks have statistically significant productivity performance than the Indian Non-FDI Banks in terms of PPE* may be accepted for (1) all banks, i.e., public and private FDI banks together but at 10% level of significance.

7.2.2 Business Per Employee

BPE is also showing mixed effects for different group of banks under study. BPE is falling in case of all FDI banks, old public sector FDI banks, new private sector FDI

Table 15 Productivity results: content dummy

Impact	PPE		BPE	
Banks	Estimate	Dummy	Estimate	Dummy
allbank	6.85E−01	0.06661.	−2840.56953	0.165511
public	−6.34E−01	0.042065*	16176.57604	0.0002776***
opub	−1.86E+00	0.09696.	−2.14E+02	0.3253002
npub	−7.34E−01	0.01327*	14397.32738	0.004037**
sbi	−1.86E+00	0.09696.	−2.13E+02	0.327529
pvt	1.06104412	0.2857	323.190672	0.4499
opvt	1.39187533	0.2364	232.18277	0.7367
npvt	−7.50E−01	0.7491119	−3.41E+02	0.0187639*
nicici	−1.16833887	0.6149573	−436.100696	0.0027576**

Signif. codes: 0 '***' 0.001 '**' 0.01 '*' 0.05 '.' 0.1 '†' 1, Yes* = Significant at 0.1 and No = Not significant

Source Consolidation of results

banks and non-ICICI and SBI bank. However, BPE is growing positively and showing statistically significant impact of content dummy in case of new public sector FDI banks and all public sector FDI banks at 10% FDI content. BPE is falling and showing statistically significant impact of content dummy in case of new private sector FDI banks and private sector group without ICICI bank at 37% FDI. So we can see that BPE is significantly falling also for and npvt 37% FDI and BPE is significantly rising in case of all pub 10%, npub at 10%.

Based on our content dummy results we can conclude that hypothesis: *Indian FDI banks have statistically significant productivity performance than the Indian Non-FDI Banks in terms of BPE* may be accepted for (1) Public sector FDI banks and (2) New Public sector FDI bank.

8 Conclusion

PPE is growing positively for Public sector FDI Banks both old and new and also for SBI. And PPE is falling both in case of new private sector and non-ICICI FDI banks. However, the coefficient is not showing a statistically significant impact of time dummy on PPE of All banks taken together both public and private FDI banks.

BPE is growing positively for Public sector FDI Banks. But BPE is falling in case of private sector FDI banks. However, PPE is showing statistically significant impact of time dummy on BPE of public sector FDI banks. PPE is also showing statistically significant impact of time dummy on BPE of both new private sector FDI banks and non-ICICI banks. But in case of private sector FDI banks BPE is falling significantly.

We, therefore, see mixed results. Since the new private sector banks are mainly the banks with more FDI than other sub groups, it is showing mixed effects of FDI time and content dummy that could be mainly due to the staff components of the productivity parameter as staff for these banks is continuously growing since they are new entrants to the business.

References

Chidambaram, P. (2005). *Finance Minister, on deregulation of FDI in India*. Indian Express, November 11, 2005.
ECONOMY WATCH. http://www.economywatch.com/foreign-directinvestment.
FDI Policy Report. (2005). Government of India, Ministry of Commerce & Industry.
Jeromi, P. D. (2002). Foreign direct investment in India—Policy, trends and impact. *Economic Development of India, 62*.
Joshi, P. N. (2001, August 11–17). Leadership in banking. *Economic and Political Weekly, 36*(32), 3023–3024. Accessed March 19, 2012 from http://www.jstor.org/stable/4410967.
OECD. (1999). Foreign Direct Investment and Economic Development, Institute for International Economics, Washington, D.C.

Is the Acquirer More Efficient Than Target? An Empirical Study from Selected Bank Consolidation in India

M. Kollapuri

Abstract This paper tries to examine whether the acquirer banks are more efficient than the target banks in 16 consolidation deals in Indian banking sector during the period 1995–2013. We find that as far as technical efficiency is concerned, the hypothesis that the acquirer is more efficient than the target bank is supported in almost all the cases except for the deal between ICICI Bank and Bank of Madura in which Bank of Madura (target) was more efficient than ICICI bank (the acquirer). Finally, both the input and output models of overall efficiency are clearly showed that the acquirer is more efficient than the target, but it does not reflect in scale efficiency.

Keywords Consolidation · Indian commercial banks · Pure technical efficiency and scale efficiency · DEA input and output-oriented models

1 Introduction

Consolidation may promote economies of scale of production and may raise the banks profit by increasing their interest rates of loans for larger clients and reducing or maintaining their interest rates of deposits that it may cause to raise their scope of economies by raising their efficiency. Efficiency means that the fractional relationship between inputs and outputs. It has included the scale and technical efficiency based on the scale and scope of economies of production. Scale of economics means that the banks are achieved the optimal size of product or services to the customer and produce these services with an optimal mix of products with their prices, is called the scope of economies. If banks fully attain scale and scope of economies then it will improve their product-mix efficiency.

M. Kollapuri (✉)
School of International Studies, Centre for International Trade and Development, Jawaharlal Nehru University, New Delhi 110067, India
e-mail: kollapuriragul@gmail.com

B. Kamaiah et al. (eds.), *Current Issues in Economics and Finance*,
DOI 10.1007/978-981-10-5810-3_10

Bank consolidation is expected to improve banking sector performance. It changes the structure of merged banks in a manner that may have a considerable effect on their management and operating cost. This may promote economies of scale and scope of consolidated banks. This paper tries to address whether the acquirer banks are more efficient than the target banks. In the Indian context, many studies examine the performance of the banking sector. However, no studies have addressed the acquirer and target bank's performance. This paper is likely to contribute to the limited literature on the acquirer and target bank's efficiency performance of Indian banking industry. Generally, the larger banks are more likely to be efficient with higher shareholder value than the smaller asset size banks. Consolidation may be a way to regain the efficiency and better management of distressed banks. A report of RBI (2013) explains that mergers and acquisitions (M&As) help to stabilize the banking sector normal that can solve financial crisis of the banking sector.[1]

This paper is structured as follows: Sect. 2 presents the review of literature of acquirer and target bank's efficiency performance of Indian commercial banks. Section 3 provides a brief discussion of consolidation in Indian banking sector. Section 4 presents the research methodology along with variables and data sources used in the study. Section 5 presents results and interpretations of acquirer and target bank efficiency performance. This section also includes the sub-section of descriptive statistics and acquirer and target efficiency comparison. Section 6 concludes the study.

2 Review of Literature

Bank consolidation causes in providing compact and stable banking services and also causes a reduction in the cost of production by reducing the operating and interest expenses. Furthermore, it is also helpful in achieving specific targets, i.e., by reducing the non-performing assets, increasing credits by efficiency, and controlling or maintaining the return on assets and the risk on assets (Peristiani 1997). Apart from that, it achieves efficiency by increasing the bank's management skills, solving the employee's issues, and quickest decision-making. Additionally, higher interest rate on higher loan for large entrepreneurs and low level of non-performing assets make a significant improvement in efficiency (Mohan 2005).

[1]An empirical study from US reveals that the consolidation of the commercial banks reduces the financial distress of merged banks (Berger and Humphery 1993).

2.1 Acquirer and Target Banks Efficiency

A few studies from foreign countries have mentioned here to understand the efficiency performance of acquirer and target banks. On the Indian context, the research based on the acquirer and target banks efficiency is scarce.

Berger and Humphrey (1993) have used cost and profit functions methodology to measure cost efficiency of U.S banks. They found that the bank efficiency improved by the direct effect of mergers and acquisitions on cost. As evident from US, bank mergers have caused to improve the cost efficiency of banks after the deal. However, it is registered with marginal improvement in during mergers and acquisitions deal. It also showed that few deals have an insignificant effect on the bank's efficiency and some mergers contributed to the bank's efficiency positively. Apart from that, the results of the study showed that there were not any upgrading income gains of banks.

Rhoades (1998) has done nine commercial bank mergers of Singapore to investigate the efficiency gains of these banks. The results of the study clearly showed that the acquirer banks in all cases were more efficient than the target banks and the branch overlap has risen in all cases after the merger activity. Singapore bank mergers found that nine out of nine mergers have achieved the cost-cutting motives; nine out of four mergers showed an efficiency gain of the banks to peers, nine out of seven mergers indicated in relation to asset peers and the nine out of five mergers revealed that the wealth effect is positive. Finally, all the nine mergers were trying to achieve cost efficiency and scale efficiency after the merger. It was apparently explained through these mergers activities.

Lim and Randhawa (2005) have analyzed the scale and technical efficiency of Singapore and Hong Kong commercial banks during mergers and acquisitions. The overall efficiency of each bank had been divided into two viz., "technical" and "scale" efficiencies. The authors have used the methodology of Data Envelopment Analysis (DEA) in illustrating the product-mix efficiency of Singapore and Hong Kong commercial banks during for the period of 1995–1999.[2] In the period of merger and acquisitions, Product-mix efficiency has been explained by using two broad approaches, viz. product and intermediation approach.[3] The results show, on the product side, the average overall efficiency score of seven local banks was 97.2% and the intermediation models overall efficiency score value of the same banks was 80.4%. It also explained that the small banks' overall efficiency is less than the large Singapore commercial banks under the product model of DEA. In the context of an intermediation approach, the overall efficiency of Singapore's larger

[2]A firm that must have a point on its production possibilities curve or that joining of services that have a superior value is called product-mix efficiency. This differswith consumer tastes and preferences, regulation policies and innovative technologies of the firm.

[3]Product method means that the banks are considered a service provider for customers and intermediate method is considered that banks have an intermediate position between borrowers and savers.

banks is very less than the smaller banks. Furthermore, it also indicated that during this period, both the ways had accepted that the technical inefficiency of Singapore commercial banks had compensated with their scale inefficiency.

Khasawneh (2006) has used a non-parametric DEA to compute the large period dynamic profit efficiency and short-time market response of merging and non-merging U.S banks from the period of 1992–2003 merger deals. The results of the study indicated that merger deals between the low efficient bidders with low efficient targets have raised their profit efficiency performance of an ongoing mergers event for this period. Another finding of the study was that merger deal between more efficient acquiring banks and less efficient target banks significantly achieved a positive Cumulative Assets Returns (CARs) and other banks have achieved negatively significant CARs due to non-merging deals.

In another study, Sufian and Majid (2007) also found that the Singapore commercial banks' overall efficiency improved during the post-merger period. By using the methodology of DEA, it suggested that Singapore commercial banks' aggregate efficiency score of 94.93% during the post-merger era was recorded higher than the 91.68% registered in the pre-merger period.[4] Finally, the results of bank-wise empirical study showed that, both the models such as product and intermediate, did not support the null hypothesis which is the acquirer more efficient than the target bank.

Chortareas et al. (2011) has taken two-stage analysis on the determinants of bank's efficiency in Mexico. By using of DEA methodology, three measures of banks efficiency were estimated. Afterward, the determinants of banks' efficiency were investigated by using a Tobit regression function with their estimated efficiency scores. The results of the study suggested that the average bank inefficiencies of the Mexican banks from the period of 2007–2009, was 15, 29, and 14% for technical efficiency (TE), pure technical efficiency (PTE), and scale efficiency (SE), respectively. Moreover, it found that the bank efficiency level has improved in the period of 2001–2006, then declined from 2006 to 2008 due to the global crisis and later recovered from 2008.

A few empirical studies explained that cost efficiency of retail banks operates below their production frontier related to an efficient frontier. Altunbas et al. (2000) explained that the difference between the best and average cost efficiency of Japanese banks are around 5–7%. It also explained that the mergers and acquisitions have brought a smaller efficiency improvement than the wider dispersion of efficiency scores. The results also tried to explain that the vast gap between the best frontiers of merged banks could be transferred to an acquirer with their superior management skills. As evidence from Japanese banks showed that the production frontier of these banks is same with a lower percentage of inputs and expenses of

[4]In spite of overall efficiency gain, has measured the usage of input to convert output. This is divided into two components pure technical efficiency and scale efficiency. Pure technical efficiency means that the banks convert its input to output in variable return to scale. Scale efficiency shows that the bank's ability to produce at maximum.

merged banks. Additionally, it was measured approximately 14% compared to before.

An empirical by Rezvanian and Mehdian (2002) have described the cost and production performance of Singaporean commercial banks with the help of a sample of selected Singaporean banks. It illustrated an average cost frontier and an efficient performance of Singapore commercial banks by using the parametric and non-parametric tactic. The results of the study explained that the small and medium scale bank mergers and acquisitions experienced and augmented with their performance of output. It also indicated that the cost-efficiency frontier of the banks was U-shaped. Furthermore, it showed that the size of banks was determining economies of scope for all Singapore banks. However, the results from the study indicated that in these Singapore commercial banks' cost of production per service declined and the overall efficiency of these banks increased. The overall inefficiency of the commercial banks included technical and distribution inefficiencies. Technical inefficiency resulted in cost inefficiencies of Singapore commercial banks.

The above-mentioned review of the literature is showing the bank's efficiency performance of acquirer and target in pre-merger. It has made clear that acquirer bank's efficiency has improved by the M&As process of the banks. The merger between the healthier and weaker banks improved target bank's efficiency positively and healthier bank's performance and decision-making unit shared by weaker banks.

3 Bank Consolidation in India

The mergers and acquisitions in the Indian banking sector have been regulated by the Banking Regulation Act (BR Act), 1949. RBI is the regulatory authority to approve and facilitate merger and acquisition processes between or among banks. However, the BR Act of mergers and acquisitions is not applicable for government owned banks viz., Public sector banks including State Bank of India (SBI) and its Associate Banks. The SBI Act 1955 regulates State Bank of India (SBI) and its Associate Banks and Banking Commercial Act 1970 regulates government owned banks effectively.[5]

The reforms of Narasimhan Committee 1991-I and 1998-II suggested that the consolidation process of the Indian commercial banks can be a way to face the challenges of banking sector liberalization. After the banking sector liberalization,

[5]Banking Regulation Act, 1949 is accessed from, https://rbidocs.rbi.org.in/rdocs/Publications/PDFs/BANKI15122014.pdf on 16-05-2014.

SBI Act 1955 is accessed from, http://financialservices.gov.in/banking/SBIActandregulation.pdf on 16-05-2014.

Banking Commercial Act, 1970 is accessed from https://www.pnbindia.in/Upload/En/Banking%20Companies%20Act%201970.pdf on 16-05-2014.

Indian commercial banks faced challenges of improved norms of prudential regulation. Altogether, the Indian banking sector witnessed 25 consolidation deals from 1991 to 2014.[6] These agreements of consolidation are determined and caused by several reasons such as synergy, poor banking efficiency, cost saving, and expansion of economies of scale and market power. Table 1 presents some details on these 25 consolidation deals.

Most of the merger and acquisition deals of Indian commercial banks were for the restructuring of weak banks and expansion of the size, scale, and scope. During 1991–2014, all but one consolidation deals were in the form of acquisition, and only one was a merger deal. In 1993, New Bank of India (NBI) merged with Punjab National Bank (PNB) due to a poor performance of NBI. It is the only merger deal that happened after the post-liberalization era, and the rest of the bank deals were based on acquisition. Also, interestingly, in 2007, the Centurion Bank acquired Lord Krishna Bank to restructure a weak bank and also make the business of the consolidated bank strong in domestic market. However, this consolidation deal did not result in better performance of the consolidated bank. Instead, the Centurion Bank was later acquired by HDFC bank in 2008. In 2010, ICICI Bank had acquired the Bank of Rajasthan due to the poor management skills and the low performance of the target bank. Additionally, State Bank of India bought State Bank of Indore for the expansion of scale and to provide wider services for different regions.

More recently, ING Bank was purchased by Kodak Mahindra Bank in 2014. In South India, more than 500 branches of ING bank were performing badly, due to lack of management skills and the increased operating cost of the banks. More recently, the finance ministry is discussing to merge all SBI and all other State Bank Associate's into one to make banking sector more stable and provide more rapid services for customers. It may generate its efficiency performance by declining its operating cost and proving more loans.

4 Methodology and Data Sources

4.1 Data Envelopment Analysis

For this paper, Data Envelopment Analysis (DEA) uses to compute efficiency of various banks. It helps to measure the profit and nonprofit organization's efficiency scores and frontier. If a bank's input–output combination lies on the frontier, it indicates that the bank is most efficient. If the bank's input–output combination lies below the efficient frontier, it implies that the bank is inefficient (Charnes et al. 1978).

[6]During the period 1961–1991, there were 59 consolidation deals. Indian banking sector experienced more than 46 consolidation deals during the period of pre-nationalization (i.e.) from 1961 to 1968. During nationalization, there were 13 consolidation deals between 1969 and 1991.

Table 1 List of selected merger and acquisitions (M&As) in India after 1991

Sl. No.	Target bank	Acquirer bank	Year	Purpose	Consolidation type
1	New Bank of India	Punjab National Bank	1993	Weak bank	Compulsory
2	Bank of Karad Ltd.	Bank of India	1994	Weak bank	Compulsory
3	Kashi Nath Seth Bank Ltd.	State Bank of India	1996	Weak bank	Compulsory
4	Bari Doab Bank Ltd.	Oriental Bank of Commerce	1997	Weak bank	Compulsory
5	Punjab Co-operative Bank	Oriental Bank of Commerce	1997	Weak bank	Compulsory
6	Bareilly Corporation Bank	Bank of Baroda	1999	Expansion of scale	Voluntary
7	Sikkim Bank Ltd.	Union Bank of India	1999	Weak bank	Compulsory
8	Times Bank Ltd.	HDFC Bank Ltd.	2000	Expansion of scale	Voluntary
9	Bank of Madura Ltd.	ICICI Bank Ltd.	2001	Expansion of scale	Voluntary
10	ICICI Ltd.	ICICI Bank Ltd.	2002	Expansion of size	Voluntary
11	Benares State Bank Ltd.	Bank of Baroda	2002	Weak bank	Compulsory
12	Nedungadi Bank Ltd.	Punjab National Bank	2003	Weak bank	Compulsory
13	South Gujarat Local Bank	Bank of Baroda	2004	Weak bank	Compulsory
14	Global Trust Bank Ltd.	Oriental Bank of Commerce	2004	Weak bank	Compulsory
15	IDBI Bank Ltd.	IDBI Ltd.	2005	Expansion of size	Voluntary
16	Bank of Punjab Ltd.	Centurion Bank Ltd.	2005	Expansion of scale	Voluntary
17	Ganesh Bank of Kurundwad	Federal Bank Ltd.	2006	Weak bank	Compulsory
18	United Western Bank Ltd.	IDBI Ltd.	2006	Weak bank	Compulsory
19	Bharat Overseas Bank Ltd.	Indian Overseas Bank	2007	Weak bank	Compulsory
20	Sangli Bank Ltd.	ICICI Bank Ltd.	2007	Expansion of scale	Voluntary
21	Lord Krishna Bank Ltd.	Centurion Bank of Punjab	2007	Expansion of scale	Voluntary

(continued)

Table 1 (continued)

Sl. No.	Target bank	Acquirer bank	Year	Purpose	Consolidation type
22	Centurion Bank of Punjab	HDFC Bank Ltd.	2008	Expansion of scale	Voluntary
23	The Bank of Rajasthan	ICICI Bank Ltd.	2010	Weak bank	Compulsory
24	State Bank of Indore	State Bank of India	2010	Expansion of scale	Voluntary
25	ING	Kodak Mahindra Bank	2013	Weak bank	Compulsory

Source Report on Trend and Progress, RBI, Table VIII, Various Issues

DEA is a non-parametric tactic used to compute input–output oriented pure technical and scale efficiency of DMUs, the commercial banks. Furthermore, production method and efficiency are based on the constant returns to scale (CRS) or variable returns to scale (VRS). This allows the overall technical efficiency to be divided into two exhaustive components: pure technical efficiency (TE) and scale efficiency (SE). It also includes the cost, profit, and allocative efficiencies.

Marginal rate of transformation of input and output combination will determine the returns to scale of the firms. The decision-making unit (DMU) frontier shows the banks' efficiency score with their ranking of performance. It also tries to explain each bank's performance with the input–output combination. Whether the input is used excessively or output is under-produced is determined by DMU frontier of the banks. Mathematical details of Data Envelopment analysis is presented in Appendix 1.

Pure Technical efficiency (PTE) = 1/measured average productivity scores. Based on this pure technical efficiency, we calculate overall efficiency and scale efficiency of the banks

Scale efficiency (SE) = Constant Returns to Scale Technical Efficiency (CRS TE)/Variable Returns to Scale Technical Efficiency (VRS TE).

Unique features of the VRS model is compared to CRS model that the DMU of banks is operated in returns to scale. It may be decreasing, constant, and increasing returns to scale (Ray 2004).

On the nature of banking technology, two approaches are used in analyzing the efficiency of banks; these are production approach and intermediate approach of analysis.[7] According to intermediation approach, while the total bank deposits ($X1$) and total expenditure ($X2$) including interest expenses are measured as input variables, the bank aggregate loans ($Y1$) and banks total income ($Y2$) including interest

[7]The production approach considers that the banks are producers of services for customers such as several transaction facilities for account holders. Based on the approach, the number of bank accounts is measured as the suitable output variable for the analysis while the physical capital and the number of bank employees is considered as the input variables.

income are measured as output variables. This paper tries to analyze the banks' efficiency with the help of DEA using intermediate method. In input-oriented model, input has assumed as constant. In an output-oriented model, output is considered as a constant. This paper shows the comparison pre- and post-merger efficiency for banks which have gone through a consolidation process.

4.2 Data

This research work is based on secondary data. The data are collected and modified from the sources "The Statistical Tables Relating to the Banks in India" of RBI, "Time Series Data of the RBI", and "Annual Publication of Banks Statistical Indicators and Performances" of RBI. The present study has excluded the regional rural and co-operative banks.

5 Empirical Results and Data Interpretation

This section analyzes the efficiency performance of acquirer and target banks and also analyzes the impact of mergers and acquisitions on efficiency of Indian commercial banks by using DEA methods such as input-oriented and output-oriented. These methods find and show clear-cut details of the bank's efficiency and it explains which firms are performing well in the banking sector by using their input and output comparing with other banks performance.

5.1 Descriptive Statistics

After the liberalization, Indian commercial banks have witnessed more than 25 consolidation deals in India. Table 2 indicates some descriptive statistics of the banking data from the period of 1995–2013, considered for this study on efficiency analysis. These are the variables of input and output which have taken for this study. In the variables, banks' total advances and total interest income are considered as output variables and banks' total deposits and interest expenditure are considered as input variables, as per the intermediation approach. Table 2 presents year-wise number of banks, maximum and minimum values of selected variables and their means. The data are for public, private, old private and foreign banks from 1995 to 2013 and all monetary values are in millions of Indian Rupees. In this statistics, the total advances of the banks included bills purchased and discounted, cash credits, overdrafts and loans, term loans and finally priority sector advances. The deposits of banks have included term deposits from the banks and included other banks term deposits. Apart from that, savings banks deposits and term deposits have included in deposits of the banks. In the term deposits, the deposits of Indian branches and outside branches such as foreign nation's branches have included in that.

The variable "interest income' is considered and included interest and discounts on advances and bills, income on investments, interest on balance with RBI and other banks funds and finally rewards from the state and central government. The final variable of the study, interest expenditure includes interest on deposits, interest on RBI, and inter banks borrowings. As the DEA efficiency scores are computed relative to all available input and output variables for the all the banks, hence these scores are very sensitive to the data being used. In preliminary exercise, it has observed that inclusion of foreign banks induces considerable instability in the efficiency scores of all banks on a year-to-year basis. As foreign banks may have very high values for the input and output variables compared to the domestic banks, therefore, inclusion of foreign banks as and when they enter in the Indian banking sector would give rise to unstable results. Hence this paper considers only 14 foreign banks that have been present in India during the entire span of 1995–2013. In 1995, 27 public sector banks, 29 private sector banks, and 14 foreign banks in India have taken for the analysis. In 1996, same public sector banks, 32 private sector banks, and 14 foreign banks have been considered for the analysis. Over a period of time, new entry and exit of domestic banks have been taken into account but foreign entries and exits have been omitted from the dataset.

If the efficiency score of any bank is equal to 1 that indicates that the bank is fully efficient. If it is below these value, the bank is inefficient and the value is equal to zero it conclude that the bank is completely inefficient.

Table 3 presents the mean efficiency scores of the banks computed by DEA using intermediary approach for three groups of banks operating in India: Public sector, Private Sector, and Foreign Banks. Table 3 presented both input-oriented and output-oriented mean efficiency scores for these bank groups. Input-oriented efficiency implies how a bank is able to minimize its inputs to produce a given level of output. Output-oriented efficiency implies banks' ability to increase output by utilizing fixed levels of inputs.

The efficiency scores have been divided into three important scales, namely, constant returns to scale, variable returns to scale, and scale efficiency.[8] In the input-oriented model of 1995, it is observed that the overall efficiency of public sector banks which have registered 0.689 ratios is less than the private and foreign sector banks which have registered 0.721 and 0.888, respectively. Among these banks, foreign banks have registered higher efficiency score in all fields. At the same period in the output-oriented model also shows same results on the aggregate mean of constant returns to scale of all sector banks but the aggregate mean score of pure technical efficiency has increased and scale efficiency has declined that is

[8]Variable return to scale tries to indicate which firm is working which return to scale. It may be increasing return to scale, decreasing return to scale, and constant return to scale (see the methodology part 3 for understanding).

Table 2 Descriptive statistics of overall banking data

Name	Advances	Int. income	Deposits	Int. exp.	Name	Advances	Int. income	Deposits	Int. exp.
Year	1995				Year	1996			
No. of banks	71	71	71	71	No. of banks	74	74	74	74
Minimum	98	23	246	3	Minimum	146	36	355	24
Maximum	485,302	106,521	851,219	66,879	Maximum	598,257	129,586	963,955	82,259
Mean	28,916	6124.01	56,180.6	4002.68	Mean	33,171.4	7399.35	60,666.4	4880.16
Year	1997				Year	1998			
No. of banks	75	75	75	75	No. of banks	77	77	77	77
Minimum	453	85	713	59	Minimum	564	102	471	37
Maximum	622,332	149,507	1,107,012	95,914	Maximum	742,373	158,789	1,310,913	104,732
Mean	35,663.3	8617.39	70,320.6	5818.19	Mean	41,128	9318.48	82,069.4	6374.55
Year	1999				Year	2000			
No. of banks	77	77	77	77	No. of banks	77	77	77	77
Minimum	509	132	407	56	Minimum	476	139	517	58
Maximum	823,598	191,075	1,690,419	130,444	Maximum	981,020	222,009	1,968,211	152,726
Mean	47,011.3	11,053.1	98,350.4	7717.6	Mean	56,710.2	12,838.4	115,460	8944.18
Year	2001				Year	2002			
No. of banks	76	76	76	76	No. of banks	78	78	78	78
Minimum	109	128	514	70	Minimum	32	141	662	66
Maximum	1,135,903	260,034	2,428,284	177,556	Maximum	1,208,065	298,101	2,705,601	207,288
Mean	68,274.6	14,852.5	137,196	10,123.9	Mean	82,381.7	16,083.8	152,779	11,093.7
Year	2003				Year	2004			
No. of banks	77	77	77	77	No. of banks	78	78	78	78
Minimum	23	123	652	54	Minimum	26	103	513	40
Maximum	1,377,585	310,870	2,961,233	211,095	Maximum	1,579,335	304,605	3,186,187	192,742
Mean	95,761.3	18,196.7	175,709	12,109.4	Mean	110,585	18,426.1	201,673	11,204.2
Year	2005				Year	2006			

(continued)

Table 2 (continued)

Name	Advances	Int. income	Deposits	Int. exp.	Name	Advances	Int. income	Deposits	Int. exp.
No. of banks	77	77	77	77	No. of banks	77	77	77	77
Minimum	24	85	482	33	Minimum	43	87	781	29
Maximum	2,023,745	324,280	3,670,475	184,834	Maximum	2,618,009	359,796	3,800,461	203,904
Mean	149,202	20,199.4	238,208	11,547.2	Mean	196,479	24,025.3	280,680	13,884.4
Year	2007				Year	2008			
No. of banks	74	74	74	74	No. of banks	73	73	73	73
Minimum	18	103	865	40	Minimum	15	112	742	31
Maximum	3,373,365	394,910	4,355,211	234,368	Maximum	4,167,682	489,503	5,374,040	319,291
Mean	266,685	31,651	363,208	19,244.8	Mean	339,075	42,218.7	454,636	28,473.6
Year	2009				Year	2010			
No. of banks	71	71	71	71	No. of banks	70	70	70	70
Minimum	19	138	608	32	Minimum	18	115	920	30
Maximum	5,425,032	637,884	7,420,731	429,153	Maximum	6,319,142	709,939	8,041,162	473,225
Mean	422,306	54,702.5	572,128	37,045.2	Mean	497,801	59,108.5	674,712	38,855.5
Year	2011				Year	2012			
No. of banks	68	68	68	68	No. of banks	66	66	66	66
Minimum	22	133	968	38	Minimum	808.745	183.307	1047.6	44.073
Maximum	7,567,195	813,944	9,339,328	488,680	Maximum	8,675,789	1,065,215	1E + 07	632,304
Mean	629,916	72,106.5	823,044	43,926.4	Mean	765,918	98,822	975,199	64,999
Year	2013								
No. of banks	66		66		66		66		
Minimum	999		242		1194		56		
Maximum	10,456,166		1,196,571		12,027,396		753,258		
Mean	887,626		115,139		1,122,634		77,601		

Source The Statistical Tables Relating to the Banks in India, RBI

Table 3 Bank group-wise mean and aggregate mean

Input-oriented						Output-oriented					
Year	Name	Public banks	Private banks	Foreign banks	All mean	Year	Name	Public banks	Private banks	Foreign banks	All mean
1995	CRSTE	0.68874	0.72143	0.88407	0.741	1995	CRSTE	0.68874	0.72143	0.88407	0.741
	VRSTE	0.89181	0.80687	0.95707	0.869		VRSTE	0.89793	0.81467	0.9595	0.875
	SE	0.77481	0.905	0.92421	0.859		SE	0.76904	0.89603	0.92193	0.853
1996	CRSTE	0.52574	0.61506	0.79036	0.616	1996	CRSTE	0.52574	0.61506	0.79036	0.616
	VRSTE	0.77967	0.67258	0.86536	0.748		VRSTE	0.80981	0.68748	0.8765	0.768
	SE	0.68089	0.92661	0.9095	0.834		SE	0.65285	0.90642	0.89971	0.813
1997	CRSTE	0.67744	0.68544	0.85914	0.715	1997	CRSTE	0.67744	0.68544	0.85914	0.715
	VRSTE	0.88067	0.72847	0.92879	0.821		VRSTE	0.89163	0.7355	0.92829	0.828
	SE	0.77141	0.94529	0.92264	0.878		SE	0.76089	0.93732	0.92421	0.871
1998	CRSTE	0.46215	0.46547	0.68856	0.511	1998	CRSTE	0.46215	0.46547	0.68856	0.511
	VRSTE	0.88944	0.67129	0.86725	0.789		VRSTE	0.89952	0.69432	0.87769	0.804
	SE	0.5217	0.70721	0.79525	0.66		SE	0.51522	0.68291	0.78363	0.645
1999	CRSTE	0.60389	0.53952	0.69312	0.596	1999	CRSTE	0.60389	0.53952	0.69312	0.596
	CRSTE	0.8963	0.69339	0.854	0.8		CRSTE	0.90374	0.712	0.86629	0.813
	SE	0.67481	0.78297	0.81165	0.751		SE	0.66881	0.76197	0.79765	0.737
2000	CRSTE	0.602	0.56153	0.74761	0.619	2000	CRSTE	0.602	0.56153	0.74761	0.619
	VRSTE	0.88085	0.71534	0.864	0.808		VRSTE	0.89333	0.72919	0.8675	0.819
	SE	0.688	0.78778	0.86917	0.772		SE	0.67737	0.77241	0.86417	0.761
2001	CRSTE	0.63241	0.60665	0.79033	0.659	2001	CRSTE	0.63241	0.60665	0.79033	0.659
	VRSTE	0.87733	0.6871	0.85817	0.795		VRSTE	0.89115	0.70519	0.86311	0.809
	SE	0.72533	0.89232	0.92467	0.841		SE	0.71296	0.86835	0.91856	0.825

(continued)

Table 3 (continued)

Input-oriented						Output-oriented					
Year	Name	Public banks	Private banks	Foreign banks	All mean	Year	Name	Public banks	Private banks	Foreign banks	All mean
2002	CRSTE	0.67841	0.63363	0.81305	0.697	2002	CRSTE	0.67841	0.63363	0.81305	0.697
	VRSTE	0.87926	0.70773	0.87138	0.811		VRSTE	0.89015	0.7194	0.87571	0.821
	SE	0.77496	0.89633	0.93419	0.865		SE	0.76456	0.88127	0.92667	0.853
2003	CRSTE	0.59893	0.56014	0.78086	0.634	2003	CRSTE	0.59893	0.56014	0.78086	0.634
	VRSTE	0.84652	0.68962	0.8721	0.794		VRSTE	0.86067	0.70638	0.8729	0.806
	SE	0.71037	0.81731	0.89376	0.801		SE	0.69793	0.7961	0.88943	0.787
2004	CRSTE	0.47511	0.4482	0.64595	0.511	2004	CRSTE	0.47511	0.4482	0.64595	0.511
	VRSTE	0.80026	0.6549	0.78962	0.742		VRSTE	0.82248	0.68043	0.79771	0.761
	SE	0.60096	0.69947	0.8139	0.696		SE	0.5837	0.66597	0.80076	0.674
2005	CRSTE	0.5067	0.49662	0.66267	0.547	2005	CRSTE	0.5067	0.49804	0.66267	0.547
	VRSTE	0.81174	0.64083	0.7909	0.744		VRSTE	0.83867	0.66943	0.79552	0.765
	SE	0.63256	0.78548	0.8349	0.745		SE	0.60981	0.75243	0.83267	0.724
2006	CRSTE	0.63896	0.63854	0.84014	0.696	2006	CRSTE	0.63896	0.62929	0.84014	0.696
	VRSTE	0.77367	0.67457	0.86705	0.764		VRSTE	0.79733	0.68104	0.86559	0.776
	SE	0.83937	0.95593	0.96836	0.919		SE	0.81337	0.93307	0.971	0.905
2007	CRSTE	0.4727	0.47832	0.67359	0.534	2007	CRSTE	0.4727	0.49128	0.67359	0.534
	VRSTE	0.7867	0.71488	0.85173	0.782		VRSTE	0.80381	0.72152	0.84614	0.792
	SE	0.60604	0.68788	0.79832	0.691		SE	0.59281	0.6906	0.80259	0.681
2008	CRSTE	0.4983	0.52913	0.78195	0.594	2008	CRSTE	0.4983	0.52492	0.78195	0.594
	VRSTE	0.80407	0.70233	0.90468	0.801		VRSTE	0.82074	0.73217	0.90477	0.813
	SE	0.62493	0.77425	0.86927	0.748		SE	0.61119	0.74038	0.87055	0.736

(continued)

Table 3 (continued)

Input-oriented						Output-oriented					
Year	Name	Public banks	Private banks	Foreign banks	All mean	Year	Name	Public banks	Private banks	Foreign banks	All mean
2009	CRSTE	0.48915	0.46909	0.71464	0.552	2009	CRSTE	0.48915	0.47113	0.71464	0.552
	VRSTE	0.82931	0.70961	0.87082	0.803		VRSTE	0.84065	0.72391	0.87636	0.814
	SE	0.59092	0.67917	0.82886	0.693		SE	0.58262	0.66587	0.82136	0.682
2010	CRSTE	0.46427	0.50365	0.71914	0.554	2010	CRSTE	0.467	0.49739	0.71914	0.554
	VRSTE	0.8315	0.7073	0.8491	0.796		VRSTE	0.84869	0.71813	0.84857	0.808
	SE	0.5615	0.73826	0.85	0.706		SE	0.55285	0.7097	0.8519	0.694
2011	CRSTE	0.38189	0.41624	0.68267	0.485	2011	CRSTE	0.38188	0.41624	0.681	0.485
	VRSTE	0.84754	0.67086	0.81224	0.782		VRSTE	0.85719	0.71005	0.8281	0.798
	SE	0.45315	0.65876	0.84924	0.639		SE	0.44762	0.6149	0.83862	0.626
2012	CRSTE	0.22835	0.2599	0.4038	0.291	2012	CRSTE	0.22835	0.2599	0.40965	0.291
	VRSTE	0.84746	0.6992	0.7682	0.779		VRSTE	0.85435	0.7532	0.75755	0.8
	SE	0.27115	0.4058	0.5781	0.405		SE	0.26877	0.35345	0.61115	0.39
2013	CRSTE	0.22835	0.2599	0.4038	0.291	2013	CRSTE	0.22835	0.2599	0.4038	0.291
	VRSTE	0.84746	0.6992	0.7682	0.779		VRSTE	0.85435	0.7532	0.77675	0.8
	SE	0.27115	0.4058	0.5781	0.405		SE	0.26877	0.35345	0.5851	0.39

Note Authors own calculation

observed in the estimators. It has registered (VRSTE) 0.875 and (SE) 0.852, respectively. It is obvious that in 1995, foreign banks were more efficient in the Indian market than their Indian counterparts. It is also observed that overall efficiency mean of foreign banks has registered 0.884 but in pure technical efficiency public sector banks have recorded 0.891 which is higher than the foreign banks. Apart from that, more interestingly, Indian private sector banks mean value of scale efficiency has recorded more than the Indian public sector banks. The results are also observed on output-oriented method of efficiency score and it is prevailing up to 2002.

In 2003, in the input-oriented model, foreign banks have recorded higher efficiency score in all returns to scale, namely, CRSTE, VRSTE, and SE and it has recorded 0.780, 0.872, and 0.893, respectively. More interestingly, it is observed that the Indian private sector banks (small assets size banks) have registered Scale efficiency of 0.817, higher than Indian public sector banks' scale efficiency of 0.710. These results also prevail in the output-oriented method that has showed in above-mentioned Table 3. In 2004, Indian public sector banks are normal to get higher variable returns to scale in both input and output model that has registered 0.800 and 0.822, respectively. However, the result is significantly higher than both private and foreign banks. In 2005, this period is also observed the same results with some deterioration in efficiency scores. In the both periods, it is shown that there is considerable and more significant result in scale efficiency. It is evident that foreign banks are much higher than the public and private sector banks. Further, public sector banks are observed less scale efficiency scores than the private sector banks.

In 2006–2010, is a global crisis and slow down year of banking performance that has observed in results. In these periods, it is shown that the public sector banks have faced low-efficiency scores of variable returns to scale 0.773, 0.7867, 0.8040, and 829 from 2006 to 2010, respectively. These are still lower than the foreign banks and higher than the private sector banks in India.

In global banking crisis which is observed 5 years in India shows that private sector banks have maintained their position in scale efficiency effectively. These results reveal that crisis would not make much difference and effects on private sectors scale efficiency and foreign banks have still continued as an efficiency determiner of Indian commercial banks. These results also observed in the output-oriented model with some effects. In this crisis period, Indian commercial banks have witnessed 8 consolidation deals in maintained their position in the banking sector. In these mergers, centurion bank has faced more effects on their scale efficiency and management. In output method, the aggregate mean of scale efficiency and variable returns to scale efficiency has registered with some effects and their scale efficiency is high in 2006 and it has increased to pure technical efficiency in 2007 that continued up to 2013.

In 2011 and after, these banks have back to normalcy compared with which has observed in the beginning and public sector banks has registered high and remarkable changes in VRSTE and it prevails up to 2013. Furthermore, the Indian private sector banks still sustain their scale efficiency from 1995 to 2013. If any changes happened in the domestic and international market and policies that would not impact more on the scale efficiency of private sector banks.

The results of Table 3 can be summarized as follows: the aggregate level clearly revealed that public sector and private sector banks are less efficient compared to foreign banks. It is found that the overall and aggregate mean value of public sector banks have registered less than the foreign banks in 1995–1998 and private sector banks are more scale efficient than the public sector banks but less than foreign banks. Public sector banks registered higher efficiency scores compared to private sector banks during 2000–2006. When crisis takes place in the banking sector, that slow down the banking performances that has witnessed for more consolidation deals in India. Namely, Indian Overseas bank takes Bharat Overseas banks, ICICI banking takes Sangli bank, Centurion bank takes Lord Krishna bank, and more interestingly HDFC bank takes Centurion bank that centurion bank becomes a target position in 2007–2008 due unexpected consolidation process with Lord Krishna bank.

In both the models, domestic public and private sector banks are performing and utilizing their resources less efficiently compared to foreign banks. In the circumstances, consolidation takes place between them that may raise their efficiency scores significantly and that would be comfortable for them to acquire new technologies and services.

The next section investigates whether the acquirer is more efficient than the target banks or not by using their pre-merger and post-merger efficiency scores by comparing between acquirer and target banks of selected mergers.

5.2 *The Acquirer is More Efficient than the Target Banks*

DEA measures the pre-merger efficiency scores of consolidated banks. These efficiency scores help for the study. The study tries in comparing the difference between the acquirer and target bank's efficiency scores to examine whether the acquirer bank is more efficient than the target bank. Theoretically, the most efficient and well managed banks take the less efficient ones as it is expected that the more efficient one better organized and more capable of handling the management issues efficiently. It is obvious that when a more efficient bank takes over a less efficient one that may lead to a improvement of the performance of the merged bank due to better management and efficient decision-making which helps in restructuring weak banks in India. The study tries to measure the selected efficiency scores pre- and post-merger for selected merger and acquisition in India and compares these pre and post-merger efficiency scores to examine whether the acquirer is more efficient than the target banks by using their overall, pure, and scale efficiency scores of the acquirer and target banks in India.

Table 4 presents the scores of overall efficiency, pure technical efficiency and scale efficiency for the both DEA Model 1(input-oriented) and DEA model 2 (output-oriented). It shows input and output models along with these efficiency scores of selected commercial banks mergers and acquisitions in India. It represents in ratios between 0 and 1 which represents the mean and aggregate mean efficiency scores of Indian commercial banks in India by using 3-year pre-merger efficiency scores and their mean value. It is evident that during the pre-merger aggregate mean value of efficiency score of selected acquirer and target banks is registered in Table 4 by using 3-year efficiency performance of consolidated banks and these efficiency scores are calculated by using all merged and non-merged Indian commercial banks from 1995 to 2013.

5.2.1 Pre-Merger

Table 4 presents the results of input and output-oriented efficiency scores for Acquirer bank (denoted by A) and Target bank (denoted by T) for 16 consolidation deals in India. Deal 1 shows that deal with the Oriental Bank of Commerce (A) and Punjab Co-Operative Bank (T). In model 1, the efficiency scores of the deal shows that overall mean value of technical efficiency score of oriental bank of commerce has registered 0.669 is higher than the Punjab co-operative bank which is registered 0.564 in overall efficiency. Apart from that, it is observed that the pure technical efficiency of the acquirer is registered 0.888 relatively lower than the target bank which is registered exactly 1. Although, the scale efficiency scores shows more favorably for acquirer banks that reveals that the acquirer bank has generated more loans/advances and services for the customers than target bank. In this particular deal, it seems that the acquirer is more efficient than the target bank except their pure technical efficiency scores. It indicates that the target banks had utilized their resources efficiently. The overall results suggest that the Oriental Bank of Commerce has utilized their resources relatively well in the basic term-shifting deposits to loans/advances with relatively minimum waste of 0.331 in both input and output model.

Deal 2 shows that the acquirer is Bank of Baroda and the target is Bareilly Corporation Bank. This is based in restructuring a weak bank in the banking sector. In model 1, it is apparent that pre-merger efficiency score on variable returns to scale and overall efficiency of Bank of Baroda is recorded 0.556 and 0.933, respectively, that is relatively higher than the target bank which is registered 0.552 and 0.595 in VRSTE and SE, respectively. More interestingly, the scale efficiency of Bareilly corporation bank has registered 0.875 that is relatively higher than the acquirer bank. Thus, the results of overall efficiency indicate that during the pre-merger period, the Bank of Baroda has produced the same output with only 0.556 amount of input which is used for the production of same level of output. In other words, Bank of Baroda could have declined their inputs by 0.444 without disturbing the amounts of production produced. In model 2, it is also obvious that pre-merger efficiency score of the deal is registered 0.556 and 0.936 and that is relatively higher than the target banks which have registered 0.522 and 0.595, respectively, in CRSTE and VRSTE. This is also identified that the scale efficiency

Table 4 Mean of efficiency scores of selected mergers and acquisitions in India 3 year pre-merger data

Deal No.	Input-oriented				Output-oriented			
	Name of the bank	CRSTE	VRSTE	SE	Name of the bank	CRSTE	VRSTE	SE
1.	Oriental Bank of Commerce (A)	0.669	0.88867	0.74967	Oriental Bank of Commerce (A)	0.669	0.89867	0.74133
	Punjab Co-Operative (T)	0.564	1	0.564	Punjab Co-Operative (T)	0.564	1	0.564
2.	Bank of Baroda (A)	0.556	0.932	0.59767	Bank of Baroda (A)	0.556	0.93633	0.59467
	Bareilly Corporation (T)	0.522	0.595	0.87467	Bareilly Corporation (T)	0.522	0.595	0.87867
3.	HDFC Bank (A)	0.66	0.81	0.81133	HDFC Bank (A)	0.66	0.81667	0.80467
	Times Bank (T)	0.51367	0.65933	0.781	Times Bank (T)	0.51367	0.66567	0.77667
4.	ICICI Banking (A)	0.492	0.67867	0.72367	ICICI Banking (A)	0.492	0.70367	0.69767
	Bank of Madura (T)	0.50933	0.707	0.72067	Bank of Madura (T)	0.50933	0.71767	0.70967
5.	Bank of Baroda (A)	0.624	0.984	0.63433	Bank of Baroda (A)	0.624	0.98467	0.634
	Benares State Bank (T)	0.49233	0.551	0.89767	Benares State Bank (T)	0.49233	0.55367	0.89467
6.	Punjab National Bank (A)	0.65033	0.987	0.65867	Punjab National Bank (A)	0.65033	0.98767	0.658
	Nedungadi Bank (T)	0.53867	0.608	0.89667	Nedungadi Bank (T)	0.53867	0.62533	0.868
7.	Oriental Bank of Commerce (A)	0.62333	0.89933	0.693	Oriental Bank of Commerce (A)	0.62333	0.911	0.68433
	Global Trust Bank (T)	0.52133	0.612	0.85033	Global Trust Bank (T)	0.52133	0.636	0.81867
8.	Centurion Bank (A)	0.53933	0.736	0.73633	Centurion Bank (A)	0.53933	0.74467	0.728
	Bank of Punjab (T)	0.53533	0.671	0.79567	Bank of Punjab (T)	0.53533	0.68233	0.78267
9.	Federal (A)	0.50367	0.68967	0.729	Federal (A)	0.50367	0.712	0.70633
	Ganesh Bank of (T)	0.379	0.39867	0.95167	Ganesh Bank of (T)	0.379	0.42833	0.887
10.	IDBI Bank (A)	0.796	0.88433	0.89733	IDBI Bank (A)	0.796	0.89633	0.887
	United Western (T)	0.47767	0.58633	0.80967	United Western (T)	0.47767	0.59967	0.792

(continued)

Table 4 (continued)

Deal No.	Input-oriented				Output-oriented			
	Name of the bank	CRSTE	VRSTE	SE	Name of the bank	CRSTE	VRSTE	SE
11.	Indian Overseas Bank (A)	0.56467	0.855	0.66433	Indian Overseas Bank (A)	0.56467	0.88033	0.644
	Bharat Overseas (T)	0.55433	0.63233	0.87733	Bharat Overseas (T)	0.55433	0.64567	0.861
12.	ICICI Banking (A)	0.479	1	0.479	ICICI Banking (A)	0.479	1	0.479
	Sangli Bank (T)	0.47333	0.55067	0.85867	Sangli Bank (T)	0.47333	0.58267	0.816
13.	Centurion Bank (A)	0.57867	0.729	0.79833	Centurion Bank (A)	0.57867	0.73967	0.78633
	Lord Krishna (T)	0.44733	0.53167	0.83633	Lord Krishna (T)	0.44733	0.561	0.797
14.	HDFC Bank (A)	0.67467	0.98567	0.686	HDFC Bank (A)	0.67467	0.99	0.68267
	Centurion Bank (T)	0.59767	0.73567	0.817	Centurion Bank (T)	0.59767	0.746	0.80567
15.	ICICI Banking (A)	0.488	1	0.488	ICICI Banking (A)	0.488	1	0.488
	Bank of Rajasthan (T)	0.44833	0.57833	0.77667	Bank of Rajasthan (T)	0.44833	0.59333	0.756
16.	State Bank of India (A)	0.525	1	0.525	State Bank of India (A)	0.525	1	0.525
	State Bank of Indore (T)	0.46967	0.75633	0.62267	State Bank of Indore (T)	0.46967	0.77133	0.61

Source Author's own calculation
CRSTE = Constant return to scale of technical efficiency ≡ OTE (overall technical efficiency)
VRSTE = Variable returns to scale of technical efficiency ≡ PTE (pure technical efficiency)
SE = Scale efficiency, (A) = acquirer, (T) = target bank

of target bank is registered higher than the acquirer. Both models support that the acquirer is more efficient than the target bank except the scale efficiency scores.

Deal 3 indicates that the acquiring bank is HDFC and the target bank is Times bank of India. This deal is based on the reason for restructuring a weak one and in achieving an economics of scale. In model 1, the results of the study show that pre-merger efficiency scores of HDFC bank in all three formats is registered higher than the target banks which is registered lower scores 0.513, 0.659, and 0.781 in CRSTE, VRSTE, and SE, respectively. In model 2, it is apparent that the output model also registered with same results that acquirer is achieved more efficient than the target bank which is considered lower scores 0.513, 0.665, and 0.77 in CRSTE, VRSTE, and SE, respectively. It is obvious that both the model support that the acquirer is more efficient than the target bank in all three formats.

Deal 4 shows that the acquirer is ICICI banking and the target bank is Bank of Madura. This deal is also motivated in restructuring a weak one and strengthens the acquirer market. In model one; it is observed that the pre-merger overall mean efficiency score of ICICI banking has registered 0.492 that is less than the Bank of Madura's efficiency scores which is registered 0.509. The model 2 shows that the ICICI banking is registered low-efficiency score relatively with target bank in all three formats that is 0.492, 0.703, and 0.697 in CRSTE, VRSTE, and SE, respectively. However, it is obvious that both the models do not support the hypothesis which is observed in that.

Deal 5 shows that the acquirer is Bank of Baroda and the target bank is Banaras State Bank. The main motivation of the deals is to regain their market power and restructure a weak bank from different financial distress. In model 1, shows that the pre-merger efficiency scores of acquirer have registered 0.624, and 0.984 in CRSTE and VRSTE, respectively, that is higher than the target banks which is registered 0.492 and 0.551 in two formats. In model 2, it is apparent that pre-merger efficiency score of the acquirer bank is registered 0.624 and 0.984 that is relatively higher than the target bank which is registered 0.492 and 0.53 in CRSTE and VRSTE. More interestingly, scale efficiency in both the model of target bank is registered higher position than the acquirer bank. Furthermore, it is clear that both the models do support the hypothesis except the scale efficiency.

Deal 6 shows that the acquirer is Punjab National Bank and the target bank is Nedungadi bank. The main motivation of the deals is in restructuring a weak bank from different financial distress. The model 1 shows that the pre-merger efficiency scores of acquirer have registered 0.650 and 0.987 in CRSTE and VRSTE, respectively, that is higher than the target bank which is registered 0.539 and 0.608 in two formats. In model 2, it is apparent that pre-merger efficiency score of the acquirer bank is registered 0.650 and 0.987 that is relatively higher than the target bank which is registered 0.538 and 0.625 in CRSTE and VRSTE. More interestingly, scale efficiency in both the model of target bank is registered higher position than the acquirer bank. Furthermore, it is clear that both the models do support the hypothesis except the scale efficiency.

Deal 7 shows that the acquirer is oriental bank of commerce and the target bank is global trust bank. This deal is also motivated in restructuring a weak one and strengthens the acquirer market. In model 1, it is observed that the pre-merger overall mean efficiency score of oriental bank of commerce has registered 0.623 that is higher than the Global trust bank's efficiency scores which is registered 0.521. This position is also observed in VRSTE. In model two, also shows that the acquirer is registered higher efficiency score relatively with target bank in two formats that is 0.623 and 0.911 in CRSTE and VRSTE, respectively. However, it is obvious that both the models do support the hypothesis which is observed in that but it is observed insignificantly in scale efficiency.

Deal 8 shows that the acquirer is Centurion Bank and the target bank is Bank of Punjab. The main motivation of the deals is to regain their market power and restructure a weak bank from financial distress. The model 1 shows that the pre-merger efficiency scores of acquirer have registered 0.539 and 0.736 in CRSTE and VRSTE, respectively, that is higher than the target bank which is registered 0.535 and 0.671 in two formats. In model 2, it is apparent that pre-merger efficiency score of the acquirer bank is registered 0.539 and 0.745 that is relatively higher than the target bank which is registered 0.535 and 0.682 in CRSTE and VRSTE. Apart from that, interestingly, scale efficiency in both the models target bank is registered higher position than the acquirer bank. Furthermore, it is obvious that both the models do support the hypothesis except the scale efficiency.

Deal 9 shows that the acquirer is Federal Bank and the target bank is Ganesh Bank of Gurudwad. The main motivation of the deals is in restructuring a weak bank. The model 1 shows that the pre-merger efficiency scores of the acquirer are registered 0.504 and 0.690 in CRSTE and VRSTE, respectively, that is higher than the target bank which is registered 0.378 and 0.399 in two formats. In model 2, it is apparent that pre-merger efficiency score of the acquirer bank is registered 0.503 and 0.712 that is relatively higher than the target bank which is registered 0.379 and 0.428 in CRSTE and VRSTE. More interestingly, scale efficiency in both the models of target bank is also registered higher position than the acquirer bank. Furthermore, it is clear that both the models do support the hypothesis except the scale efficiency.

Deal 10 shows that the acquirer is IDBI Bank and the target bank is United Western Bank. This deal is based on the reason for restructuring a weak one and in achieving an economics of scale. In model 1, the results of the study show that pre-merger efficiency scores of IDBI bank in all three formats is registered higher than the target bank which is registered lower scores 0.478, 0.586, and 0.810 in CRSTE, VRSTE, and SE, respectively. In model 2, it is apparent that the output model also registered with same results that acquirer is achieved more efficient than the target bank which is considered lower scores 0.477, 0.560, and 0.792 in CRSTE, VRSTE, and SE, respectively. It is obvious that both the model support that the acquirer is more efficient than the target bank in all three formats.

Deal 11 shows that the acquirer is Indian Overseas Bank and the target bank is Bharat Overseas Bank. The main motivation of the deals is in restructuring a weak bank. The model 1 shows that the pre-merger efficiency scores of the acquirer are registered 0.565 and 0.855 in CRSTE and VRSTE, respectively, that is higher than the target bank which is registered 0.554 and 0.632 in two formats. In model 2, it is apparent that pre-merger efficiency score of the acquirer bank is registered 0.564 and 0.880 that is relatively higher than the target bank which is registered 0.554 and 0.645 in CRSTE and VRSTE. Apart from that, scale efficiency in both the models target bank is registered higher position than the acquirer bank. Furthermore, it is clear that both the models do support the hypothesis except the scale efficiency.

Deal 12 shows that the acquirer is ICICI Banking and the target bank is Sangli Bank. The main motivation of the deals is to regain their market power and restructure a weak bank. The model 1 shows that the pre-merger efficiency scores of acquirer have registered 0.479 and 1 in CRSTE and VRSTE, respectively, that is higher than the target bank which is registered 0.473 and 0.550 in two formats. In model 2, it is apparent that pre-merger efficiency score of the acquirer bank is registered 0.479 and 1 that is relatively higher than the target bank which is registered 0.473 and 0.582 in CRSTE and VRSTE. Apart from that, it shows that scale efficiency in both the models of target bank is registered higher position than the acquirer bank. Furthermore, it is obvious that both the models do support the hypothesis except the scale efficiency.

Deal 13 shows that the acquirer is Centurion Bank and the target bank is Lord Krishna Bank. The main motivation of the deals is in restructuring a weak bank. The model 1 shows that the pre-merger efficiency scores of the acquirer are registered 0.578 and 0.729 in CRSTE and VRSTE, respectively, that is higher than the target bank which is registered 0.447 and 0.531 in two formats. In model 2, it is apparent that pre-merger efficiency scores of the acquirer bank is registered 0.578 and 0.740 that is relatively higher than the target bank which is registered 0.447 and 0.561 in CRSTE and VRSTE. Apart from that, it indicates that scale efficiency in both the models of target bank is registered higher position than the acquirer bank. Furthermore, it is clear that both the models do support the hypothesis except the scale efficiency.

Deal 14 shows that the acquirer is HDFC Bank and the target bank is Centurion Bank. The main motivation of the deals is to regain their market power and restructure a weak bank. The model 1 explains that the pre-merger efficiency scores of acquirer have registered 0.674 and 0.986 in CRSTE and VRSTE, respectively, that is higher than the target bank which is registered 0.597 and 0.736 in two formats. In model 2, it is apparent that pre-merger efficiency score of the acquirer bank is registered 0.674 and 0.99 that is relatively higher than the target bank which is registered 0.597 and 0.746 in CRSTE and VRSTE. Apart from that, it shows that scale efficiency in both the model of target bank is registered higher position than the acquirer bank. Furthermore, it is obvious that both the models do support the hypothesis except the scale efficiency.

Deal 15 shows that the acquirer is ICICI Banking and the target bank is Bank of Rajasthan. The main motivation of the deals is in restructuring a weak bank. The model 1 gives that the pre-merger efficiency scores of acquirer is registered 1 in VRSTE that is higher than the target bank which is registered 0.578 in VRSTE. In model 2, it is apparent that pre-merger efficiency scores of the acquirer bank is registered 1 that is relatively higher than the target bank which is registered 0.593 in VRSTE. Apart from that, it indicates that scale efficiency in both the model of target bank is registered higher position than the acquirer bank. Furthermore, it is observed that the overall efficiency of Bank of Rajasthan is registered significantly higher than the acquirer. It is also clear that both the models do not support the hypothesis except the VRSTE efficiency.

Deal 16 shows that the acquirer is State Bank of India and the target bank is State Bank of Indore. The main motivation of the deals is to regain their market power and restructure a weak bank. The model 1 explains that the pre-merger efficiency scores of acquirer have registered 0.525, and 1 in CRSTE and VRSTE, respectively, that is higher than the target bank which is registered 0.469 and 0.756 in two formats. In model 2, it is apparent that pre-merger efficiency score of the acquirer bank is registered 0.525 and 1 that is relatively higher than the target bank which is registered 0.469 and 0.771 in CRSTE and VRSTE. Apart from that, it shows that scale efficiency in both the model of target bank is registered higher position than the acquirer bank. Furthermore, it is obvious that both the models do support the hypothesis except the scale efficiency.

According to these consolidation deals, it is clearly observed that the deal between HDFC and Times Bank and the deal between IDBI and United Western Bank have supported the hypothesis that the acquirer is more efficient than the target bank, in all aspects of efficiency, viz., overall efficiency (technical efficiency) and scale efficiency. Most of the consolidation deals have witnessed improvement of the overall efficiency for the acquirer but not necessarily their scale efficiency. Thus, as far as technical efficiency is concerned, the hypothesis that the acquirer is more efficient than the target bank is supported in almost all the cases except for the deal between ICICI and Bank of Madura has not supported the hypothesis. In this particular deal, the Bank of Madura (Target) was more efficient than ICICI bank (the acquirer). Finally, both the input and output models of overall efficiency are clearly showed that the acquirer is more efficient than the target but it is not reflected in scale efficiency which is observed in Table 4.

6 Conclusion

Using, the non-parametric DEA methods, this paper analysis the overall, pure technical and scale efficiency of Indian commercial banks over the period of 1995–2013. This paper examines the target and acquirer bank's efficiency performance and effects of consolidation on efficiency. The results show the acquirer and target bank's efficiency comparison before the merger deal. The results also show that the selected acquirer efficiency performance of selected 3-year average mean efficiency scores has comparatively higher than target bank's efficiency performance except some deals which has happened in the crisis period. However, the results of the study directly accept our objective-based hypothesis that the acquirer is more efficient than the target bank. The result has observed from the comparison of pre-merger effects of selected consolidation deals with input and output comparisons. Thus, it will show that the consolidation of selected banks will improve its input usage effectively to produce more outputs.

The findings suggest that the consolidation of banks improves its efficiency by generating synergy situation among the services and by using their input and output combination effectively. More interestingly, well defined voluntary consolidation makes the acquirer efficiency positively and uncertain deals go negative results on its efficiency. Thus, observed in Centurion Bank with uncertain conglomeration with Lord Krishna Bank.

The results of DEA scores, Most of the consolidation deals have witnessed improvement of the overall efficiency for the acquirer but not necessarily their scale efficiency. It is clearly observed that the deal between HDFC and Times Bank and the deal between IDBI and United Western Bank have supported the hypothesis that the acquirer is more efficient than the target bank, in all aspects of efficiency, viz., overall efficiency (technical efficiency) and scale efficiency. Finally, both the input and output models of overall efficiency are clearly showed that the acquirer is more efficient than the target but it is not reflected in scale efficiency which is observed in Table 4. Better management and solving the bank distress generated banks efficiency. More recently, the finance ministry is discussing to merge all state bank groups into one to make banking sector more stable. It must scrutinize by RBI to make banking system more efficient.

Acknowledgements I am grateful to my supervisor Dr. Mandira Sarma, who has cared about my research work and given full support to me to finish this so early.

Appendix 1: Mathematical Form of DEA

The average productivity of the banks is measured as the ratio of outputs to inputs (Ray 2004). If firm t uses n inputs to produce m outputs, then its average productivity is given

$$\mathrm{AP}_t = \frac{\sum_{r=1}^{m} v_{rt} y_{rt}}{\sum_{i=1}^{n} u_{it} x_{it}} \tag{1}$$

m	No. of outputs;
n	No. of inputs;
AP_t	Average Productivity of tth bank;
u_t (shadow prices of inputs)	$(u_{1t}, u_{2t}, \ldots, u_{nt})$;
v_t (shadow prices of outputs)	$(v_{1t}, v_{2t}, \ldots, v_{mt})$;
x_{it} (input bundle)	$(x_{1t}, x_{2t}, \ldots, x_{nt})$;
y_{it} (output bundle)	$(y_{1t}, y_{2t}, \ldots, y_{mt})$.

In the shadow prices, two conditions are imposed. First, all the shadow prices of input and output bundles are nonnegative values. Second, the shadow prices of input and output bundles result in Average Productivity (AP) lower than unity ($AP_t \leq 1$) for not only the *t*th bank but also for all other banks.

$$\text{Maximize}\, AP_t = \frac{\sum_{r=1}^{m} v_{rt} y_{rt}}{\sum_{i=1}^{n} u_{it} x_{it}}$$

Such that

$$\begin{aligned} AP_j &= \frac{v^{t'} y^j}{u^{t'} x^j} = \frac{\sum_{r=1}^{m} v_{rt} y_{rj}}{\sum_{i=1}^{n} u_{it} x_{ij}} \leq 1; \quad (j = 1, 2 \ldots, N) \\ u_{it} &\geq 0; \quad (i = 1, 2, \ldots, n); \\ v_{rt} &\geq 0; \quad (r = 1, 2, \ldots, m); \end{aligned} \tag{2}$$

This is a fractional functional programming problem. To transform this into a linear programming problem (LPP) by using Charnes and Cooper model (1962). However, when all the shadow prices of input and output bundles are multiplied by a non negative factor ($k > 0$), that will not affect our objective function (AP_t) as well as constraints.

$$w_{it} = k u_{it} \quad (i = 1, 2, 3, \ldots, n) \tag{2a}$$

$$p_{rt} = k v_{rt} \quad (r = 1, 2, 3, \ldots, m.) \tag{2b}$$

Then, the optimization function is,

$$\begin{aligned} &\max \frac{p^{t'} y^t}{w^{t'} x^t}; \\ &\text{s.t.}\ \frac{p^{t'} y^t}{w^{t'} x^t} \leq 1; \quad (t = 1, 2 \ldots N); \\ &p^t \geq 0; \\ &w^t \geq 0; \end{aligned} \tag{3}$$

Now, we set $k \equiv \frac{1}{\sum_{i=1}^{n} u_{it} x_{it}}$. Then, $w^{t'} x^t = 1$ and then the objective problem turns into

$$
\begin{aligned}
&\max \sum_{r=1}^{m} p_{rt} y_{rt} \\
&\text{s.t.} \quad \sum_{r=1}^{m} p_{rt} y_{rt} - \sum_{i=1}^{n} w_{it} x_{it} \leq 0; \\
&\sum_{i=1}^{n} w_{it} x_{it} = 1 \\
&P_{rt} \geq 0; \quad (r = 1, 2, \ldots m) \\
&W_{it} \geq 0; \quad (i = 1, 2, \ldots n)
\end{aligned} \tag{4}
$$

This linear programming problem can be solved using the simplex method. In this paper, we have used two-input and two-output model. y^t (output bundle) = (y_{1t}, y_{2y}) and x^t (input bundle) = (x_{1t}, x_{2t}). Then, the linear programming problem (LPP) is,

$$
\begin{aligned}
&\max p_{1t} y_{1t} + p_{2t} y_{2t} \\
&\text{s.t.} \quad p_{1t} y_{11} + p_{2t} y_{21} - w_{1t} x_{11} - w_{2t} x_{21} \leq 0; \\
&p_{1t} y_{12} + p_{2t} y_{22} - w_{1t} x_{21} - w_{2t} x_{22} \leq 0; \\
&p_{1t} y_{1t} + p_{2t} y_{2t} - w_{1t} x_{1t} - w_{2t} x_{2t} \leq 0; \\
&p_{1t} y_{1N} + p_{2t} y_{2N} - w_{1t} x_{1N} - w_{2t} x_{2N} \leq 0; \\
&w_{1t} x_{1t} - w_{2t} x_{2t} = 1; \\
&p_{1t}, p_{2t}, w_{1t}, w_{2t} \geq 0.
\end{aligned} \tag{5}
$$

This is a primal LPP and it is difficult to solve because this LPP includes $N + 1$ constraint (the additional constraint is $w_{1t} x_{1t} - w_{2t} x_{2t} = 1$). The primal of the LPP problem is duel. In variable return to scale (VRS), the above-mentioned linear programming problem is used with additional constraint λ which is equal to 1. Scale efficiency of banks has been measured by using the ratio of Constant Returns to Scale technical efficiency and Variable Returns to Scale technical efficiency.

References

Altunbas, Y., et al. (2000). Efficiency and risk in Japanese banking. *Journal of Banking & Finance, 24*(10), 1605–1628.

Berger, A. N., & Humphrey, D. B. (1993). *Bank scale economies, mergers, concentration, and efficiency: The U.S. experience* (pp. 1–34). Wharton School University of Pennsylvania, Financial Institutions Centre working paper, No. 94-25.

Charnes, A., & Cooper, W. W. (1962). Programming with linear fractional functionals. *Naval Research Logistics Quarterly, 9*(3–4), 181–186.

Charnes, A., et al. (1978). Measuring the efficiency of decision-making units. *European Journal of Operational Research, 2*, 429–444.

Chortareas, G. E., et al. (2011). Banking sector performance in Latin America: Market power versus efficiency. *Review of Development Economics, 15*(2), 307–325.

Khasawneh, J. A. (2006). *Bank efficiency dynamics and market reaction around merger announcement*. University of New Orleans theses and dissertations 1031. http://scholarworks.Uno.edu/td/1031. Accessed on July 23, 2014.

Lim, G. H., & Randhawa, D. S. (2005). Competition, liberalization and efficiency: Evidence from a two-stage banking model on banks in Hong Kong and Singapore. *Managerial Finance, 31* (1), 52–77.

Mohan, T. T. R. (2005). Bank consolidation issues and evidence. *Economic and Political Weekly, 40*(12), 1151–1159.

Peristiani, S. (1997). Do mergers improve the X-efficiency and scale efficiency of U.S. banks? Evidence from the 1980s. *Journal of Money, Credit and Banking, 29*(3), 326–337.

Ray, S. C. (2004). *Data envelopment analysis: Theory and techniques for economics and operations research*. Cambridge: Cambridge University Press.

Reserve Bank of India (RBI). (2013). *Banking structure in India—The way forward*. Discussion paper, Department of Banking Operations and Development (DBOD) and Department of Economic and Policy Research (DEPR), Mumbai, August 2013.

Rezvanian, R., & Mehdian, S. (2002). An examination of cost structure and production performance of commercial banks in Singapore. *Journal of Banking & Finance, 26,* 79–98.

Rhoades, S. A. (1998). The efficiency effects of bank mergers: An overview of case studies of nine mergers. *Journal of Banking & Finance, 22,* 273–291.

Sufian, F., & Majid, M.-Z. A. (2007). Deregulation, consolidation and banks efficiency in Singapore: Evidence from event study window approach and Tobit analysis. *International Review of Economics, 54,* 261–283.

Part IV
Agriculture and Food Security

Foreign Exchange Rate and Agricultural Performances: A Time Series Exercise for India

Madhabendra Sinha and Partha Pratim Sengupta

Abstract The paper attempts to investigate and analyze the causal linkage between movements of foreign exchange rate and agricultural performances in terms of production and export empirically in India. Agricultural is described as the backbone of India, contributed largest but continuously declining share of national income. Indian agricultural exports, contribute a significant share of total exports, an important earner of foreign exchange. So foreign exchange rate can have a relationship with worldwide exports and well as output of India's agricultural and allied commodities. In this context, the current paper explores the underlying long-term causal relationships among India's foreign exchange rate and productions of exports of agricultural and allied commodities to fill gaps in the available literature. Yearly data on agricultural exports is calculated from DGCIS, Government of India over the period 1970–2015. Reserve Bank of India provides the yearly data on foreign exchange rate and data on GDP of agricultural and allied activities is collected from CSO, Government of India over the same period. The stochastic properties of variables are checked by applying ADF and PP unit root tests. Johansen cointegration test is employed followed by vector error correction mechanism (VECM) to find the long run dynamics. Our findings imply unidirectional long run causality between agricultural exports and India's foreign exchange rate.

Keywords Foreign exchange rate · Agriculture export · Agricultural production
Unit root test · Johansen cointegration test · VECM

M. Sinha (✉) · P.P. Sengupta
Department of Humanities and Social Sciences, National Institute of Technology Durgapur, Durgapur 713209, West Bengal, India
e-mail: madhabendras@gmail.com

B. Kamaiah et al. (eds.), *Current Issues in Economics and Finance*,
DOI 10.1007/978-981-10-5810-3_11

1 Introduction

Foreign exchange rate is a vital macroeconomic variable for an open economy like India influencing international trade mainly through exports and imports. It is obvious that movements of foreign exchange rate are linked with worldwide exports of agricultural and other primary products from India. Agricultural and others exports can affect equilibrium exchange rate in two ways, either through appreciation or depreciation of domestic currency depending on volume of trade. Oppositely appreciation or depreciation of foreign exchange rate makes exports of primary and other products more costlier or cheaper. So, Due to stronger the Indian rupee, exports become more expensive in foreign countries, and the costs of imported commodities will reduce to India. Alternatively, a weaker the Indian rupee inversely impacts, enhancing exports and lowering imports. By and large, currency appreciations and depreciations both are transient in nature. The difference in relative prices in domestic and foreign markets reflected by foreign exchange rate determines the pattern of trade of agrarian and other products between the nations.

Agriculture and allied activities have been portrayed as the foundation of Indian economy due to several reasons. First, agriculture has constituted the biggest share of gross domestic product (GDP) in India, though the share follows a declining trend to around 30% in early 1990s and less than 20% in 2014–2015 from almost 55% in early 1950s. Second, more than 70% of workforce in India had been employed in agriculture and allied sectors till 1971, and also during current period almost 52% of total workforce is engaged with primary activities in India. Finally, growths of secondary and tertiary sectors also depend on performance of agriculture and allied sectors to a large extent. Indian agriculture is also identified as a consistent foreign exchange earner. Exports of agricultural and allied products contribute a significant share of India's total export though its trend is declining. In early 1990s share of agriculture and allied products to total export was around 20% but declined to about 10% in 2005–2006. Still, this sector directly contributes around 16% of export earnings for the year 2014–2015 and indirectly promotes overall exports through others sectors in India.

The policy of economic liberalization in 1991 has brought some revolutionary changes in India with a swing from import substituting inward looking to an outward looking and export promoting policies, more liberalized and competitive approach to integrate the economy with global. Foreign exchange rate is an important macroeconomic variable, influenced by worldwide export of India's agricultural and other commodities and services. Export of agricultural commodities can affect equilibrium currency exchange price in both ways, either appreciation or depreciation of domestic currency depending on the volume of exports as well as imports. On another side appreciation or depreciation of Indian currency makes its exports more costlier or cheaper to other countries and reduces or enhances the cost of imports. In this way, foreign exchange rate fluctuations can also impact agricultural exports. Since economic reform in India, exchange rate of Indian rupee compare to US dollar is continuously depreciating except some periods. But the movements of India's foreign exchange rate follow a slight fluctuating path due to unequal rate of growth at different times. In this context, the current paper explores the underlying long-term cointegrating relationship between foreign exchange rate and exports of agricultural and allied commodities in case of India to fill the different gaps in available literature on the basis of suitable time series econometric methodology. We collect the yearly data of foreign exchange rate measured by exchange rate of Indian rupee compare to US dollar from Reserve Bank of India over the 1970–2015 as available. Yearly data of agricultural export for the same period has been calculated from DGCIS, Government of India by maintaining the rules of measurement of export of agricultural and allied products as mentioned in exports of principal commodities, and agricultural GDP data has been collected from Central Statistics Office, Government of India. We carry out ADF and PP unit root tests for the variables followed by Johansen cointegration test and mechanism of vector error correction to explore the long run dynamics among the variables. The rest of the paper is structured as follows. Next section briefly reviews the existing literature followed by a discussion about the Indian scenario of agriculture and dynamics of foreign exchange rate. After documenting the hypotheses to be tested in the study with the data sources, we discuss the methodological issues followed by empirical results. Our final section concludes the paper.

2 Review of Literature

The area of existing theoretical and empirical evidences related to existing study for Indian context and other developing countries is not so large. A very few studies have identified the agricultural sector by exploring the dynamic causality among foreign exchange rate, and production and trade performances of agricultural and allied sectors. Vellianitis-Fidas (1976) investigated the hypothesis that changes in foreign exchange rate significantly impact the agricultural exports from USA and got the possible satisfactory results. Johnson et al. (1977) put together the impact of foreign exchange rate versus overseas commercial policy in the wheat pricing in USA. A study by Hughes and Penson (1985) observed a remarkable increase in volume as well as value of agricultural exports over the years with a significant relationship with agricultural output and exchange rate. Oyejide (1986) examined the impacts of international trade and foreign exchange rate strategies on agricultural export for Nigeria by utilizing the method of ordinary least squares (OLS) over the period from 1960 to 1982. Empirical results of the study implied that appreciation of real exchange rate has some violent impacts on exports of non-oil, particularly during the oil boom period.

Schwartz (1986) analyzed the impact of changes in foreign exchange rate with other macro variables in a simple competitive versus noncompetitive wheat market, and found some significant results. Bradshaw and Orden (1990) observed some possible findings by exploring the Granger causality test of foreign exchange rates on prices and exports of agricultural commodities. Chambers and Just (1991) pointed out that while some studies observed that exchange rate plays a vital role in exports of agricultural products, still other researchers explained the relatively slight effect of exchange rate on the agriculture sector in the economy. Paarlberg et al. (1994) documented the economic theory behind the effect of foreign exchange rates movements on some basic macroeconomic variables like prices, productions and consumptions. They reported that various studies measured the impacts of movements of exchange rate on agriculture. Khan et al. (1995) examined the direction of causality between exports and economic growth by using Granger causality test and cointegration technique. They discovered the bi-directional causality between export and economic growth.

An analytical testing of the hypothesis of export-led growth has been conducted by Khalafalla and Webb (2001) in Malaysia. They found a significant relationship between exports and GDP growth using the quarterly data over the period from 1965 to 1996. Chandra (2002) found a short run bi-directional causal linkage between export and GDP growth in India. On investigating the impacts of economic reforms as well as trade liberalization on the performance of agricultural exports in case of Pakistan, Bashir (2003) referred that export of agricultural products more sensitive to the factors in domestic market, and that varies due to economic reforms. Shirazi and Manap (2004) re-investigated the nexus between export and annual economic growth over the period from 1960 to 2003. Their results strongly aided a long run relationship among export, import and output. It is also observed that exports cause economic growth, but the converse is not true.

In the context of Indian economy, Sharma and Panagiotidis (2005) tested the hypothesis of export-led growth, and their outcomes strengthened the arguments against the export-led growth in India. After discussing the relationship between export growth and GDP growth in India over the period from 1960 to 1992, Raju and Kurien (2005) used the Granger causality approach and found a unidirectional causal linkage between exports and economic growth, with and without an error correction term. Shombe (2008) investigated causal relationships among agricultural, manufacturing production and exports in Tanzania using data over the period from 1970 to 2005. The empirical results confirmed the Granger causality where agriculture causes both manufacturing production and exports. Dash (2009) examined the causality between exports and economic growth in India during the post-liberalization period from 1992 to 2007 and observed a unidirectional long run relationship running from exports to output growth. Against this back drop, it can be argued that impact of the export of agricultural and allied products on the foreign exchange rate is almost under investigated empirically in the post reform India with large data sets that the paper tries to complete by using the yearly data for a significant time period.

3 Indian Agriculture and Foreign Exchange Rate Dynamics: A Brief Scenario

Agriculture has been identified as backbone of Indian economy, but it is consistently losing its importance in the process of economic growth compare to other sectors. Agriculture and allied sectors including forestry, fishing, livestock, etc., have contributed around 17% of GDP in India for the period 2015–2016, and still more than 50% of the population directly and indirectly depends on them. Also an increasing trend of GDP of agriculture and allied activities in India has been found during post reform period as shown in Fig. 1. Indian agro industry has been divided into various sub-segments like dairy, canned, frozen and processed fishes, poultry, meat, and food grains. Different departments, bodies and research units have been established to develop these sectors.

India ranks first in production, consumption and export of spices and related products. During last quarter of the year 2016, export of spices from India has grown by 9% in volume to 660,975 tonnes. Fruits productions in India grow faster than vegetables items, which help to hold the second largest position of fruit production in the world. The estimated figure of horticulture production in India is around 260 million tonnes in 2015–2016. Exports of basmati rice are expected to increase to about Rs 22,000 crore by 2017–2018 and Groundnut export may cross 700,000 tonnes during 2017–2018 from India. Agricultural export is the fourth-largest exported items of principal commodity. Expected increase in grapes export to China and Europe is around 20% during the current period. Food grains production in India has reached to 264 million tonnes in 2014 by the more than twice increment, but it is not profit enhancing to farmers. Still good yield in India depends upon rainfall and climatic conditions.

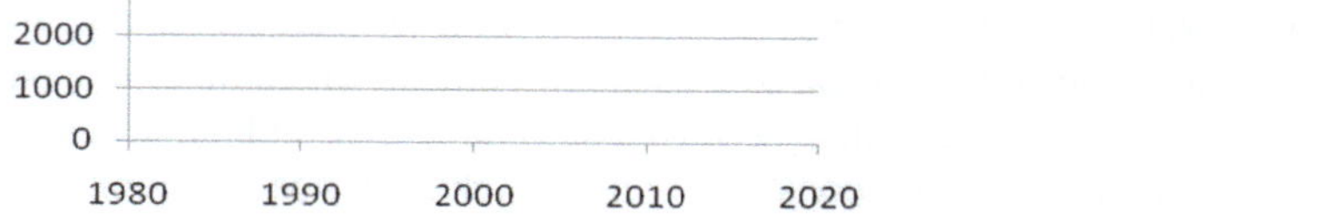

Fig. 1 GDP of agriculture and allied activities. *Source* CSO, Government of India, annual data from 1990 to 2015

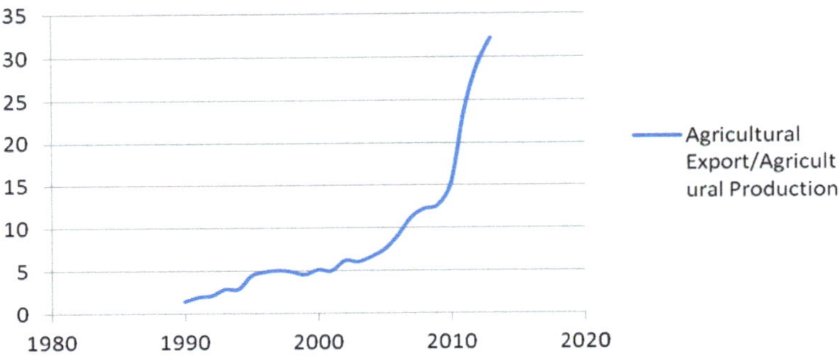

Fig. 2 Agricultural export as a share of agricultural GDP. *Source* DGCIS and CSO, Government of India, annual data from 1990 to 2015

As export is one of components of GDP, the growth by export-led hypothesis postulates that export expansion is one of the main determinants of growth. India's export performance is fluctuating in nature from 1990 to 2015. Agricultural export of India faces the impact of negative growth in the year 1999–2000 than previous year. The next major setback for India's exports was the global crisis of 2008. The dampened trade deficit in India in 2009–2010 with a negative import growth (−0.78%) was also impacted with a negative growth rate of 2.9% in 2008–2009 than previous years. India has been following overall an increasing path in agricultural exports throughout the period from 1990 to 2015 except the years 1999–2000 and 2009–2010. The share of agricultural export to agricultural GDP follows rising trends since 1990 in India, and the share is sharply increasing from 2010 as Fig. 2 represents.

Some commodities such as wheat, sugar, cotton, edible oil, rubber, etc., are directly related to the government's trade decisions and control. It is observed that in the past few years, the government's approach to deal with the trade of the commodities has been widely exposed. Indian Government has to adopt bottom-up agricultural approaches which emphasize the involvement of the rural people and first prioritize the concerns of our own farmers. Exports compositions refer the commodities, which are sold to other nations. During the early 1950s, India's exports were consisted of various agricultural commodities like tea, tobacco, spices etc. India also exported jute and allied products and cotton textiles in a large extent.

Foreign exchange rate is a key financial as well as macroeconomic variable which influences the choices made by traders, foreign exchange investors, bankers, financial institutions, businessmen, policymakers and tourists in both developed and developing countries. Fluctuations in foreign exchange rate also influence the estimates of global investment portfolios, trade competitiveness in terms of exports and imports, currency value of debt payments, value and volume of international reserves and costs to tourists. Figure 3 clearly indicates that except the recession period in last decade, India's foreign exchange rate is rising over the period of time since 1990.

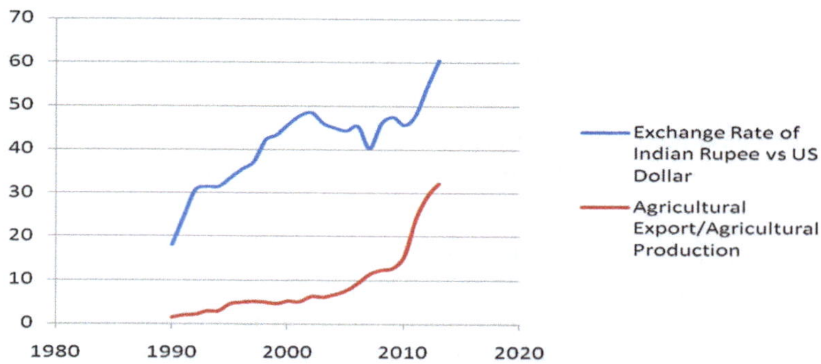

Fig. 3 Trends of exchange rate and agricultural exports in India. *Source* Handbook of Statistics for Indian Economy, RBI, annual data from 1990 to 2015

Movements in foreign exchange rates hence have important ramifications for the economy's business cycle, trade and are therefore crucial for understanding financial improvements and changes in economic policy also with the reverse effect on it from the same macroeconomic factors. India has been experiencing a controlled but floating foreign exchange rate regime since March 1993, which denotes an era of a market determined foreign exchange rate regime of Indian rupee with the provision of time to time intervention by the central bank that is Reserve Bank of India (RBI). Under the floating exchange rate regime worldwide, RBI is actively participating in market dynamics of foreign exchange for signaling its position and keeping up the efficient conditions.

4 Hypotheses and Data

As the foreign exchange rate is a major macroeconomic variable to be affected by the exports of agricultural and allied products in the economy simply as the exchange rate is the price of domestic currency in terms of foreign currency. It is expressive of economy's external competitiveness and a reflection of balance of payments position. Exchange rate fluctuations can deeply affect on the banking and financial sectors of the economy when the fluctuations are high and sudden. An improvement in the export scenario of agricultural goods causes the real exchange rate to appreciate due an increase in the amount of dollars vis-à-vis the Indian rupee. The supply of dollars increases as a consequence of which the dollar debilitates opposite the Indian rupee. This implies the Indian rupee appreciates in value. As our exports become relatively more expensive, an appreciation in Indian rupee has a negative impact on exports. This in turn impacts the aggregate demand of the economy and subsequently exchange rate is an important macroeconomic variable for the growth and development of the economy.

In this background the two null hypotheses to be tested for achieving the above-mentioned objective of the study are categorized for Indian economy as follows:

(a) Agricultural production and export do not cause foreign exchange rate and;
(b) Foreign exchange rate do not have any impact on agricultural production and export.

We collect the yearly data of foreign exchange rate measured by exchange rate of Indian rupee compare to US dollar (EXRT) from Reserve Bank of India over the period 1970–2015. Yearly data of agricultural export (AEXP) for the same period has been calculated from Directorate General of Commercial Intelligence and Statistics (DGCIS), Government of India by maintaining the rules of measurement of export of agricultural and allied products as mentioned in exports of principal commodities. Central Statistics Office (CSO) (2016), Government of India provides the estimates of the GDP of agricultural and allied activities (AGDP) in India over the same period of time.

5 Methodology

A very common property of macro data or time series data is the existence of correlation across observations, not usually present in cross-sectional data. For example, income of a country in present year is very much correlated with the same of the last year. Thus, a time series variable tends to exhibit trend behaviour and to be highly correlated over time. The non-stationary time series which contains a unit root, gives a stochastic trend. We examine the stochastic properties of the time series variable by carrying out Augmented Dickey Fuller (ADF) and Phillips–Perron (PP) unit root tests. After incorporating both intercept and trend components in the ADF estimated relation for the time series variables agricultural export (AEXP), foreign exchange rate (EXRT) and agricultural production (AGDP) used in our study can be presented as following:

$$\Delta \text{AEXP}_t = \phi_0 + \beta t + \rho \text{AEXP}_{t-1} + \sum_{i=1}^{P} \gamma_i \Delta \text{AEXP}_{t-1} + \varepsilon_t \tag{1}$$

$$\Delta \text{EXRT}_t = \phi_0 + \beta t + \rho \text{EXRT}_{t-1} + \sum_{i=1}^{P} \gamma_i \Delta \text{EXRT}_{t-1} + \varepsilon_t \tag{2}$$

$$\Delta \text{AGDP}_t = \phi_0 + \beta t + \rho \text{AGDP}_{t-1} + \sum_{i=1}^{P} \gamma_i \Delta \text{AGDP}_{t-1} + \varepsilon_t \tag{3}$$

Eqs. (1–3) show the ADF unit root test equation for the variables AEXP, EXRT and AGDP, respectively. The ADF statistic is the t value of the estimated coefficient of ρ. The PP test is nothing but the non-parametric extension of the Dickey Fuller (DF) unit root test with adding a correction factor to the t statistic of DF test. The tests will be performed their first differences, and we cannot perform the tests for all logarithmic series. The lag length choice is very much crucial and the number of lags used in ADF regressions has to be selected by the Akaike (1969) Information Criterion (AIC).

We apply Engle and Granger (1987) cointegration theory by utilizing the methodology developed by Johansen and Juselius (1990). The concept of cointegration, first developed by Granger (1981), is relevant to the problem of the determination of long run equilibrium relationships in economics in the sense that as variables move together over time so that disturbances in short term will be corrected from the long-term trend. Engle and Granger (1987) showed that if two time series are cointegrated then there will be a causal relation in at least one direction. For three variables AEXP, EXRT and AGDP, where we can have maximum two cointegrating equations, the model can be written either of the following form:

$$\mathrm{AEXP}_t = \theta_1 + \sum_{i=1}^{p} \pi_{1i}\mathrm{AEXP}_{t-i} + \sum_{j=1}^{q} \phi_{1j}\mathrm{EXRT}_{t-j} + \sum_{K=1}^{r} \gamma_{1j}\mathrm{AGDP}_{t-K} + u_{1t} \quad (4)$$

$$\mathrm{EXRT}_t = \theta_2 + \sum_{i=1}^{p} \pi_{2i}\mathrm{AEXP}_{t-i} + \sum_{j=1}^{q} \phi_{2j}\mathrm{EXRT}_{t-j} + \sum_{K=1}^{r} \gamma_{2j}\mathrm{AGDP}_{t-K} + u_{2t} \quad (5)$$

$$\mathrm{AGDP}_t = \theta_3 + \sum_{i=1}^{p} \pi_{3i}\mathrm{AEXP}_{t-i} + \sum_{j=1}^{q} \phi_{3j}\mathrm{EXRT}_{t-j} + \sum_{K=1}^{r} \gamma_{3j}\mathrm{AGDP}_{t-K} + u_{3t} \quad (6)$$

or,

$$\begin{aligned}\Delta\mathrm{AEXP}_t = {} & \theta_1 + \sum_{i=1}^{p} \pi_{1i}\Delta\mathrm{AEXP}_{t-i} + \sum_{j=1}^{q} \phi_{1j}\Delta\mathrm{EXRT}_{t-j} \\ & + \sum_{K=1}^{r} \gamma_{1j}\Delta\mathrm{AGDP}_{t-K} + \lambda_1\mathrm{ECM}_{t-1} + u_{1t}\end{aligned} \quad (4.a)$$

$$\begin{aligned}\Delta\mathrm{EXRT}_t = {} & \theta_2 + \sum_{i=1}^{p} \pi_{2i}\Delta\mathrm{AEXP}_{t-i} + \sum_{j=1}^{q} \phi_{2j}\Delta\mathrm{EXRT}_{t-j} \\ & + \sum_{K=1}^{r} \gamma_{2j}\Delta\mathrm{AGDP}_{t-K} + \lambda_2\mathrm{ECM}_{t-1} + u_{2t}\end{aligned} \quad (5.a)$$

$$\Delta \mathrm{AGDP}_t = \theta_3 + \sum_{i=1}^{p} \pi_{3i} \Delta \mathrm{AEXP}_{t-i} + \sum_{j=1}^{q} \phi_{3j} \Delta \mathrm{EXRT}_{t-j} + \sum_{K=1}^{r} \gamma_{3j} \Delta \mathrm{AGDP}_{t-K} + \lambda_3 \mathrm{ECM}_{t-1} + u_{3t}, \quad (6.a)$$

where u_{it} are random disturbances with zero mean and not serially correlated. The ECM denotes error correction mechanism. When the variables are not cointegrated, we have to look at the short run dynamic relationships among them by applying the unrestricted vector auto regression (VAR) structure.

6 Empirical Results

On the basis of methodology taken in our study as discussed in earlier, we present the results of unit root test.

6.1 *Unit Root Test*

Table 1 represents the ADF and PP test statistics for testing unit roots of all the series. Like most of the time series analysis, here the null hypothesis of the presence of unit roots cannot be rejected in the original series indicating that all the series are non-stationary at level in case of both ADF and PP tests. But all the variables are stationary at first difference.

To find the dynamic relationships among agricultural production, export and measure of India's foreign exchange rate as mentioned above we have used cointegration theory developed in Engle and Granger (1987). The ADF and PP unit root tests suggest that the all the series of the variables are integrated of order one, i.e., I(1). All the stationary variables at same order of integration may have a

Table 1 Estimated statistics of unit root tests

Series	Augmented Dickey–Fuller test statistics		Phillips Perron test statistics	
	Level	First difference	Level	First difference
AEXP	3.71	−6.89***	−3.10	−6.97***
EXRT	−1.71	−5.94***	−2.11	−7.19***
AGDP	−1.84	−7.01***	−1.98	−5.89***

Source Authors' estimation by using data from CSO and DGCIS in E-views 7

***, ** and * denote the level of significance at 1, 5, and 10%, respectively

common trend and it is reasonable to search for a possible cointegrating relationship among them. In this context we plan for cointegration test. We can also argue that all the variables used here continuously follow a time trend.

6.2 Cointegration Test

The estimated results of Johansen's cointegration tests have been shown in Table 2. In this table, both the trace or LR test statistic and the eigenvalues are used for testing the hypothesis of presence of cointegrating relation, against the alternative hypothesis of full rank. Findings suggest that there are two cointegrating equations as trace and maximum eigenvalue test statistics report at 5% level. So we think about a long run relationship among India's agricultural output, export and foreign exchange rate.

Now we have to test the long run dynamic relationship among the variables by utilizing the structure of vector error correction mechanism (VECM) by incorporating two period lag as suggested by the minimum AIC rule.

Table 3 shows the estimation of coefficients with corresponding *t* statistics in from the mechanism of vector error correction. Results indicate that only the exchange rate of Indian rupee versus US dollar is significantly determined by the India's agricultural export with one period lag.

Table 2 Estimated statistics of Johansen cointegration test

Unrestricted cointegration rank test					
Tests	Hypothesized no. of CE(s)	Eigenvalue	Statistic	5% Critical value	Prob.[b]
Trace	None[a]	0.2615	27.1149	28.2131	0.0189
	At most 1[a]	0.2063	18.7415	17.5122	0.0291
	At most 2[a]	0.1157	6.1133	3.9124	0.0159
Maximum eigenvalue	None[a]	0.2611	24.2301	20.6621	0.0125
	At most 1[a]	0.2124	17.9593	14.2646	0.0105
	At most 2[a]	0.1201	6.7934	3.8414	0.0121

Source Authors' estimation by using data from CSO and DGCIS in E-views 7
Trace test indicates 2 cointegrating eqn(s) at the 0.05 level
Max-eigenvalue test indicates 2 cointegrating eqn(s) at the 0.05 level
[a]Rejection of the hypothesis at the 0.05 level
[b]MacKinnon–Haug–Michelis (1999) *p* values

Table 3 Vector error correction model

Error correction	D(AEXP)	D(EXRT)	D(AGDP)
CointEq1	0.136331	−0.210324	1.491757
	[0.40173]	[−3.79521]	[1.62302]
D(AEXP(−1))	−0.567609	0.197455**	−1.157333
	[−3.22642]	[3.28108]	[−1.48145]
D(AEXP(−2))	−0.39494	0.03073	−0.395151
	[−2.44982]	[0.34332]	[−0.55198]
D(EXRT(−1))	0.53144	−0.215037	0.338056
	[1.92940]	[−1.18748]	[0.23341]
D(EXRT(−2))	0.965519	0.130901	1.17242
	[3.03410]	[0.74088]	[0.82968]
D(AGDP(−1))	0.074281	−0.000473	0.056518
	[1.37404]	[−0.01575]	[0.23543]
D(AGDP(−2))	0.049528	0.00992	0.015062
	[1.36229]	[0.49144]	[0.09329]
C	0.003051	0.001007	−0.000229
	[0.50684]	[0.30139]	[−0.00856]
R-squared	0.306223	0.328827	0.241821
Adj. *R*-squared	0.286562	0.303621	0.221642
Sum sq. resids	0.068523	0.021123	1.351208
S.E. equation	0.041389	0.212981	0.183794
F-statistic	2.642655	4.845018	6.757499
Log likelihood	89.13378	117.3769	17.57580

Source Authors' estimation by using data from CSO and DGCIS in E-views 7

***, ** and * denote the level of significance at 1, 5, and 10%, respectively

7 Concluding Remarks

The findings from our study suggest that agricultural export and foreign exchange rate in India are cointegrated, so there exists a long run causal relationship between agricultural export and exchange rates measured by Indian rupee versus US dollar. To find the long run relationship between the variables we employ the model of VECM, and then this model also implies that there is a long run equilibrium relation between the variables, showing that agricultural export with one period lag is significantly determining the Indian foreign exchange rate in post reform period. It can be viewed that foreign exchange rate is a good indicator to predict future volume of agricultural exports. Depreciation of home currency contributes towards the increase in export earnings. Like several third world nations, Indian authority devalues local currency against US dollar to place export.

To have the price elastic agricultural exports from India, several policies which help to increase the share of domestic products in exportable goods by expanding the production base and also help diversify the pattern of the exporting items should be prioritized. Though, exchange rate depreciation may not have same impacts for all export sub-sectors, and that is why the relationship between foreign exchange rate and different sub-sectors of export should be considered and analyzed separately. Additionally, a careful investigation of different incentive options is compulsory for selecting a pragmatic and effective policy to support exports. Furthermore, the terrible impacts of depreciation on other sectors also should be seriously considered before taking any policy towards helping the depreciation. The policy of foreign exchange rate in India, which aims to support agricultural exports, has to be re-evaluated. Exchange rate policy ought to balance exports and imports growth, and that will in turn to support Indian firms to export more with achieving the higher level of productivity and efficiency.

During the changing scenario of agricultural and allied sectors in India, this paper has tried to identify that why agricultural export from India to international market follows the declining path. Since two and half decades India is experiencing the phase of liberalization with WTO agreement. The paper on the basis of some empirical exercise with time series India data reveals the significant negative impacts of agricultural production on its export performances where domestic consumption plays an insignificant role. We have clearly mentioned the crisis with the challenges of the Indian agricultural sectors in the present context.

Low productivity with high cost of production and absenteeism of labour are the important barriers of the Indian agricultural. Though many measures are taken to solve these types of constrains, India is unable to enhance production of agricultural. However, the one and only way to market the agricultural is the value addition in the production in global market. Also due to high demand in domestic market India's export performance is slowing down than other exporter of agricultural. Kenya leads the position of agricultural exports and captures most of the major global markets due to the production of agricultural at lower cost of production. As we find the countries like Vietnam, Argentina and Indonesia are also increasing progressively its share in the world primary product market with high productivity and lower cost of production. Currently India is facing some problems in productivity gain and in lowering cost of production. According to Food and Agricultural Organization (FAO) on the side of supply, the unit cost must be reduced through productivity gain.

Acknowledgements Authors are thankful to the organizers and participants of 5th International Conference on Applied Econometrics held on 22–23 July 2016 at IBS Hyderabad, India. Authors are also grateful to the editors for including this paper as a chapter in this book. Important comments made by Session Chairs are gratefully acknowledged. Useful disclaimers apply.

References

Akaike, H. (1969). Fitting autoregressive models for prediction. *Annals of the Institute of Statistical Mathematics, 2,* 243–247.

Bashir, Z. (2003). The impacts of economic reforms and trade liberalisation on agricultural export performance in Pakistan. *Pakistan Development Review, 42*(4), 941–959.

Bradshaw, G., & Orden, D. (1990). Granger causality from the exchange rate to agricultural prices and export sales. *Western Journal of Agricultural Economics, 15*(1), 100–110.

Central Statistics Office (CSO). (2016). *National Accounts Statistics*. New Delhi: MOSPI, Government of India.

Chambers, R. G., & Just, R. E. (1991). Effects of exchange rate changes on U.S. agriculture. *American Journal of Agricultural Economics, 73,* 33–43.

Chandra, R. (2002). Export growth and economic growth: An investigation of causality in India. *Indian Economic Journal, 49,* 64–73.

Dash, R. K. (2009). Revisited export-led growth hypothesis: An empirical study on India. *South Asia Economic Journal, 10*(2), 305–324.

Engle, R. F., & Granger, C. W. (1987). Cointegration and error correction: Representation. *Estimation and Testing, Econometrica, 55*(2), 251–276.

Granger, C. W. J. (1981). Some properties of time series data and their use in econometric model specification. *Journal of Econometrics*, 121–130.

Hughes, D. W., & Penson, J. B., Jr. (1985). Effects of selected macroeconomic policies on agriculture: 1984–1990. *Agricultural Financial Review, 45,* 81–91.

Johansen, S., & Juselius, K. (1990). Maximum likelihood estimation and inference on cointegration—With applications to the demand for money. *Oxford Bulletin of Economics and Statistics, 52*(2), 169–210.

Johnson, P. R., Grennes, T., & Thursby, M. (1977). Devaluation, foreign trade control, and domestic wheat prices. *American Journal of Agricultural Economics, 59,* 619–627.

Khalafalla, K. Y., & Webb, A. J. (2001). Export-led growth and structural change: Evidence from Malaysia. *Applied Economics, 33*(13), 1703–1715.

Khan, A. H., Hasan, L., & Malik, A. (1995). Exports, growth and causality: An application of co-integration and error-correction modelling. *Pakistan Development Review, 11,* 1–19.

Oyejide, T. A. (1986). *The effects of trade and exchange rate policies on agriculture in Nigeria.* IFPRI Research Report No. 55.

Paarlberg, P. L., Webb, A. J., Morey, A., & Sharples, J. A. (1994). *Impacts of policy on U.S. Agricultural Trade*. United States Department of Agriculture Economic Research Service.

Raju, S. S., & Kurien, J. (2005). Exports and economic growth in India: Cointegration, causality and error-correction modeling: A note. *Indian Journal of Economics and Business, 4*(1).

Schwartz, N. E. (1986). The consequences of a floating exchange rate for the U.S. wheat market. *American Journal of Agricultural Economics, 68,* 428–433.

Sharma, A., & Panagiotidis, T. (2005). An analysis of exports and growth in India: Some empirical evidence. *Review of Development Economics, 9*(2), 232–248.

Shirazi, N. S., & Manap, T. A. A. (2004). Export and economic growth nexus: The case of Pakistan. *Pakistan Development Review, 43*(4), 563–581.

Shombe, N. H. (2008). *Causality relationships between total exports with agricultural and manufacturing GDP in Tanzania*. Discussion Paper No. 136, Institute of Developing Economies—Japan External Trade Organization.

Vellianitis-Fidas, A. (1976). The impact of devaluation on U.S. agricultural exports. *Agricultural Economics Research, 28,* 107–116.

Assessing Nutritional Intake from a Field Study in Odisha

Bhabani Prasad Mahapatra and Bhagabata Patro

Abstract Nutritional Intake Assessment is still a popular method to measure household food security through food intake surveys. This measurement primarily detects the presence of inadequate intake among individuals and population groups. Even though, a sufficient intake of a nutrient does not guarantee adequate nutrition status for an individual, and an insufficient intake does not always indicate a deficiency, but such findings warn of possible problems. This article is a part of the doctoral research on Sustainable Food and Nutritional Security in Odisha-A Research Study on Nayagarh District by the first author. Data on daily food intake was collected from the 400 sample families. The data on cereal, pulses, vegetables, edible oil, milk&milk products and flesh food which includes meat/fish/egg. Then using dietary guidelines of National Institute for Nutrition (NIN), the energy from the food has been converted into energy in terms of Kilo Calorie, Separate conversion of energy from fat, protein and carbohydrates were also done. The research study has found that diversification of diet, percentage of family members working in agriculture, share of non-food essentials significantly affect the average food intake at the household level. The article is divided into four parts. Section 1 provides the introduction and review of literature on nutritional intake at household level. Section 2 has outlined the status of nutritional security at household level. Section 3 analyses various determining variables affecting food intake and the last section concludes the article. This study takes on average nutritional intake at household level as the measure of nutritional status at household level.

Keywords Nutritional intake · Food security · Household

B.P. Mahapatra (✉) · B. Patro
Department of Economics, Berhampur University, Berhampur, Odisha, India
e-mail: bhabanimilu@gmail.com

B. Patro
e-mail: patro_b1957@rediffmail.com

B. Kamaiah et al. (eds.), *Current Issues in Economics and Finance*,
DOI 10.1007/978-981-10-5810-3_12

1 Introduction

Food is a basic need for nutrients that human beings obtain through food have vital effects on physical growth and development, maintenance of normal body function, physical activity and health and hence helps in sustaining life and activity. Our diet must provide all essential nutrients in the required amounts. Requirements of essential nutrients vary with age, gender, physiological status and physical activity. Dietary intakes lower or higher than the body requirements can lead to two types of malnutrition: under nutrition (deficiency diseases) or over nutrition (diseases of affluence), respectively. Under nutrition is defined as failure to consume adequate energy, protein, and micronutrients to meet basic requirements for body maintenance, growth, and development. This is the leading nutrition problem in low-income countries and is characterized by low height for age (stunting), low weight for height (wasting), and low weight for age (underweight). The second type of malnutrition involves two issues: overweight (excessive weight relative to height) and obesity (excessive body fat content). There are numerous methods to measure the food and nutritional security. One such measurement is Nutritional Intake Assessment, which is done through food intake survey at individual or household level. This article is a part of the doctoral research on Sustainable Food and Nutritional Security in Odisha-A Research Study on Nayagarh district by the first author. The objective of the article is to understand the food intake at household level in rural Odisha and find out the determining variables affecting it.

1.1 Review of Literature

Research shows that there has been an apparent increase in the prevalence of under nutrition over time in rural India, while in urban areas, the prevalence has remained unchanged, or has declined (Viswanathan and Meenakshi 2006; Deaton and Dreze 2009). Similarly, Subramaniam and Deaton (1996) are of the opinion that nutritional issues are more important for rural area. There is some evidence that, despite declining energy intakes in rural areas, there has also been some dietary diversification.

While analyzing the National Nutrition Monitoring Bureau (NNMB) reports, Ravi and Radhakrishna (2004) identified eight states—Andhra Pradesh, Bihar, Gujarat, Madhya Pradesh, Maharashtra, Rajasthan, Uttar Pradesh and West Bengal—as accounting for 77% of malnourishment in children. They explain that the efficient conversion of food into energy is dependent on access to safe drinking water, healthcare and environmental hygiene because these reduce food wastage from diarrhoea and dysentery. States like Kerala and Tamil Nadu have low levels of malnutrition even when their food energy intake is low, while states like Rajasthan and Uttar Pradesh have higher malnutrition even with higher levels of food intake.

Radhakrishna (2006) reviews the trends over three decades in the consumption of cereals, calories and micronutrients and nutritional status based on anthropometric measures using the data sets of National Sample Survey (NSS), National Nutritional Monitoring Bureau (NNMB) and National Family Health Survey (NFHS). He calls for improving the income of a household along with improving the health and educational status of mothers. Food inflation would affect the nutritional well-being of the population. Both cereal price and non-food cereal price are negatively associated with the consumption of food and calories. With economic growth, urbanization, the supply source of calories is likely to diversify, and non-cereal food may emerge as a major source of supply. Along with improving their diet, it is necessary to improve the health and educational status of mothers. India has put in place a number of nutrition intervention programmes to reduce the incidence of malnutrition but their impact so far seems to be marginal. They need to be scaled up and their governance requires substantial improvement.

1.2 *Calorie Puzzle*

Before going to understand the calorie puzzle, if we observe the trend of calorie intake in rural Odisha and Rural India (Table 1), we shall find that the calorie intake has been increasing from 1995 kcal in 27th round of NSS (1972–1973) to 2199 kcal in 50th NSS round (1993–1994) in rural Odisha. But from 50th NSS round to 61st round (2004–2005), the calorie intake has been declining from 2199 to 2023 kcal in the rural Odisha. However, again in 66th NSS round in 2009–2010, the calorie intake has been increasing to 2126 kcal in rural part of the state. However, for rural India, the calorie intake has been declining since 1972–1973 which is evident from the various NSS reports. For rural India, the calorie intake was 2266 kcal in 1972–1973 and it has been declining to 2020 kcal in 2009–2010. Observers describe such phenomenon as calorie consumption puzzle as Indian economy is being faced with peculiar paradox of declining calorie intake and rising undernourishment in the face of rapid economic growth and declining poverty.

Table 1 Nutritional intake in rural Odisha and Rural India

Various rounds of NSS	Rural Odisha			Rural India		
	Calories (kcal)	Protein (g)	Fat (g)	Calories (kcal)	Protein (g)	Fat (g)
1972–1973 (27th)	1995	49	8	2266	62	24
1983 (38th)	2103	51	13	2221	62	27
1993–1994 (50th)	2199	52.7	14.8	2153	60.2	31.4
1999–2000 (55th)	2119	49.9	16.3	2149	59.1	36.1
2004–2005 (61st)	2023	48.3	17.8	2047	57.0	35.5
2009–2010 (66th round)	2126	49.7	23.2	2020	55	38.3

Source NSS Report no. 540. Nutritional intake in India, 66th Round 2009–2010

There are three schools of thought to explain the causes of declining calorie intake in India. The first puzzle, noted by Deaton and Dreze (2009), is that societies undergoing rapid growth and structural transformation have often seen stagnant caloric intake despite rapid growth of incomes. This is quite puzzling because cross-sectional data from poor countries always reveal a strong positive relationship between household expenditure and caloric intake, but expenditure growth over time is not reflected in higher caloric intake. This general pattern also appears to be existing when comparing urban and rural sectors within a country or rich and poor countries—the richer and more developed the area, the lower is caloric intake for household holding real expenditures constant.

The second puzzle is that holding per capita expenditure constant, larger households have lower food expenditure and lower caloric intake than smaller households. However, the theory says the opposite. The classic model of Barten (1964) predicts that larger households would be better off and would consequently consume more food per capita. Deaton and Paxson (1994) found that the negative relationship between household size and private food expenditure per capita is stronger for food and for poor countries, including India, suggesting that there may be something special about food demand in poor countries. The third puzzle is that food expenditure falls significantly for older households in India contradicting the permanent-income life-cycle hypothesis that predicts smooth consumption despite the income that varies over the life-cycle.

According to Eli and Li (2012), the factor which can explain the three puzzles is calorie needs across the households. According to them, decreasing food expenditure and caloric intake should be interpreted as raising household welfare by freeing up resources for higher quality food or non-food expenditures. Due to a structural transformation, i.e., from movement of labour from physically demanding sectors like agriculture and manufacturing to less physically demanding sectors like service sector combined with labour-saving appliances, the need of calorie has been lower. This phenomenon also explains the differences in consumption pattern between rural and urban India. Larger households are able to lower their caloric requirements through specialization and household scale economies—they lower the amount of market work required to generate a given level of expenditures and they also decrease the amount of home production, leading to significantly higher leisure per member. Older households in India experience a sharp drop in caloric intake but an even sharper drop in caloric needs due to lower biological metabolism needs caused by a reduction in activity levels.

In the opinion of Basu and Basole (2012), calorie consumption puzzle in India can be explained through the operation of coercive and non-coercive factors. Due to the influence of coercive factors like adoption of neoliberal policies, households are not allowed to consume the preferred number of calories and hence there is a welfare loss. Prominent believers of this thought are Mehta and Venkatraman (2000), Chandrasekhar and Ghosh (2003), and Patnaik (2010). On the other hand, calorie consumption declines due to operation of non-coercive factors like urbanization, diversification of diet, market integration and development of supply networks, improvement of epidemiological environment (improved access to safe drinking water), changes in occupational structure, mechanization of agriculture work. These factors necessitated a decline in calorie needs and hence to a decline in calorie intake. Prominent believers of this line of thought are Deaton and Dreze (2009) and Eli and Li (2012). In this context, we try to examine the determining variables of food intake in rural Odisha by including both coercive and non-coercive factors in our empirical model.

1.3 Research Methodology

Data on daily intake on cereal, pulses, vegetables, edible oil, milk&milk products and flesh food which includes meat/fish/egg were collected in the month February 2015 from the 400 sample families in five villages-Gohirabadu, Mardakota, Barkola, Nuagaon and Barpalla of Nayagarh District in Odisha. From each village, 80 families were randomly chosen for the study. Then using dietary guidelines of National Institute for Nutrition (NIN), Hyderabad, the energy from the food has been converted into energy in terms of Kilo Calorie. However, no attempt was made to find out the food intake for the individual members like pregnant women, lactating mothers, pre-school children, etc. This may be a limitation of the study. Ordinary least square method was applied to find out the significant variables of food intake at household level. Before going for the analysis of the nutritional intake at sample household level, a summary demographic profile of the sample households will provide an outline of the status of the population. The profile is provided in Table 2.

2 Status of Nutritional Security at Household Level

Intake of dietary energy per person continues to be the most widely used indicator of the level of nutrition of a population (National Sample Survey Organisation 2012). Following the NSS methodology, this study has also taken intake of dietary energy per consumer unit along with per capita calorie intake. The per consumer unit calorie intake gives a much better idea of adequacy of calorie intake at the level of the individual household. From the 26th round, NSS tables on nutritional intake have expressed observed calorie intakes per consumer unit of different segments of population as percentages of a level of 2700 kcal per consumer unit per day. This practice is continued in this report for convenience in making comparisons.

As explained in Table 3, the average energy intake per capita and per CU has been 1926 and 2511 kcal, respectively, in the sample area. The average protein per capita and per CU has been 76 and 100 g, respectively. Similarly, the fat consumption per capita and per CU has been 38 and 51 g, respectively. Among all the villages, the energy intake is the highest in Mardakota village and the lowest intake was in Barapalla village.

Table 2 Summary demographic profile of the sample households

Indicators	Gohirabadu	Mardakota	Barkola	Nuagaon	Barapalla	All five villages
Total population	316	282	299	283	343	1523
Female	151	128	149	141	160	729
Male	165	154	150	142	183	794
Average family size	3.95	3.5	3.7	3.5	4.3	3.8
Average consumer unit	3.19	2.79	2.99	2.74	3.53	3.048
ST (%)	38.75	22.5	18.75	17.5	20	23.5
SC (%)	41.25	42.5	36.25	2.5	37.5	32
Others (%)	20	35	45	80	42.5	44.5
Female literacy (%)	84.06	63.21	81.62	66.15	59.60	71.10
Male literacy (%)	91.50	86.13	93.53	85.48	77.01	86.38
Landless (%)	52.5	73.75	67.5	71.25	22.5	57
Marginal (%)	27.5	25	30	27.5	72.5	36
Small (%)	16.25	1.25	1.25	1.25	3.75	5
Others (%) (large and semi-medium)	3.75	0	0	0	0	2

Source Field survey

Table 3 Average nutritional intake in field area (village wise)

	Energy (kcal)		Protein (g)		Fat (g)	
	Per capita	Per CU	Per capita	Per CU	Per capita	Per CU
Gohirabadu	2002	2582	76	98	36	48
Mardakota	2088	2712	86	112	41	54
Barkola	1918	2599	77	105	40	57
Nuagaon	1972	2652	83	112	39	53
Barapalla	1648	2012	59	73	34	41
All villages	1926	2511	76	100	38	51

Source Field survey

As per the social category, the energy intake among SC has been the lowest with 1939 kcal per capita where as the energy intake as per CU has been the lowest among ST families. The nutritional intake as per social category has been explained in Table 4.

An attempt has been made to understand the dietary energy intake among the economic categories of the sample households. As explained in Table 5, no pattern has been visible on nutritional intake so far as energy intake is concerned. It indicates that energy intake has nothing to do with the land ownership of the families.

Table 4 Nutritional intake in sample villages of Nayagarh District (as per social category)

Social category	Energy (kcal)		Protein (g)		Fat (g)	
	Per capita	Per CU	Per capita	Per CU	Per capita	Per CU
Others (SEBC&General)	1945	2526	79	102	39	51
SC	1939	2570	73	97	39	53
ST	1872	2414	76	99	36	46

Source Field survey

Table 5 Nutritional intake in sample villages of Nayagarh District (as per land holding)

Economic category	Energy (kcal)		Protein (g)		Fat (g)	
	Per capita	Per CU	Per capita	Per CU	Per capita	Per CU
Landless	1977	2641	79	106	40	54
Marginal	1822	2303	72	91	36	46
Small	1996	2484	73	91	34	43

Source Field survey

2.1 Calorie Intake as Per MPCE Decile Classes

Now a day, instead of income, expenditure has been taken as a proxy variable to understand its linkage to energy intake. More concrete picture emerges when the energy intake has been calculated as per the decile class of the total consumption expenditure.

If energy intake with lowest decile and top decile is compared, we can find the pattern of energy intake with variability of consumption expenditure. As found in Table 6, the per capita energy intake is the lowest among the 1st decile and the highest intake is found in the 9th decile and 10th decile class. It indicates that lower is the standard of living, lower will be the intake of energy and in that sense it may be inferred that poorer people are nutritionally insecured as energy intake is considered as an important indicator of nutritional security

An attempt has been made to find out the share of expenditure on food, percent expenditure on cereal and percent calories from cereal with the variation of level of living. It has been found from Table 7 that share of food expenditure in the bottom decile is the highest with 66% and among the top decile, the share is the lowest. Similarly, less preference on cereal among the richer section is visible in that table. When the share of expenditure among the second lowest decile class (2nd decile) and third lowest decile class (3rd decile) are higher (18 and 32%, respectively) than the share among the bottom decile with 14%.

Table 6 Distribution of calorie intake: variation with level of living in the sample area

MPCE Decile classes	Energy intake (kcal)		Protein intake (g)		Fat intake (g)	
	Per capita	Per CU	Per capita	Per CU	Per capita	Per CU
1	1736	2459	63	89	37	54
2	1881	2409	68	87	36	47
3	1864	2374	69	88	36	46
4	1803	2336	67	89	35	48
5	1826	2257	73	90	32	40
6	1921	2429	77	98	36	46
7	1912	2479	80	104	38	49
8	2045	2628	87	113	39	50
9	2177	2976	91	125	44	62
10	2090	2767	88	116	46	63

Source Field survey

Table 7 Share of food expenditure, share of cereal expenditure and percent of calories in cereal as per MPCE Decile classes in sample area

MPCE Decile classes	% expenditure on food	% expenditure on cereal	% of calories from cereal
1	66	18	76
2	70	32	78
3	68	33	78
4	65	29	78
5	62	25	76
6	62	24	74
7	59	20	71
8	55	18	70
9	53	17	72
10	49	14	71

Source Field survey

3 Variables Affecting Calorie Intake at Household Level

One of the indicators of the nutritional status of the population is the calorie intake at household level. To examine the various determining variables of calorie intake, this article has used energy intake per capita as dependent variable. We used OLS method of estimation by taking various independent variables (both quantitative and dummy) like monthly per capita expenditure (MPCE) for cereal, non-cereal and non-food essential; share of agricultural workers and share of earning members in the family, size of the household, age of the head of the household, per capita income, drinking water status, gender of the head of the household, social category of the family, land holding status of the family, occupation of the head of the household and education of the head of the household. Identification of these variables is based on literature review and also on the basis of personal interaction with the respondents. Thus, our model to be estimated may be written as follows:

$$Y = a_0 + \beta_1 X + \varepsilon,$$

where, Y is energy intake per capita, X is the vector of regressors to be included unconditionally (as discussed above), a_0 is an constant, and ε represents the net effect of omitted variables which may affect energy intake (which is often referred as residual). Finally, to ensure that the estimated model is a good fit and meets all OLS assumptions we conducted several diagnostic tests such as VIF-to test the problem of multi-collinearity, Ramsey RESET test to test whether the model is correctly specified. The detailed description of the explanatory variables and the theoretical justification for inclusion in the model is given below.

3.1 Description of Independent Variables

3.1.1 Independent Quantitative Variables

Monthly Per Capita Expenditure (MPCE) and Per Capita Income (PCM Income): In recent times, expenditure replaces income as a better indicator of standard of living (NSS reports). The expenditure has been taken in terms of monthly per capita, which is indicated by MPCE. The MPCE for food has been divided into MPCE for cereal and non-cereal food items. Cereals being the main staple food in Odisha and expenditure on cereal food are dominating in various NSS reports, it will be interesting to find the relationship between the average food energy intake and cereal food expenditure. The dietary diversity of the population can be understood from the expenditure on non-cereal food (NCF) items. We have considered MPCE for non-food essential like education, electricity, medicines, conveyance, etc. Besides, we have also considered household income as one of the explanatory variables to assess its impact on the food intake.

Share of workforce engaged in agriculture: The share of the workforce engaged in agriculture is included in our model to capture the effect of activity levels on calorie needs and hence calorie intake. It is well known that agricultural work is, on average, far more physically demanding than that of industrial or service sector work.

Share of earning members: The access to food is determined by the capacity to earn and the number of earning members in the family. In a family especially in rural areas of Odisha, the people are dependent on agriculture and hence it is included in the model.

Household (HH) Size: It is included to take account of the economies of scale and congestion effects.

Age of the Head of the Household: It is included to examine the effect of age on food intake.

3.2 Dummy Variables of the Model

Landholding status: The financial status of the household is of importance in determining the quality of food consumed. The status of land holdings by the households provides some idea on financial status in rural areas. A household that possess land is obviously better off than a household not possessing land. In the OLS model, two dummies are used to capture the effect of land holdings. The dummy landless D5 = 1, 0 otherwise, and marginal & small land holdings D5 = 1, 0 otherwise so that we could get the separate effects for both landless households and for marginal and small farming households.

The sex and literacy of the head of the household: Women empowerment has been one of the major determining variables which influence household food intake and food security at household level. Female headed household is assumed to have a positive impact on the food intake. Similarly, literacy of the household head is also assumed to have a positive impact on food intake. The dummy variable for gender is defined as D2 = Female, 0 for male. The dummy variables for literacy is defined as D6 = 1 if the head of the family is illiterate, 0 otherwise. Specifically, we define D6 = 1 if the head of the family has primary education, 0 otherwise, and in another specification we define D6 = 1 if the head of the family has middle and secondary education, 0 otherwise.

Safe drinking water: The proportion of households with access to safe drinking water (from tap, tube well or hand pump) is meant to capture the epidemiological environment. In our study, it is hypothesized that safe drinking water has a positive effect on food intake. The dummy variable is defined as D1 = 1 for safe drinking source, 0 otherwise.

Occupation of the Household Head: The occupation of the family head is included in the model as the type of occupation can have an effect on calorie consumption. The dummy variable considers three types of occupations: cultivator, agricultural labour, and non-agricultural labour. The dummy variables are D3 = 1 if cultivator, 0 otherwise, D3 = 1 if agriculture labour, 0 otherwise and D3 = 1 if non-agriculture labour, 0 otherwise.

Social category of the household: It is assumed that food security among the backward category is inferior to the general category. If food intake is considered as an indicator of food security, then it is quite interesting to find the impact of social group on food intake. Therefore, social category as a dummy variable is included in this model. If the household belongs to a backward social group, i.e., Scheduled Castes (SC), Scheduled tribe (ST) and, Socially and Educationally Backward Class (SEBC), then the dummy variable D4 takes the value 1 and 0 otherwise.

3.3 *Regression Results*

Summary statistics of various important variables has been mentioned in Table 8. Important measures of statistics taken are mean, median and standard deviation. The MPCE for cereal food, non-cereal food, non-food essential and per capita monthly income have been measured in terms of Indian Rupee (INR). The age of the head of household is measured in year. When the average energy intake per capita of all the 400 sample households is 1926 kcal, the average MPCE for non cereal food, cereal food, non-food essential are INR 361, INR 211.51 and INR 359, respectively.

The results of the OLS estimates are reported in Table 9. We have estimated the results for all 400 sample observations and the adjusted R^2 value is around 0.25.

Monthly per Capita Expenditure (MPCE): As per Table 9, food expenditure on non-cereal and cereal food is positively significant affecting the energy intake. However, the cereals expenditure is more influential in affecting the average energy intake per capita. It can be interpreted that for one unit increase in monthly per capita expenditure on non-cereal foods, the increase in average food intake calorie per capita will be 0.66 units. This phenomenon explains the existence of dietary diversity in the consumption pattern of rural Odisha. On the other hand, by increasing one unit of MPCE for cereal food, the average food intake increases by 1.21 units. This shows that cereal is still the dominant contributor of energy intake in rural Odisha. On the other hand, MPCE for non-food essential is negatively affecting the food intake. This is indicative of the working of food budget squeeze which results in declining the food intake. One unit increase in MPCE for non-food essential results 0.22 units decline in average food intake per capita among the sample households. However, the influence is significant only at 5%.

The Share of agricultural workers: In the model, the share of agriculture workers has a negative influence on the average energy intake per capita at household level.

Share of earning members: The influence of the share of earning members in the family is not a significant determining factor of energy intake at household level.

Household Size: As the size of the members in the household increases, normally the per capita consumption of energy falls. The result shows that the size of the household is significantly affecting the energy consumption per capita in the family.

Per capita Income: The result shows that per capita income is not a significant factor affecting the energy consumption. Our result is also supported by the findings of the NSS reports which give emphasis on consumption expenditure rather than income.

Age of the Household head: The results show a highly significant result of this variable which influences the energy consumption. When the age of the household head increases by one unit, the per capita food intake will increase by a large unit.

Table 8 Summary statistics of variables

Statistics	Energy intake per capita (Kcal)	MPCE non-cereal food (INR)	MPCE for cereal food (INR)	MPCE non-food essential (INR)	Share of agricultural workers (%)	Share of earning members (%)	Family size (no.)	Per capita monthly income (INR)	Age of the household head
Mean	1926	361	211.51	359.07	24.575	39.35	3.81	1809.18	47.69
Median	1924	347	213.33	300	0	33.33	4	1587.5	48
SD	534.48	160.86	124.51	261.81	40.38	24.22	1.43	1148.18	13.86

Source Compiled by the authors

Table 9 OLS, using observations (sample n = 400)

Variable	Coefficient	SE	t-Statistic	p value
Constant	1913.01	382.946	4.996	8.97e −07***
MPCE for non-cereal	0.66	0.197147	3.372	0.0008***
MPCE for cereal	1.21	0.375955	3.243	0.0013***
MPCE for non-food essential	−0.22	0.109048	−2.05	0.0408**
Share of agricultural workers	−2.37	1.33498	−1.78	0.0754 *
Share of earning members	−0.60	1.32306	−0.45	0.6482
Household (HH) size	−98.8	22.7587	−4.34	0.0000***
Per capita monthly income	0.006	0.0225465	0.31	0.7577
Age of the head of HH	5.62	2.03990	2.757	0.0061***
Drinking water (safe) (dummy D1)	99.27	56.1904	1.767	0.0781*
Gender of the head of HH (female) (D2)	137.13	105.055	1.305	0.1926
Occupation of head of HH (cultivator) (D3)	−54.30	137.319	−0.3955	0.6927
Occupation of the head of HH (agri. labour) (D3)	−21.25	124.444	−0.17	0.8645
Occupation of the head of HH (non-agri labour) (D3)	−134.04	75.3877	−1.778	0.0762*
Social category (D4)	52.76	50.7730	1.039	0.2994
Landholding (landless) (D5)	−331.57	249.222	−1.330	0.1842
Landholding (marginal& small) (D5)	−423.63	248.605	−1.704	0.0892*
Education of head of HH (illiterate) (D5)	186.13	110.697	1.681	0.0935*
Education of head of HH (primary) (D6)	73.71	102.395	0.719	0.4720
Education of head of the HH (D6) (Middle &secondary)	69.71	98.9644	0.704	0.4813
R^2	0.291080	SE of regression	461.1371	
Adjusted R^2	0.255634	F statistic	5.060426(8.86e−11)	

Dependent variable: Y (Energy kcal intake per capita)
***, ** and *Significance at 1, 5 and 10 pc, respectively. Adj. R^2 0.25

Drinking water: The result shows that better availability of safe sources of drinking water enhances the per capita energy intake by 99 units. These results are significant at the 10% level.

Gender of the Household head: It is assumed that if the head of the household is a woman, the food in the family is consumed with more equitably. But the result presented in Table 9 shows that female headed household has not having any effect on the energy intake.

Occupation of household head: The result shows that the occupation as non-agricultural labour (employees in public and private sector, service sector) has a significant negative influence on energy intake while the influence of the occupation-cultivator and agricultural labour is not significant.

Social Category of the Household: Our result shows that energy intake is not affected by the social category. This is substantiated by the results reported in Table 9.

Landholding status of the Household: In our analysis, an attempt was made to understand the influence of the land holding status of the family on the energy intake of the family. It was found that marginal & small families have a negative influence on the energy intake as found in Table 9.

Education of the household head: As per the Table 9, illiterate head of the household influences the food intake positively and significantly. However, the improvement of literacy status of the head of the family does not significantly influence the average energy intake per capita in the family.

4 Conclusion

Food Intake at household level is an input indicator of food and nutritional security of the population. In order to understand the determining variables of the average nutritional intake, food intake survey was conducted among 400 sample households in rural area of Nayagarh district of the Odisha state. Then using the conversion table of National Institute of Nutrition (NIN), Hyderabad, food consumption has been converted to energy. The average daily intake of energy per capita is the dependent variable. OLS regression model has been used to understand the influence of the set of independent variables (both quantitative and qualitative) on the energy intake per capita. It has been found that food expenditure on non-cereal and cereal food is positively significant affecting the energy intake. However, the cereals expenditure is more influential in affecting the average energy intake per capita. It can be interpreted that for one unit increase in monthly per capita expenditure on non-cereal foods, the increase in average food intake calorie per capita will be 0.66 units. This phenomenon explains the existence of dietary diversity in the consumption pattern of rural Odisha. Similarly, cereal continues to be the dominant food of Odisha as food intake is increased by 1.21% with one unit increase of cereal expenditure. Food budget squeeze is also influencing the energy intake. This is evident from the regression results. One unit increase in MPCE for non-food essential results 0.22 units decline in average food intake per capita among the sample households. Among other independent variables, share of agricultural workers, household size, age of the head of the household, access to drinking water, occupation of the head of the household as non-agricultural labourers, land holding status and educational status of the head of the household are significantly affecting the average daily food intake among the sample households. Many important independent variables like gender of the head of the household and social category of the family have no influence on the food intake.

The finding from the model is having policy implications. More public investment on cereal production as well as non-cereal production is essential to bring the much needed diversity in the food baskets of the household members. Preference of non-agricultural occupation indicates that agriculture is not an attraction of the population in rural Odisha. Access to drinking water from safe sources needs to be universal as it is having significant positive influence on enhancing the food intake at household level. The relationship between food intake and other independent variables is not linear. Therefore, linear regression model used in this article may be replaced by non-linear regression model to get a more realistic assessment of the influence of various independent variables on food intake.

References

Barten, A. P. (1964). Family composition, prices and expenditure patterns. In G. Mills, P. E. Hart, & J. K. Whitaker (Eds.), *Econometric analysis for national economic planning*. London: Butterworths.

Basu, D., & Basole, A. (2012). The calorie consumption puzzle in India: An Empirical investigation. In *PERI working paper series 285*. Amherst: Political Economy Research Institute, University of Massachusetts.

Chandrasekhar, C. P., & Ghosh, J. (2003). The calorie consumption puzzle. *The Hindu Business Line*. http://www.thehindubusinessline.in/2003/02/11/stories/2003021100210900.htm.

Deaton, A., & Dreze, J. (2009). Food and nutrition in India: Facts and interpretations. *Economic and Political Weekly, 44*(7), 42–65.

Deaton, A., & Paxson, C. (1994). Intertemporal choice and inequality. *Journal of Political Economy, 102*(3), 437–467.

Eli, S., & Li, N. (2012). Can calorie needs explain three food consumption puzzle? Evidence from India'. University of Toronto https://www.dartmouth.edu/~neudc2012/docs/paper_263.pdf.

Mehta, J., & Venkatraman, S. (2000). Poverty statistics: Bermicide's feast. *Economic and Political Weekly, 35*(27), 2377–2382.

National Sample Survey Organisation. (2012). Nutritional Intake in India. Report No. 540, 66th Round July 2009–June 2010, Ministry of Statistics and Programme Implementation, New Delhi.

Patnaik, P. (2010). Left approach to development. *Economic and Political Weekly, 45*(30), 33–37.

Radhakrishna, R. (2006). Food consumption and nutrition status in India: Emerging trends and perspectives. In *Working paper* 2006–008, Mumbai, IGIDR.
Ravi, C., & Radhakrishna, R. (2004). Malnutrition in India. *Economic and Political Weekly, 39*(7), 671–676.
Subramaniam, S., & Deaton, A. (1996). The demand for food and calories. *Journal of Political Economy, 104*(1), 133–162.
Vishwanathan, B., & Meenakshi, J. V. (2006). The changing pattern of under nutrition in India: A comparative analysis across Regions. Research paper no 2006/118, United Nation University-WIDER.

Dynamics of Food Grains Production in Telangana

S. Indrakant

Abstract Problem of food insecurity is a multi-dimensional, multi-faceted and multi-causal problem. Food grain production can be increased either by increasing the area under food grains or by improving the yield rate. Expansion and sustainability in the growth of food production is a big challenge as demand for land for non-agricultural purposes is bound to increase in the days to come. Expansion of urban agglomeration, growth of smaller towns, need for provision of physical and social infrastructures result in the decline in land available for agricultural purpose. The problem gets aggravated when there is a shift in cropping pattern from food crops to non-food crops. In this background, adequate food production can be maintained mostly by improving the yield of food grains. Against this backdrop, an attempt is made in this Paper to estimate the contribution of the 'increase in area under food grains' and 'improvement in technology' to the growth of food grain production in Telangana using Simple Decomposition Technique and to estimate the influence of determinants of per capita availability of food grains using Multiple Regression Technique. The results of the Study indicate that generally the yield effect is stronger than the area effect on growth of food grains, Cereals and Rice. However, yield effect seems to be declining with passage of time which casts shadow on the sustainability of food grain production. Improvement in productivity and extension of cropped area have positive influence on per capita availability of food grain while higher density of population would result in decline in per capitaavailability of food grains.

Keywords Food security · Cropping pattern · Urban agglomeration
Simple decomposition technique · Agricultural productivity

Earlier version of the Paper was presented at 5th International Conference on Applied Econometrics (ICAE-V) held at IBS Hyderabad, India during July 22–23, 2016.

S. Indrakant (✉)
Council for Social Development, Hyderabad 500030, India
e-mail: indrakant_s@yahoo.com

B. Kamaiah et al. (eds.), *Current Issues in Economics and Finance*,
DOI 10.1007/978-981-10-5810-3_13

1 Introduction

Problem of food insecurity is a multi-dimensional, multi-faceted and multi-causal problem. Production of adequate food is necessary but not sufficient condition for ensuring food security. Food grain production can be increased either by increasing the area under food grains or by improving the yield rate. Expansion and sustainability in growth of food production is a big challenge as demand for land for non-agricultural purposes is bound to increase in days to come. Expansion of urban agglomeration, growth of smaller towns, need for provision of physical and social infrastructures like roads, railway lines, bus station, railway station, airport, education and technical institutes result in decline in the land available for agricultural purpose. The problem gets aggravated when there is a shift in cropping pattern from food crops to non-food crops. In this background, adequate food production can be maintained mostly by improving the yield of food grains. In other words, technological development plays a dominant role in agriculture transformation. Further, results of technology can be enjoyed only when the growth rate of population or the density of population is under control. In this context, it is of crucial importance to look at the past track record. Further, both demand and supply factors influence the availability of food grains in a region.

2 Objectives

The main aim of this paper is to examine the dynamics of food grain production in Telangana. The specific objectives of the study are:

1. To estimate the contribution of 'increase in area under food grains' and 'improvement in technology' to the growth of food grain production in Telangana.
2. To estimate the influence of important determinants on per capita availability of food grains both at State and District level.

3 Methodology

The contribution of 'increase in area under food grains' and 'improvement in technology' to the growth of food grain production in Telangana has been estimated by using Simple Decomposition Technique. Symbolically

$$\Delta Q = (A_1 - A_0)Y_0 + (Y_1 - Y_0)A_0 + (A_1 - A_0)(Y_1 - Y_0),$$

where

ΔQ Change in output
A_0 Area under food grains in the initial year
A_1 Area under food grains in the terminal year
Y_0 Yield of food grains in the initial year
Y_1 Yield of food grains in the terminal year

Now,

$$\text{Area effect} = \frac{(A_1 - A_0)Y_0}{\Delta Q}$$

$$\text{Yield effect} = \frac{(Y_1 - Y_0)A_0}{\Delta Q}$$

$$\text{Interaction effect} = \frac{(A_1 - A_0)(Y_1 - Y_0)}{\Delta Q}.$$

The time period selected for the Study is two decades, i.e. 1993–1994 is 2014–2015. To even out the fluctuations in annual agricultural production 3-year averages for both initial and terminal years have been taken. For better understanding, the total study period has been classified into two sub-periods namely sub-period I, i.e. 1993–1994 to 2004–2005 and sub-period II, i.e. 2004–2005 to 2013–2014. The exercise has been done for Telangana as a whole and for nine districts only Hyderabad is excluded as it is basically a consumption centre and not a production centre. To get better picture, the analysis, besides food grain has been carried out for cereals, rice and jowar.

4 Determinants of Per Capita Food Grain Production

Food security can be ensured when there is an adequate production of food grains. To boast food grain production, it is essential to know it's important determinants. Improvement in method of cultivation and an increase in area under food grain are likely to contribute positively to the per capita food grain production of a region. While an increase in density of population of a region is likely to bring down the per capita food grain production of a region. To know the influence of these factors on per capita food grain production of a region multiple regression technique has been used. As districts differ in size, the analysis has been made in per capita terms. The per capita food grain production is regressed on productivity of food grain per hectare, per capita cropped area under food grain and density of population. The first two independent variables namely productivity of food grain per hectare and per capita cropped area under food grains are expected to have positive sign, while the third variable namely the density of population is expected to have negative sign. Six different specifications of equation have been tried. Variables not having statistically significant estimated co-efficient were dropped. Therefore, the specification of selected regression equation varies from one district to another district.

5 Results

5.1 Role of Technology in Production

Technology brings in dynamism in the economy. Transformation of agricultural sector is possible only when technology plays a dominant role in the growth of production. The area under food grains in Telangana during the study period, i.e. 1993–1994 to 2014–2015 generally varied in a narrow range of 28–32 lakh hectares. Only exception years being 2013–2014 when the area under food grains shot up to over 34 lakh hectares and 1997–1998 when the area touched a rock bottom level, i.e. below 26 lakh hectares. It is heartening to note that the yield with some fluctuation has increased from 1.4 tonnes per hectare to 3 tonnes per hectare. Consequently, the production of food grains has more than doubled, i.e. from 40 lakh tonnes to over 80 lakh tonnes. In fact, in 2013–2014 production of food grains registered a record level of 106 lakh tonnes.

Decomposition analysis reveals that about 90% of increase in production of food grains is due to 'yield effect', i.e. improvement in technology (Table 1). This is true for the whole period as well as for both the sub-periods. Similar pattern is observed in the case of cereals. In fact, during first sub-period, the area effect was negative as area under cereals registered a decline. In case of rice both area effect and yield effect are substantial. It is a matter of concern to note that the contribution of the technology to the increase in production of rice has declined from 75% during the first sub-period to only 22% during the second sub-period. This raises doubts about sustainability in the growth process. In contrast a different pattern is observed in the case of jowar. The area under jowar has drastically declined from 7 lakh hectares to about one lakh hectares. This is reflected in sharp decline in output from 5 lakh tonnes to one lakh tonne. Only silver lining in the dark clouds is the marginal improvement in yield rate from 0.7 tonne to over one tonne per hectare. If there was no improvement in yield rate, the production of jowar would have been still lower. The positive sign to the area effect only indicates that the decline in area under jowar has positively contributed to the decline in the output of jowar while the negative sign to the yield effect indicates that improvement in yield rate has prevented the decline in output of jowar.

Districtwise analysis reveals that in all the districts, yield effect with reference to food grain production is positive and much more than the area effect (Table 2). It implies that the farmers in all the districts are adopting improved method of production. In some districts, area effect is negative indicating a decline in area under food grains. Districts having stronger yield effect have registered negative area effect. For instance, Adilabad, Rangareddy and Khammam have recorded stronger yield effect but negative area effect. Perhaps farmers in Adilabad and Khammam

Table 1 Decomposition of growth in production of principal food grain crops in Telangana

S. no.	Principal crops	Sub-period I			Sub-period II			Total period		
		Area effect	Productivity effect	Interaction effect	Area effect	Productivity effect	Interaction effect	Area effect	Productivity effect	Interaction effect
1	Rice	20.35	75.74	3.91	67.61	22.33	10.07	48.34	33.86	17.80
2	Jowar	132.87	−63.69	30.82	108.65	−31.35	22.69	108.93	−62.63	53.70
3	Cereals	−3.525	104.98	−1.45	27.77	62.85	9.38	11.29	78.38	10.33
4	Foodgrains	6.39	91.18	2.43	6.83	89.96	3.21	5.47	88.90	5.63

Note

1. For sub-period I initial year is average of 1993–1994, 1994–1995 and 1995–1996, terminal year is average of 2003–2004, 2004–2005 and 2005–2006
2. For sub-period II initial year is average of 2003–2004, 2004–2005 and 2005–2006, terminal year is average of 2012–2013, 2013–2014 and 2014–2015
3. For total period initial year is average of 1993–1994, 1994–1995 and 1995–1996, terminal year is average of 2012–2013, 2013–2014 and 2014–2015

Table 2 Decomposition of growth in production of food grains in Telangana by districts

S. no.	District	Sub-period I			Sub-period II			Total period		
		Area effect	Productivity effect	Interaction effect	Area effect	Productivity effect	Interaction effect	Area effect	Productivity effect	Interaction effect
1	Adilabad	−203.11	392.19	−89.08	433.67	−482.99	149.32	−1431.38	2868.13	−1336.75
2	Karimnagar	35.42	52.93	11.65	38.58	51.24	10.18	31.75	46.66	21.59
3	Khammam	−27.5	138.00	−10.5	179.96	357.44	−77.47	−63.91	226.64	−62.72
4	Mahabubnagar	17.22	70.99	11.78	21.66	67.73	10.61	14.70	63.25	22.04
5	Medak	17.25	77.79	4.95	−4.475	108.255	−3.78	1.84	95.62	2.53
6	Nalgonda	−27.43	130.18	−2.74	8.32	88.4	3.28	2.74	95.80	1.46
7	Nizamabad	−2.40	103.07	−0.67	37.89	42.32	19.79	24.89	51.51	23.60
8	Rangareddy	−25.42	141.74	−16.31	−587.00	831.36	−144.00	−54.34	210.97	−56.63
9	Warangal	25.00	61.18	13.82	20.46	73.50	6.04	19.58	60.62	19.81
10	Telangana	6.39	91.18	2.43	6.83	89.96	3.21	5.47	88.90	5.63

Note

1. For sub-period I initial year is average of 1993–1994, 1994–1995 and 1995–1996, terminal year is average of 2003–2004, 2004–2005 and 2005–2006
2. For sub-period II initial year is average of 2003–2004, 2004–2005 and 2005–2006, terminal year is average of 2012–2013, 2013–2014 and 2014–2015
3. For total period initial year is average of 1993–1994, 1994–1995 and 1995–1996, terminal year is average of 2012–2013, 2013–2014 and 2014–2015
4. Hyderabad is deleted as data set is incomplete

districts may have shifted to cotton crop from food grain cultivation. In Rangareddy, the demand for land for non-agricultural purpose is responsible for the observed pattern. In most of the districts, the yield effect during second sub-period has declined which raises doubts about the sustainability of the growth process. Similar pattern is observed in the case of production of cereals (Table 3). The yield effect in the case of cereals is generally not as strong as observed in the case of food grains. Area effect especially during first subperiod is negative in many districts. Even in well irrigated Nalgonda District there is a substantial decline in area under cereals. It is disturbing to note that the contribution of improvement in technology to the growth of cereal production is not impressive in agriculturally developed districts like Nalgonda, Nizamabad and Karimnagar. This is true even in the case of rice production (Table 4). Further, Nizamabad and Nalgonda have registered a decline in area under rice during the first sub-period. Perhaps farmers may be finding it unprofitable to cultivate paddy. In short, the contribution of improvement in technology to production of rice is lower than that in the case of production of cereals which, in turn, is lower than that in the case of production of food grains.

6 Technology Vis-a-Vis Population Density

Growth in population/increase in internal migration (which is more true at sub-national level) reflected in terms of an increase in density of population is likely to restrict the benefit of improvement in technology. For Telangana results of two alternative forms namely one without per capita cropped area under food grains (Alt-I) and the other with per capita cropped area under food grains (Alt-II) are presented in Table 5. The results of regression analysis reveal that in Telangana per capita monthly food grain production increases by 10 kg in response to increase in yield by one tonne per hectare. On the other hand, an increase in density of population by 100 persons per sq. km., as expected, would bring down per capita monthly food grain production by 3 kg.

District level analysis reveals that generally density of population is not a significant variable. Only in Adilabad, Karimnagar and Rangareddy Districts the density of population turns out to be a significant variable. The impact of improvement in food grains production across the districts varies between 6 and 11 kg. The impact of increase in per capita cropped area varies widely across the districts. It is as high as 224 kg in Nizamabad District and as low as 30 kg in Rangareddy District. This may be due to differences in the quality of land, method of production and input mix.

Table 3 Decomposition of growth in production of cereals in Telangana by districts

S. no.	District	Sub-period I			Sub-period II			Total period		
		Area effect	Productivity effect	Interaction effect	Area effect	Productivity effect	Interaction effect	Area effect	Productivity effect	Interaction effect
1	Adilabad	−679.74	1131.79	−352.05	267.26	−260.61	93.34	590.99	−1110.39	619.4
2	Karimnagar	51.67	36.17	12.17	58.58	31.63	9.79	49.23	29	21.76
3	Khammam	0.68	99.12	0.2	−14.83	117.85	3.02	−4.53	107.06	−2.53
4	Mahabubnagar	5.41	90.33	4.26	13.96	78.15	7.89	6.87	80.78	12.35
5	Medak	−22.95	133.36	−10.4	17.6	71.68	10.77	4.07	90.46	5.47
6	Nalgonda	−411	589.7	−78.8	18.77	73.34	7.89	18.77	73.34	7.89
7	Nizamabad	−27.82	137.91	−0.1	47.43	33.31	19.26	25.66	50.83	23.51
8	Rangareddy	−52.24	194.04	−41.79	−159.27	299.82	−40.55	−60.41	236.42	−76.01
9	Warangal	34.33	49.7	16.04	46.39	44.75	8.86	33.06	42.22	24.72
10	Telangana	−3.525	104.98	−1.45	27.77	62.85	9.38	11.29	78.38	10.33

Note

1. For sub-period I initial year is average of 1993–1994, 1994–1995 and 1995–1996, terminal year is average of 2003–2004, 2004–2005 and 2005–2006
2. For sub-period II initial year is average of 2003–2004, 2004–2005 and 2005–2006, terminal year is average of 2012–2013, 2013–2014 and 2014–2015
3. For total period initial year is average of 1993–1994, 1994–1995 and 1995–1996, terminal year is average of 2012–2013, 2013–2014 and 2014–2015
4. Hyderabad is deleted as data set is incomplete

Table 4 Decomposition of growth in production of rice in Telangana by districts

S. no.	District	Sub-period I			Sub-period II			Total period		
		Area effect	Productivity effect	Interaction effect	Area effect	Productivity effect	Interaction effect	Area effect	Productivity effect	Interaction effect
1	Adilabad	0.52	99.29	0.19	29.64	66.3	4.07	11.64	81.64	6.72
2	Karimnagar	28.78	65.83	5.39	78.76	11.59	9.66	59.89	20.22	19.89
3	Khammam	50.6	43.4	6	−41.89	145.78	−3.89	30	63.4	6.60
4	Mahabubnagar	40.25	46.78	12.97	70.99	19.16	9.84	17.79	61.35	20.86
5	Medak	−1706.4	1979.67	−373.27	47.42	30.18	22.4	26.72	51.75	21.53
6	Nalgonda	−133	241.1	−8.1	82	12.2	5.8	69.2	21.8	9.00
7	Nizamabad	−49	169.28	−20.28	10.12	77.99	11.89	0.69	97.87	1.44
8	Rangareddy	−74.26	188.35	−14.08	224.75	−109.99	−14.75	30.2	66.48	3.32
9	Warangal	53.89	35.37	10.75	75.25	20.5	4.25	57.73	26.86	15.50
10	Telangana	20.35	75.74	3.91	67.61	22.33	10.07	48.34	33.86	17.8

Note

1. For sub-period I initial year is average of 1993–1994, 1994–1995 and 1995–1996, terminal year is average of 2003–2004, 2004–2005 and 2005–2006
2. For sub-period II initial year is average of 2003–2004, 2004–2005 and 2005–2006, terminal year is average of 2012–2013, 2013–2014 and 2014–2015
3. For total period initial year is average of 1993–1994, 1994–1995 and 1995–1996, terminal year is average of 2012–2013, 2013–2014 and 2014–2015
4. Hyderabad is deleted as data set is incomplete

Table 5 Determinants of per capita food grains production by districts

S. no.	Districts	Intercept	Co-efficient of independent variable			*R* square	Adjusted *R* square	*F*
			FG PRDTY	PC CRA	DoPOP			
1	Adilabad	49.88	10.60		−0.33	76.41	73.93	30.78
		(9.32)	(7.48)		(7.59)			
2	Karimnagar	2.12	12.02	139.88	−0.11	93.44	92.35	85.44
		(0.18)	(5.54)	(4.30)	(2.14)			
3	Khammam	−17.86	5.46	130.23		84.04	82.36	50.03
		(4.30)	(8.33)	(6.60)				
4	Mahabubnagar	−11.43	10.15	51.26		98.29	98.11	544.72
		(6.27)	(32.65)	(6.76)				
5	Medak	−25.62	8.89	155.62		96.61	96.25	270.75
		(5.56)	(20.09)	(6.32)				
6	Nalgonda	−19.88	7.55	125.31		87.13	85.78	64.32
		(4.64)	(5.88)	(4.76)				
7	Nizamabad	−30.62	7.48	224.11		97.18	96.89	327.65
		(10.78)	(6.49)	(7.79)				
8	Rangareddy	2.85	2.96	30.43	−0.01	88.02	86.02	44.07
		(1.63)	(6.87)	(2.99)	(3.72)			
9	Warangal	−24.02	7.66	137.79		94.53	93.96	164.30
		(6.81)	(12.19)	(6.26)				
10	Telangana-Alt-I	22.28	10.64		−0.10	90.06	89.02	86.11
		(4.61)	(9.74)		(4.28)			
	Telangana-Alt-II	−4.73	7.51	93.99	−0.03	93.00	92.00	83.68
		(0.49)	(5.34)	(2.96)	(1.09)			

Note
1. Figures in bracket are *t*-ratios
2. PC FG PRO = Per Capita Food Grains Production in kg per month which is the dependent variable
3. FG PRDTY = Food Grains Productivity in tonnes per hectare
4. PC CRA = Per Capita Cropped Area in hectares
5. D o POP = Density of Population in persons per square kilometre
6. Time period for the study is 1993–1994 to 2014–2015
7. Hyderabad district is deleted as data set is incomplete

Source
(a) Statistical Abstract of Andhra Pradesh (various years), Directorate of Economics and Statistics, Government of Andhra Pradesh, Hyderabad
(b) Records of Directorate of Economics and Statistics, Government of Telangana

7 Conclusion

Production of food grains in Telangana during the two decades (1993–1994 to 2014–2015) has doubled. This is brought about mainly by the improvement in technology as decomposition analysis reveals that the yield effect is stronger than the area effect in the growth of production of food grains, cereals and rice. However, the impact of technology seems to be declining with passage of time which casts shadow on the sustainability of food grain production. There is a drastic reduction in area and production of jowar. Improvement in productivity and extension of cropped area have positive influence on per capita availability of food grain while higher density of population would result in decline in per capita availability of food grains. Results of multiple regression analysis reveal that in Telangana per capita monthly food grain availability increases by 10 kg in response to increase in yield by one tonne per hectare. This is broadly true even at district level. On the other hand, an increase in density of population by 100 persons per km^2, as expected, would bring down per capita monthly food grain availability by 3 kg.

MIX
Papier aus verantwortungsvollen Quellen
Paper from responsible sources
FSC® C105338

If you have any concerns about our products,
you can contact us on
ProductSafety@springernature.com

In case Publisher is established outside the EU,
the EU authorized representative is:
Springer Nature Customer Service Center GmbH
Europaplatz 3, 69115 Heidelberg, Germany

Printed by Libri Plureos GmbH
in Hamburg, Germany